MORAL DEMANDS IN NONIDEAL THEORY

OXFORD ETHICS SERIES

Series Editor: Derek Parfit, All Souls College, Oxford

THE LIMITS OF MORALITY
Shelly Kagan

PERFECTIONISM
Thomas Hurka

INEQUALITY
Larry S. Temkin

MORALITY, MORTALITY, Volume I
Death and Whom to Save from It
F. M. Kamm

MORALITY, MORTALITY, Volume II
Rights, Duties, and Status
F. M. Kamm

SUFFERING AND MORAL RESPONSIBILITY
Jamie Mayerfield

MORAL DEMANDS IN NONIDEAL THEORY
Liam B. Murphy

MORAL DEMANDS IN NONIDEAL THEORY

Liam B. Murphy

OXFORD

UNIVERSITY PRESS

2000

OXFORD
UNIVERSITY PRESS

Oxford   New York
Athens   Auckland   Bangkok   Bogotá   Buenos Aires   Calcutta
Cape Town   Chennai   Dar es Salaam   Delhi   Florence   Hong Kong   Istanbul
Karachi   Kuala Lumpur   Madrid   Melbourne   Mexico City   Mumbai
Nairobi   Paris   São Paulo   Singapore   Taipei   Tokyo   Toronto   Warsaw

and associated companies in
Berlin   Ibadan

Copyright © 2000 by Liam B. Murphy

Published by Oxford University Press, Inc.
198 Madison Avenue, New York, New York 10016

Oxford is a registered trademark of Oxford University Press.

Library of Congress Cataloging-in-Publication Data
Murphy, Liam B., 1960–
Moral demands in nonideal theory / Liam B. Murphy.
p.   cm.—(Oxford ethics series)
Includes bibliographical references and index.
ISBN 0-19-507976-0 (alk. paper)
1. Benevolence. 2. Social ethics. 3. Utilitarianism. I. Title. II. Series.
BJ1474 M87 2000
170'.42—dc21   99-029459

9 8 7 6 5 4 3 2 1

Printed in the United States of America
on acid-free paper

For my parents

Betty Murphy and Leo J. Murphy

ACKNOWLEDGMENTS

My first thanks go to Barry Taylor for his extraordinary teaching at the University of Melbourne, the inspiring example of his philosophical mind, and his judicious but kind encouragement.

I first wrote about the issues of this book in my doctoral dissertation at Columbia University; scarcely a line of the dissertation remains, but my understanding of these issues has been fundamentally shaped by the suggestions and criticisms of my advisers, Charles Larmore and Thomas Pogge. I have also been greatly influenced by conversations with Robert Myers that began while I was finishing my dissertation and, happily, have continued since.

In writing the book I have also been helped by the comments of many other people, including members of audiences at various colloquia and workshops; I would like to thank in particular Richard Arneson, Ruth Chang, Frances Kamm, Muhammad Ali Khalidi, Lewis Kornhauser, Jeff McMahan, Tim Mulgan, Joseph Raz, Amélie Rorty, Carlos Rosenkrantz, Lawrence Sager, Samuel Scheffler, Gisela Striker, William Talbott, and especially Ronald Dworkin and Thomas Nagel.

Special thanks are due to Sibylle Fischer for her comments on many drafts and for almost ten years of discussions of the themes of this book; I have not managed to convince her of the wisdom of my ways, but the attempt has made the book much better.

The readers for Oxford University Press were Shelly Kagan and Larry Temkin. Their extensive and extremely insightful comments on both details and fundamental issues helped me to improve every chapter in important ways. I am immensely grateful to them both.

My greatest debt is to Derek Parfit. From his early enthusiastic encouragement, without which I probably would not have written this book, to his more recent voluminous comments on my manuscript, which corrected several important errors and led to improvements on almost every page, his generosity to me has been literally astonishing.

I am grateful to Columbia University's Society of Fellows in the Humanities and the Mellon Foundation for a Teaching Fellowship, to Harvard University's Society of Fellows for a Junior Fellowship (and to Diana Morse for making life at the Society of Fellows so easy and so happy), to the Filomen d'Agostino and Max E. Greenberg Research Fund of New York University School of Law for financial support, and to my colleagues at NYU for their kind encouragement. Some passages from my article "The Demands of Beneficence," *Philosophy & Public Affairs* 22 (1993): 267–92 (© 1993 Princeton University Press), appear in different places in this book; I thank Princeton University Press for permission to reprint this material. Finally, I would like to thank Elizabeth Newman for allowing me to reproduce her photograph of the corner of Barkly and Canning Streets, Carlton, Melbourne, circa 1979.

New York City   L. B. M.
September 1999

CONTENTS

MORAL DEMANDS IN NONIDEAL THEORY

1

INTRODUCTION

I. The Puzzle of Beneficence

In some areas of moral and political thought, something like a consensus exists. No one denies that it is wrong to kill a person for the sake of stealing his car. Other areas of normative thought, by contrast, are characterized by great disagreement and uncertainty. The issue of required beneficence is a salient example.* Most well-off people feel that they should "do something" to alleviate severe suffering, such as that caused by famine. But there is certainly no agreement about the extent of this obligation to promote the well-being of total strangers. Furthermore, and more important, most individuals have no settled view of their own about the question.

Of course, disagreement and individual uncertainty are found in other areas of normative thought as well. The issue of beneficence, however, is distinctive in a further respect, marking a striking contrast with issues such as abortion or euthanasia. For on the question of the shape of required beneficence, people not only tend to be uncertain but also appear to be quite content about this condition of uncertainty.[1]

How can this be? If I can greatly reduce people's suffering, and I believe that it can sometimes be wrong for me not to greatly reduce people's suffering, how is it that I can remain contentedly unsure, in any

---

*Beneficence is distinct from benevolence. The latter is about being well-disposed toward others, caring about their well-being; the former is about actually promoting others' well-being. Different accounts of beneficence employ different accounts of well-being (see chapter 2, section I) and differ further over whether "others" includes non-human animals (I do not discuss this issue). Strictly, "beneficence" is about doing *good*, which may involve more than promoting well-being; however, the narrower sense of the term, which I will use throughout, seems closer to ordinary usage.

given case, whether failing to help is or is not wrong? As moral questions go, this one would seem to be very important, for the decision I arrive at is of immense significance for the people who are suffering. Since we typically care rather a lot about not doing even trivially wrong things of other kinds, such as stealing an apple from a market stand, or missing appointments without apology, our complacency about the question of required beneficence needs some explanation.

One possible explanation turns on empirical beliefs. Sidgwick observed that there seemed to be no "*consensus* as to what each man owes to his fellow-men, as such."[2] He also claimed that "each person is for the most part, from limitation either of power or knowledge, not in a position to do much good to more than a very small number of persons."[3] Given that very badly off strangers lived in Sidgwick's vicinity, and that organized efforts to assist the poor were not unknown in Victorian England, this claim seems wrong even for Sidgwick's time. A hundred years later, when efficient international humanitarian aid organizations and public and private agencies within our own countries can very effectively transform the surplus money of the well-off into greatly improved prospects for the very badly off, the claim is fairly clearly wrong.* But Sidgwick's view about the severe practical limits to any one person's ability to benefit other people is still widely held, and no doubt at least partly explains the prevailing complacency about beneficence.

However, a much more significant part of the explanation seems to be normative. It is widely believed that when it comes to the well-being of strangers, the question is not so much one of what people should do directly, but rather one of which institutional regime they should support. One way of developing this idea leads to Rawls's division of normative theory into individual morality for people and political justice for institutions.[4] I myself reject this division, but even if we were to grant it, the underlying problem of the extent of people's responsibility for the well-being of mere strangers would not go away.[5] As I explain in section III, whether our responsibility for the well-being of others is mediated by institutional structures or not, we still have to know what the shape and extent of that responsibility is.

In any case, the thought that beneficence is "for the government" suggests not just an institutional focus; more important in the current context, it also suggests that we tend to view beneficence in terms of collective responsibility. In this respect beneficence is different from other moral obligations, such as the obligation not to kill someone for monetary gain. This further distinctive feature of beneficence may do a lot to explain most people's complacency about it. For though each person is not sure what her responsibility is, what does seem evident enough is that

*See further chapter 2, section I.

most *other* people are falling short of whatever *their* responsibility may be. The practically relevant question of the shape of required beneficence is thus a question of "nonideal theory"—a question, that is, of what a given person is required to do in circumstances where at least some others are not doing what they are required to do.[6] This question of nonideal theory is especially puzzling in the context of collective responsibility, and a person may justify her neglect of it by noting the absence of any sign that others are prepared to do their part, whatever it may be.

But that is not a good reason to avoid the question. We need to focus more than we traditionally have on the practically urgent problems of nonideal moral and political theory.

II. The Problems of Moral Demands

Whatever the reason for most people's contentment with not knowing what they owe other people as such, it is certainly the case that it is very difficult to come up with plausible answers to the question. Of course everyone accepts that it is morally good to promote the interests of worse-off people; "charity" brings social honor. But our question is what beneficent acts are required of us: When do we act wrongly for not promoting someone else's interests? If we limit ourselves to charity, the answer is "never"—beneficence is always supererogatory. I take it that it is not especially controversial to reject this view; as I have said, most of us believe that well-off people—or at least their representative institutions—do have to do *something*. A "principle of beneficence," as I understand it, is a moral principle that sets out what beneficent action is required of people. The charity view thus presents no principle of beneficence at all—indeed, it denies that there is such a thing.

One of my two main aims in this book is to suggest a plausible principle of beneficence. The normative question to which such a principle is an answer is urgent and weighty, but there are no natural candidates. And thus my own suggestion—the "collective principle of beneficence" introduced later in this section—is offered in the spirit of exploring neglected possibilities. I believe that the collective principle of beneficence is more plausible than the alternatives I am aware of; but this does not mean that I find it overwhelmingly compelling considered on its own. In all parts of normative theory we must make arguments of relative plausibility.* This cautious methodology is especially important in a case like

---

*See Rawls, *A Theory of Justice*, 52: "Objections by way of counterexamples are to be made with care, since these may tell us only what we know already, namely that our theory is wrong somewhere. The important thing is to find out how often and how

this, where disagreement and uncertainty make it abundantly clear that there is no default view on the subject, no view that stands unless rebutted.

In making the argument of relative plausibility for the collective principle of beneficence, much of my attention is devoted to the best-known principle of beneficence—that embraced in the utilitarian tradition. The "optimizing principle of beneficence" requires agents always to do the best they can for others. It requires us to keep benefiting others until the point where further efforts would burden us as much as they would help the others.* This principle has the virtue of simplicity, but the demands it makes strike just about everyone as absurd—as we say, a principle that makes such demands "just *couldn't* be right."[7] Explaining why the demands of the optimizing principle of beneficence are absurd, if they are, is the second main aim of this book.

The most obvious explanation is that the demands of the optimizing principle are simply *excessive*. I discuss this problem of over-demandingness in chapter 2, arguing as well that some other objections that can be raised against the optimizing principle may reduce in the end to the same issue of excessive demands. But having thus argued that the simple problem of over-demandingness is most likely what is really of concern even for those who raise more sophisticated objections, I turn in chapter 3 to cast doubt on that concern. The very idea of excessive moral demands turns out to be unclear. Efforts to introduce clarity, and to rescue the idea from the accusation that it simply states a bias in favor of the moral and political status quo, in the end serve only to undermine the initial intuitive force of the problem of over-demandingness.

This collapse of the most natural explanation for the apparent absurdity of the demands of the optimizing principle of beneficence lends support to the alternative diagnosis I offer in chapters 5 and 6. I argue that

---

far it is wrong. All theories are presumably mistaken in places. The real question at any given time is which of the views already proposed is the best approximation overall. To ascertain this some grasp of the structure of rival theories is surely necessary."

*According to utilitarianism, the optimizing principle of beneficence is the only moral principle there is. Some writers use the word "consequentialism" for what I call utilitarianism. I understand consequentialism more broadly, as any view that assesses the rightness of action in terms of the goodness of consequences, where the goodness of consequences is not necessarily solely a function of well-being. (On the terminological issues discussed here and in the note on p. 3, I follow suggestions made by Derek Parfit.)

I should point out here that talk of moral "theories" and "principles" in this book is meant to imply neither any particular metaethical commitments, nor any assumption that normative thought can be reduced to something like a decision procedure. As I understand it, a moral principle is just a representation, at whatever level of specificity is possible, of a particular area of moral thought; and a moral theory is just a representation, at whatever level of specificity is possible, of the whole of moral thought.

the optimizing principle of beneficence imposes its demands unfairly in situations of partial compliance; the true problem with the demands of the optimizing principle thus does indeed arise in the realm of nonideal theory. If I am complying with the optimizing principle but others are not, I not only have to do my own fair share, I have to take on as much of the shares of the noncomplying others as is optimal as well. This, I argue, is unfair.[8] I suggest a "compliance condition" on principles of beneficence: very roughly, the idea is that the demands on a complying person should not exceed what they would be under full compliance with the principle. My diagnosis of the apparent absurdity of the optimizing principle of beneficence is thus that it violates the compliance condition. As I explain in chapter 5, the compliance condition does not apply to so-called deontological obligations, such as the obligation not to kill for monetary gain, but rather only to principles that can be understood in terms of collective responsibility. Thus this diagnosis explains why it is never argued that extremely demanding deontological requirements are for that reason absurd.

The collective principle of beneficence is designed to satisfy the compliance condition; roughly, it requires agents to promote the well-being of others up to the level of sacrifice that would be optimal under full compliance. More accurate formulations of the principle are quite complicated, and I devote chapter 7 to sketching how the principle might be employed by agents in practice.

The other main alternative to the optimizing principle of beneficence is found in a group of principles I call "limited principles of beneficence." These principles, all of which hold that there is a limit to the size of the burden people need to sustain for the sake of benefiting others, are appealing if we accept that the problem of over-demandingness provides the right diagnosis of the apparent absurdity of the optimizing principle of beneficence. But their familiarity makes them worth discussing even if that diagnosis is rejected; I discuss limited principles of beneficence in chapter 4.

III. Politics, Morality, and Nonideal Theory

Though most of my discussion will focus on questions of what people might be required to do to benefit others directly, examples from politics are also invoked at crucial points. Indeed, I believe that almost all of the argument in this book is as relevant to political theory as to moral theory.

As I have indicated, I believe that principles of justice apply not just to institutions but also to personal conduct. I am also inclined to believe, furthermore, that the best theoretical account of political justice is grounded in a principle of weighted beneficence—one that gives additional weight to benefits to worse-off people.[9] In this account of justice, the principle of weighted beneficence requires us both to design institutions and also to act so as to promote overall weighted well-being. Rawls would reject not just the content of this view—weighted beneficence—but its very structure. On his view, it is institutions alone that have responsibility for promoting the aims of justice; people's responsibilities in respect of justice are to support and promote just institutions.[10] From this perspective, this book's discussion of people's responsibilities of beneficence could be thought to be relevant only to the subject of individual morality, and indeed the discussion could be thought to be rather unimportant, on the ground that most of the work of making others' lives go better should be done by institutions, the design of which requires distinct normative principles.

But even if we accepted Rawls's dualist view about normative theory, the problems about the demands of beneficence discussed in this book would nevertheless arise in closely analogous form. The point is clearest and strongest if we focus on what Rawls deliberately did not focus on: nonideal theory. In Rawls's view, political theory must first produce an account of just institutions as they would be under conditions of full compliance, and then, having established the appropriate ideal, turn to questions of nonideal theory.[11] Rawls himself has not devoted much attention to nonideal theory. But it is clear that he believes that doing so would involve attention to the issue of the sacrifices that could be demanded of people. In discussing the operation of the "natural duty of justice" in nonideal circumstances, Rawls says that "we are to assist in the establishment of just arrangements when they do not exist, at least when this can be done with little cost to ourselves."[12] Obviously enough, there are many possible views about the shape of the responsibilities of people to bring about just institutions. Any discussion of what Rawlsian justice requires of people in an unjust world will need to cover pretty much the same territory as this book's discussion of the demands of beneficence, including, especially, the discussion of the problem of demands under partial compliance.[13] Since we *do* live in an unjust world, and since indeed we are doomed always to apply nonideal theory only, this is hardly an insignificant political issue.

2

OVER-DEMANDINGNESS, ALIENATION, AND CONFINEMENT

In the next few chapters my aim is not to solve the familiar problem of over-demandingness but rather to undermine its force. As a first step, I offer in this chapter a detailed interpretation of the problem.* This involves describing two other potential problems concerning the demands of the optimizing principle of beneficence. These are, first, the problem of alienation, which concerns the idea that compliance with the optimizing principle alienates agents from ethically significant aspects of their own lives; and, second, the problem of confinement, where the idea is that the optimizing principle narrows the options available to complying agents in an objectionable way. I argue that both of these problems may be compelling only to the extent that they are aspects of the problem of over-demandingness.

I. The Demands of the Optimizing Principle of Beneficence

The over-demandingness problem has its origin in a traditional objection to utilitarianism. Richard Brandt puts that objection succinctly: "Act utilitarianism makes extreme and oppressive demands on the individual,

---

*I see the problem of over-demandingness as arising within morality, rather than as a problem about the authority of moral reasons. For the latter view, see Susan Wolf, "Moral Saints," *Journal of Philosophy* 79 (1982): 419–39, and "Above and Below the Line of Duty," *Philosophical Topics* 14 (1986): 131–48; David O. Brink, "Utilitarian Morality and the Personal Point of View," *Journal of Philosophy* 83 (1986): 417–38. For defense of the approach I adopt, see Samuel Scheffler, *Human Morality* (New York: Oxford University Press, 1992), esp. chap. 4.

so much so that it can hardly be taken seriously; like the Sermon on the Mount, it is a morality only for saints."[1] This objection to utilitarianism has been familiar at least since Sidgwick,[2] but it has been much revived in recent decades, due in large part to the work of Bernard Williams.[3]

Now our interest is not limited to utilitarianism. Utilitarianism presents the optimizing principle of beneficence as the whole of morality; but a pluralist moral conception that *includes* the optimizing principle of beneficence, such as that of W. D. Ross, is likely also to be very demanding.[4] Indeed, extreme demands can also come from parts of morality other than beneficence. This fact will be important in the next chapter, where I note that if extreme demands are objectionable, they presumably are so whatever their provenance. In the meantime, however, I will limit my discussion of the problem of over-demandingness to the context of beneficence. One reason for this is just that the optimizing principle of beneficence gives us the clearest case of an extremely demanding moral principle. More important, this focus allows us to pursue at the same time our project of developing a potentially plausible principle of beneficence.

The remainder of this section describes the demands that would be made by the optimizing principle of beneficence standing alone—as the whole of morality. But the aim is to provide a rough outline of the demands made by the optimizing principle of beneficence wherever it is found. The reason our outline can be only rough for principles of beneficence that are part of pluralist moral theories is that the principles of a pluralist theory may be ranked in various ways that effectively reduce the demands of some of them. For example, the optimizing principle of beneficence may make lesser demands on a person also subject to various prior special obligations. Furthermore, in a pluralist moral theory the requirements of the optimizing principle of beneficence may overlap with those of various other principles of the theory, and in such a case it would be arbitrary to assign demands to one principle rather than another. These points show that the proper object for investigation is the demands of entire moral theories, not moral principles considered in isolation. However, it would be tedious to discuss in turn the demands of each of the various possible theories that might contain the optimizing principle of beneficence. Moreover, I do not believe that anything in the subsequent discussion is undermined by my simplifying assumption that the impact the optimizing principle of beneficence has on demands is roughly the same whatever the overall moral theory.[5]

What, then, are the demands of the optimizing principle of beneficence? Such a principle requires each person to act such that she will produce as great an expected overall benefit, given what she has reason to believe, as she would acting in any other way available to her.* So the optimizing principle requires each agent to go on promoting well-being until the point where further efforts would burden the agent as much as they would benefit others. Depending on the circumstances, the loss sustained by the time this point is reached could be very great; moreover, the agent's resulting level of expected well-being could be very low in absolute terms. In certain circumstances, then, the optimizing principle is extremely demanding.

The importance of this fact for moral theory depends in part on the nature of the relevant circumstances. If extreme demands occurred under only very exotic circumstances, it could plausibly be thought that no pressing normative problem was raised. But of course the circumstances under which the optimizing principle of beneficence imposes extreme demands need be no more exotic than those that currently obtain.

The most obvious aspect of the problem is world poverty. Determining the best way to promote the well-being of the poorest people in the long term is of course an extremely difficult and complex matter.[6] Nevertheless, individual agents need not, and, if they accept the optimizing principle, ought not, wait until the various issues involved are definitively settled. Each moderately well-off person is already in a position to save many thousands of lives by donating money to efficient aid organizations that provide cures for various childhood diseases.[7] And there is money that could provide food for people who would otherwise die of starvation. Beyond saving lives, each person who has resources in excess of what is needed for health, food, shelter, and those extras that might be needed to keep income flowing could best promote overall well-being by giving the surplus to those who are sick, hungry, or homeless. Here it should be clear, moreover, that there is actually no need to bring up *world* poverty. A restricted optimizing principle, requiring agents to promote the good in their own country, would also be very demanding in most countries, including some Western industrial countries at the end of the twentieth century.

---

*This states the principle's subjective criterion of right action, which, in practice at least, is the only criterion we need. I follow Derek Parfit, "What We Together Do" (unpublished ms., 1988), and Allan Gibbard, *Wise Choices, Apt Feelings* (Cambridge, Mass.: Harvard University Press, 1990), 42–43. The phrase "expected overall benefit" masks the extremely difficult issue of whether agents should choose the action that will lead to the greatest increase in the expected total level of well-being, or the greatest increase in the expected average level of well-being. See, on this question, Parfit, *Reasons and Persons*, pt. IV. Note, finally, that though I take principles of beneficence to be about the promotion of expected well-being, for the sake of simplicity I will from now on typically write simply about the promotion of well-being, or benefiting people. On the importance of choosing the action productive of the optimal increase in overall *expected* well-being, rather than the action that has the best chance of bringing about the greatest benefit that any action available to the agent could bring about, see Frank Jackson, "Decision-Theoretic Consequentialism and the Nearest and Dearest Objection," *Ethics* 101 (1991): 461–82.

The demands of the optimizing principle are not just financial. In addition to the loss of the pleasures both high and low that extra money can bring, there are the losses involved in not being able to live the life of one's choice. For most of us it would be hard to show that there is no alternative to our way of earning a living that would better promote the good, perhaps just because it would bring in more money. But switching to that alternative could bring a great loss in well-being. It might do this because it would make it not feasible to have children, for example, or simply because we would have to give up what we enjoy doing for something we do not. And even if it would be best if I kept my current job or project, I have leisure time that could be spent volunteering in homeless shelters or in political campaigning. Of course I need some time to relax, or I might run out of steam and be able to do less good on the whole, but it is obvious enough that most moderately well-off people could absorb a substantial loss of leisure time without any reduction in their efficiency in promoting the good.

I should emphasize that I am not claiming that it would best promote overall well-being if *all* of us gave away all our surplus money, changed jobs, gave up on leisure time, and so on; rather, I am claiming that each moderately well-off agent could now best promote overall well-being if *she* did these things—the assumption being, of course, that not many others are likely to do the same.[8] The question of what the better-off as a group could do to promote the best outcome raises distinct issues about the overall economic effects of widespread changes in the behavior of skilled people and widespread changes in what the rich do with their money. So the question raises all the problems facing development policy generally, and more. Nevertheless, it is safe to assume that the greater the number of people trying to act optimally, the lower the sacrifice required of each person trying to act optimally. That this is so is most clear for the purely financial demands of the optimizing principle, and for the demands on leisure time, but it is also plausible for the demands on careers and projects—it would very likely not make the outcome best if everyone in the industrialized world gave up their jobs and tried to promote overall well-being in some more direct way. Thus we can assume that with full compliance the demands of the optimizing principle of beneficence on each agent would drop drastically, and they would continue to drop as this high level of beneficence reduced the need for further beneficence. Indeed, it is plausible to guess that in what we can call "optimal full-compliance"—full compliance in an optimally improved world with vastly less need for beneficence—the demands of the optimizing principle of beneficence would be rather moderate. (I will say a little more about this point later.)

So it is important to remember that the extreme demands the optimizing principle of beneficence makes of an individual agent in our current situation are due as much to the fact of minimal expected compliance with any such principle as to current levels of need. Neglect of this fact can easily lead to an underestimation of the demands the optimizing principle makes on individual agents.

A related matter is the impact of political institutions on the demands of beneficence. It is often said that in a just political order where the government shouldered most of the burden that would otherwise fall to individuals, the demands of beneficence would be much decreased.[9] This is surely right, but it is of little relevance to the question of how demanding the optimizing principle of beneficence is in a situation (such as our own) that lacks such ideal institutions. An agent who reflected on the advantages of coordinated action through political institutions over "free-lance good-doing"[10] might conclude, perhaps often correctly, that the best way for her to promote the long-term good is to involve herself in political struggle for institutional reform. But even if so, this would not necessarily mean that the costs to her would be less than if she engaged in more direct efforts to promote the good. It is quite clear that in our current situation the optimizing principle of beneficence requires more than mere *support* for better political arrangements.[11]

We need now to consider briefly two arguments against my claim that the optimizing principle of beneficence is extremely demanding (at least under partial compliance). The first, which has been very influential, is practical. Part of Sidgwick's response to the concern that "Utilitarianism seems to go beyond the standard of duty commonly prescribed under the head of Benevolence" is to point out that since we know more about our own good, and have greater opportunities to promote it, than we do for people far removed from us, we can typically expect to produce most overall goodness by aiming at our own good (and at the good of those close to us who we know well).[12] Only doubtfully plausible for Sidgwick, this argument seems rather clearly not to survive twentieth-century technological and organizational developments.[13] It is in any case an entirely contingent response to the claim of extreme demands, since it obviously cannot be ruled out that changing circumstances will make it possible for individuals to do great good for others at great (though lesser) cost to themselves.

The second argument turns on the fact that different versions of the optimizing principle of beneficence employ different conceptions of well-being; there are both different possible accounts of well-being and different views about which aspects of well-being agents are required to promote (these issues are discussed further in section III). If we are required to promote all aspects of well-being, and well-being is understood in terms of the fulfillment of an agent's desires whatever they are, then any principle of beneficence requires us to promote the satisfaction of all the desires of all people. This might seem extravagant, and it could be thought that where the optimizing principle of beneficence imposes extreme demands this can be blamed on some such extravagance in its account of the good to be promoted; more plausible versions of the principle, employing reasonable accounts of well-being, will not impose extreme demands.[14]

In a similar vein, my claim that the optimizing principle imposes extreme demands might be said to rest on a failure to recognize that there are principled limits to the *ability* of one person to promote the well-being of another. Joseph Raz's account of well-being could be appealed to here; on that account the most that beneficent agents can do is create the conditions under which a person might be able to make a success of her life—the rest is necessarily up to the person herself.[15]

But in claiming that the optimizing principle of beneficence imposes extreme demands, I have not needed to make any assumptions about the account of well-being employed. A rather austere account of human well-being and a rather minimal view about which aspects of it we are required to promote would suffice for the examples I have discussed—all of which concern issues of life and death, or, most extravagantly, the needs for food, basic health, and shelter. There may be good reasons to avoid a desire fulfillment account of well-being, or to adopt a principle of beneficence that requires promotion of only some part of what makes people's lives go better. And there may also be good reasons to think that agents can in principle do no more than help create the conditions under which a person might be able to make her life go well. But the truth of any of these views about well-being would have only a slight impact on the extent of the demands of the optimizing principle.* This is clearly so in our current situation of minimal compliance. It would even be so under (nonoptimal) full compliance, where the basic needs of large numbers of people would remain unmet, and the conditions allowing for a successful life unrealized. Where different theories of well-being might make a difference to the demands of beneficence is in a situation of optimal full compliance. In such a situation it might, for example, make a big difference to the extent of demands if the most anyone could do for another was to promote the conditions of a successful life—for we stipulate that under optimal full compliance such conditions already obtain for most people.** But as the problem of over-demandingness is not

---

*It should also be noted here that it makes little or no difference to the discussion of the extent of the demands of principles of beneficence that a plausible principle of beneficence will either be accompanied by some principle of equality, or, in my view more plausibly, be itself sensitive to the distribution of well-being in that it weights benefits to worse-off people higher in importance than benefits to better-off people. See, on these issues, Parfit, *Equality or Priority?* Thus, though I favor a weighted principle of beneficence, I will for the most part ignore the complications this weighting introduces; an exception is the first section of chapter 6.

**This point is actually misleading in an important way, as one can always "benefit" someone by not harming them, and thus the demands of beneficence could be high even on such a view of well-being and in such a world. I ignore these demands here

to be solved by imagining a situation of optimal full compliance, our discussion can continue to be neutral among the various possible conceptions of well-being that the optimizing principle of beneficence might use.

II. Over-demandingness

The optimizing principle of beneficence imposes extreme demands. Why does this raise a problem for moral theory? One possible response to the fact of extreme demands is to hold tight: "If morality is demanding, it is demanding."[16] Another is to suspend judgment, and look for some underlying rationale for the thought that extreme demands are objectionable; if there is no such rationale, there is no problem for moral theory. This is in effect Shelly Kagan's position in his discussion of the "appeal to cost" as a justification for "options" not to promote the greater good.[17] Neither of these responses seems right. Virtually no one believes that people act wrongly if they fail to live up to the demands just described.[18] And to explain this, it seems to me that the right thing to do is to state the obvious. The objection to extreme demands is based on the simple belief that there is a limit to how much morality can demand of people.[19] The prima facie plausibility of this belief is very high; it stands in no obvious need of a deeper rationale.*

It is of course true that we have one clear ground for *suspicion* of the belief that there is a limit to the demands of morality, particularly in the case of beneficence: such a limit is very much more in the interests of the best-off than of the worst-off.[20] For not only do the best-off not need the beneficence of others nearly as much as the worst-off do, the demands of the optimizing principle of beneficence are much greater for the best-off as well. Nevertheless, though this point gives us reason to investigate the idea of a limit to the demands of beneficence as deeply as we can, it is not in itself enough to rob the belief in a limit of its initial force. It is a belief anyone could reasonably hold, whatever their relative level of well-being.[21] So though in the next two chapters I will argue against the idea of a limit to moral demands, my arguments will turn on difficulties that emerge when we try to make the idea more concrete. I will not be suggesting that the idea is insufficiently motivated philo-

---

because this is an area of overlap with various deontological constraints, and the demands of such moral principles are, as we will see in the next chapter, usually tolerated by the critics of beneficence.

*This does not mean that no deeper rationale is possible. One such rationale can be found in Nagel's influential discussion of the problem of over-demandingness in terms of a clash between the personal and impersonal points of view; see *The View from Nowhere*, 202–3.

sophically to begin with, or that its asymmetrical impact on people with different levels of well-being disbars it from serious consideration.

We cannot yet move on, however; for there is an indirect way of arguing in support of a limit to moral demands that must be mentioned. The indirect argument focuses on the gap between typical human motivation and the requirements of extremely demanding moral principles. Philosophers with different views about the nature of morality and about moral psychology put this fact to different uses. But the general structure of the indirect argument is that for one or another philosophical reason there is a "motivational condition" that moral principles must meet, and that the optimizing principle of beneficence, because it is so demanding, does not meet it.[22] For example, J. L. Mackie, who holds that morality is "invented" by people, rejects utilitarianism on the ground that it is "impracticable"—no one is likely to follow the theory, so it is pointless to propose it for general adoption.[23] The issues involved in this and other versions of the indirect argument are extremely difficult and controversial. And so though I am inclined to agree with Kagan that any plausible motivational condition would in fact be met by the optimizing principle of beneficence,[24] I cannot attempt to discuss all the possibilities here. Fortunately, this is not necessary, since on my understanding of the problem of over-demandingness the success or failure of the indirect argument is actually of no relevance. It is clear that the failure of the argument does not dispose of the problem: the belief that extreme demands are intrinsically objectionable remains. But since it is just this idea of an intrinsic problem with extreme demands that we are interested in, the success of the indirect argument would also be beside the point. Suppose that there is some plausible motivational condition that rules out the optimizing principle of beneficence given some account of typical human motivation. We could then imagine that people were different, that they would be quite likely to act in accordance with the optimizing principle if only they believed that this was required of them. The direct intuitive objection to extreme demands need not be any the weaker in this hypothetical world.

III. Demands and Well-Being

The problem of over-demandingness is that certain otherwise appealing moral principles are objectionable for imposing extreme demands on complying agents. The problem apparently could not be more straightforward.

But the problem of over-demandingness is not straightforward, for the reason that the very idea of a moral demand is not straightforward. So far we have operated with apparently uncontroversial intuitive ideas of what moral demands are, and of how they are assessed. Further investigation of these matters will lead us, in the next chapter, to have serious doubts about the problem of over-demandingness. For now, I will offer just enough clarification of the idea of a moral demand to allow proper comparison of the over-demandingness problem with the problems of alienation and confinement.

In a natural, loose sense a demand is made whenever an agent is morally required to do something; in this sense, "demand" is just a mildly pejorative variation on "requirement." But the sense of "demand" relevant to the over-demandingness objection is clearly narrower than this. Our interest here is in just those demands that involve a loss to the agent—if meeting a moral requirement would not bring a loss, we would say that no demand, in the relevant sense, is made. Thus we should say that the demand a requirement makes is greater or less depending on the extent of the loss of well-being sustained by a complying agent.*

The assessment of the demands of a moral principle therefore requires an account of well-being. It may seem that there is no question to be raised about *which* account of well-being should be used—we should simply use whichever is the best account. But different accounts of well-being may be appropriate in different contexts; in particular, the best *general* account of well-being may not always be the appropriate account. By a "general" account of well-being, I mean an account of "what it is for a single life to go well";[25] it is the account we use when we ask straightforward questions about people's actual levels of well-being. Different moral contexts may require restricted versions of the general account.[26] We therefore do need to decide which is the appropriate account of well-being for the specific purpose of assessing moral demands.

To see that the account of well-being appropriate for a given moral context is not necessarily the general account, we can suppose first that we are deciding which account of well-being should be employed by a principle of beneficence. Adapting T. M. Scanlon's well-known example, it is very plausible to hold that it would contribute to my well-being if I were to build a monument to my god—because it would bring me immense satisfaction—while at the same time denying that this interest of mine is part of what a principle of beneficence requires other people to promote.[27] More generally, it is possible that the best general account of well-being will have a preference-hedonist component but the account of

*This means that prudence, which requires a person to optimize his own self-interest over time, makes no demands. If this seems wrong, it may be because of issues related to the problem of confinement, discussed in section VII. Another relevant issue is that of the appropriate time period for the assessment of demands, discussed in chapter 3, section II.

well-being appropriate for a principle of beneficence will not—the latter could be a "substantive good" account that does not count hedonistic preference satisfaction as a relevant good.*

Supposing this to be the case, which of the two accounts of well-being should we use to measure the demands of a principle of beneficence? The answer must be that we should use the best general account. We are interested in the loss that in fact flows from following a given principle; the content of the principle does not determine how it is appropriate to measure that. We must measure actual loss in well-being with the best account of actual well-being.**

Now of course some moral theories or principles do make use of a general account of well-being, and this may differ from what we (assessors of demands) take to be the best general account. This shows that we cannot claim that the mere assessment of the demands of a theory is fully neutral with respect to the merits of that theory; to the contrary, it imposes a prior conclusion on the extremely controversial question of what is the best general account of well-being. Nevertheless, controversy about the nature of well-being need not place the whole problem of over-demandingness on hold. For the assessment of demands can proceed without an exhaustive and complete account of general well-being—if indeed such a thing is available, even in principle. When it is a question of which moral theories impose *extreme* demands, all plausible accounts of loss are likely to yield the same verdict, and so we can proceed on the basis of this overlapping consensus. This is the analogue of the point made in section I that a version of the optimizing principle of beneficence employing even the most austere account of well-being will nevertheless impose extreme demands on agents in current circumstances, where basic needs for health, shelter, and so forth, remain unmet for millions of people. The analogy is not exact, since the losses sustained by agents complying with the optimizing principle of beneficence have not been

---

*Preference hedonism holds that a person's well-being is a matter of the satisfaction of preferences that concern introspectively discernible features of his conscious states. Substantive good accounts of well-being may include a preference-hedonist component; they may also hold that aspects of a person's life contribute to his well-being irrespective of any of his preferences; knowledge could be an example of this kind of substantive good. See Parfit, *Reasons and Persons*, Appendix I; Scanlon, "Value, Desire, and the Quality of Life."

**Liberal political theory is rightly wary of the imposition, by way of policy choice, of any particular view of "actual" well-being on persons who hold a different view. And Scanlon rightly extends this concern to the use of any particular account of well-being in the context of moral reasoning; he might thus say that the demands of moral theories should be assessed according to an account of general well-being that no one could reasonably reject. See "Value, Desire, and the Quality of Life," 195–99. My remarks about controversy over conceptions of well-being that follow in the text show that I am actually in rough agreement with Scanlon here.

described in terms of basic needs, but rather in terms of pleasures forgone, lost leisure time, career dissatisfaction, and the like. But it is hardly more plausible to deny that these latter reduce actual well-being than it is to embrace a principle of beneficence that does not require us to promote basic human needs. And to accept this claim about what counts as a demand is not to adopt preference hedonism as our general account of well-being, for such goods would surely figure in any plausible substantive-good account of well-being.[28]

There are, however, views that cut across the various accounts of well-being that I have been discussing and that raise some doubts of a different kind. One might, for example, allow that as a hypothetical matter complying with the optimizing principle of beneficence would reduce most people's well-being, but insist that the only people who actually *will* comply are in fact likely not to live a worse life because of it. For the only people likely to be able to bring themselves to comply with the optimizing principle of beneficence are those who already have preferences, desires, or projects that are compatible with the principle's requirements.[29] This should not be confused with a claim of psychological egoism, which asserts the impossibility of doing what is worse for oneself. The claim is just that the really dramatic requirements of the optimizing principle of beneficence would in practice only be met by people whose personal good for the most part coincides with those requirements. This claim seems plausible, but it does not undermine my claim that the optimizing principle of beneficence is extremely demanding, in that compliance with it would bring great loss for most people. The fact that for most people the principle is so demanding that they are very unlikely ever to comply with it does not undermine the claim that the principle is, indeed, so very demanding.

A somewhat similar idea might seem to lead to a more damaging conclusion. People whose preferences, goals, and projects are quite contrary to what the optimizing principle requires may be able to change their lives without much loss, for they may be able to identify with the life that is required of them—in part for the very reason that they believe that it is morally required—embracing its goals and projects and developing preferences in harmony with it. On this story many complying agents will suffer no more than the transitional losses of disruption.[30] But whatever may be the typical case, it seems to me clear that people are capable of living their lives, and continuing to do so over long periods, with the awareness both that this is ethically good or required and that it is disastrous for their well-being. Consider someone who has a child that is so severely handicapped that it both needs constant attention and lacks any emotional life. The parent might think, rightly, that it would be better for him if the child lived elsewhere. It is simply not true that his own self-interest argues in favor of caring for the child at home; he cares for the child himself because he believes that it is better for the child, and that it would be "a terrible thing" to send the child to an institution.

My preliminary discussion of the assessment of demands has thus provided no reason to retract the claim that in the actual world of minimal compliance with the optimizing principle of beneficence, most agents would, if they complied, sustain great losses in well-being.

IV. Losses or Absolute Level?

As I have presented it, the problem of over-demandingness concerns the size of the losses that can flow from compliance with certain moral principles. But there is an importantly different way to think about the problem. In addition to, or instead of, a concern with the size of losses, there might be a concern about complying agents' falling below a certain absolute level of well-being.[31] On the absolute-level view, certain moral theories are unacceptable because they leave complying agents at a level of well-being below a certain minimum; being left below the minimum is in itself objectionable, even if in a particular case the losses sustained were fairly small.*

In recent discussion of the problem of over-demandingness the absolute limit version is quite popular. For much of that discussion focuses on a particular conception of the minimally acceptable level—it is a life in which it is possible to enjoy close personal relationships and pursue personal projects. This focus on projects and relationships can be partly explained by the connection (discussed in the next section) between the problem of over-demandingness and that of alienation, and partly by the fact that Williams, whose writings are at the center of both discussions, restricts his own discussion of over-demandingness to the very special issue of "ground projects."[32] In any case, it is notable that one recent discussion styles the objection to the excessive demands of utilitarianism as the "nearest and dearest objection."[33]

Absent strong conclusions in the domain of the alienation problem, however, it is not obvious that compliance with the optimizing principle of beneficence is incompatible with the enjoyment of personal relationships. And once we move away from Williams's special notion of a "ground project," it is not obvious that the idea of a project is well enough defined to mark out a special aspect of human well-being. In any case, it is hard to see what would warrant exclusive focus on projects and relationships in defining the minimally acceptable level. Without dis-

---

*It might well be wondered by now what kind of baseline I have in mind for the measurement of the losses of compliance. The next chapter is devoted to that question.

cussing these issues further here, let me just state my view that a plausible minimum level of well-being would be understood in more general terms, placing more mundane goods such as health, pleasure, and absence of suffering in the same league as the goods of relationships and projects; I will return to the question of how the minimum level might be formulated in chapter 4.

In the critical discussion of the over-demandingness problem in the next two chapters, I will keep in mind both the losses and the absolute-level versions. Yet for the most part I will focus on the losses version, for the reason that it seems to me to be the more plausible. A huge loss in well-being that leaves me just above the minimum acceptable level seems much more objectionable prima facie than a very small loss that takes me just below the cutoff point. Of course if the minimal level is described in terms of some special goods that are lexically prior to all other aspects of my well-being, then falling from above to below that level will also be a great loss, and the two versions of the problem will coincide.[34] In any case, we do not have to decide between these two versions, for most of the criticisms of the next chapters will apply to both of them.

V. Alienation

The problem of alienation concerns motivations. Specifically, the worry is that the motivations modern "impartial morality" requires us to have are at odds with the motivations appropriate to personal relationships, or indeed to any activity regarded as intrinsically valuable.[35] By "impartial morality" is meant on the one hand utilitarianism, and on the other hand Kantianism or some other deontological account; the main contrast here is with "virtue ethics" of some form. Simplifying greatly, the idea is that when an agent complying with an impartial moral theory engages in some desirable activity, she must have as at least one of her motivations the thought that the activity is required or permissible; and though motivations directly aimed at the activity may be present, the fact that these direct motivations are accompanied by and contingent on thoughts of obligatoriness or permissibility means that agent cannot be committed to the activity as in itself valuable or indeed derive full value from it.

Let us suppose for a moment that this characterization of the motivational state of a complying modern moral agent is correct, and let us focus on the popular case of friendship. Suppose, then, that a complying modern moral agent is permitted to have friends, but that his motivations within the friendships are always accompanied by thoughts of permissibility. Suppose finally that genuine friendship is therefore simply not available to him.

If morally required motivations do ruin friendships in this way, our agent's life will go worse than it might, since the good of friendship should presumably be recognized by any plausible general account of well-being. Perhaps the complying agent should not be said to lack the good of friendship altogether, but rather to enjoy it to a lesser degree than someone whose motivations do not include the thought of permissibility. In either case the upshot would be that we had found a special and important way in which compliance with a moral theory can reduce the well-being of a complying agent. Thus we would be able to fold concerns about alienation into the problem of over-demandingness.

But it would be wrong to think that a special kind of effect on agents' well-being exhausts philosophers' interest in alienation. Consider what Williams says about the man who has "one thought too many"—he rescues his wife rather than someone else in part because he recognizes that it is permissible for him to do so. Williams emphasizes not that the man has a worse life than he might, but that his wife might have hoped that he had not had the extra thought.[36] Here, as in some other discussions of alienation, the point seems to be not that alienated people are worse-off, but that they are worse people. And perhaps they are worse not just in the sense that they make the people around them (in particular their spouses) worse-off; rather, the idea might be that a world of such people is a worse world in a sense not reducible to its having a lower aggregate level of well-being. If this is right, at least part of the problem of alienation cannot be seen just as a special aspect of the problem of over-demandingness.

I do not find this more ambitious interpretation of the problem of alienation especially compelling, but I will not try to do it justice here. Let me just point out that the characterization of the motivations of moral agents granted previously, and relied on as a premise in any interpretation of the alienation problem, is in fact highly contestable. In general, the question of the appropriate motivations of a complying agent is open to a variety of answers.[37] And the answers given will be determined by considerations specific to particular moral conceptions. Thus while the problem of alienation may be real for Kantians, it is not likely to be so for ordinary deontologists with no special interest in the moral worth of action done from the motive of duty.[38] Utilitarians will tell a different story again. Given our interest in beneficence, it is appropriate to have an outline of that story before us.

Utilitarianism requires us to have motives such that there is no other set of motives that it would be better for us to have; the optimizing principle of beneficence imposes the same requirement. Now utilitarianism would potentially face a problem of alienation if it required all agents always to be consciously disposed to do whatever will bring about the best outcome. But such "pure do-gooders," as Parfit calls them, are unlikely to have a high level of well-being, since so much of human well-being depends upon partiality for particular people and projects. This provides one reason that it would not be best for us all to be pure do-gooders; if we all always aimed for the best, we would be worse-off than we could be if we had different motives. In addition to impartial benevolence, then, it would be better if we also had some strong partial motives, and thus this is what utilitarianism and the optimizing principle of beneficence require.[39]

Now utilitarianism does not need to make the alienating requirement that people acquire partial motives out of a desire to promote general well-being. What is required is that the motives we in fact have are not ones it would be best for us to try to replace with others; and as it happens, partial motives come naturally.

Are the utilitarian's motivations appropriate to friendships and the like? According to this account, the partial motives are not always consciously accompanied by an impartial motive of, say, permissibility; but they do remain contingent, or conditional, and this may seem to raise a further objection. As Peter Railton puts it, the motivational structure of a utilitarian agent meets a counterfactual condition: "While he ordinarily does not do what he does simply for the sake of doing what's right, he would seek to lead a different sort of life if he did not think his were morally defensible."[40] Does the conditional nature of the utilitarian's partial motives show that the problem of alienation persists? The question is whether I can be committed to something as intrinsically valuable and derive full value from it even though my commitment is conditional and thus overridable. I agree with Railton that I can.[41]

Obviously, I have not done justice to the issues raised by the problem of alienation. But I hope I have said enough to suggest that so long as a moral theory can allow its complying agents to have and act on partial motives, and barring special views about the worth of the motive of duty or the like, it is as controversial to assert as it is to deny that there is a residual problem of alienation—either as an aspect of the problem of over-demandingness or as a separate, more exotic problem.

It must be noted, however, that it is not necessarily the case that the optimizing principle of beneficence *does* allow its complying agents to have and act on partial motives. As Parfit points out, in a situation of minimal compliance, such as currently prevails, it would be better for some of us to become pure do-gooders.[42] This would be another source of extreme demands from the optimizing principle of beneficence under partial compliance, which would of course need to be recognized as an important aspect of the problem of over-demandingness.

VI. A Digression:
Blameless Wrongdoing

I have said that part of the problem of alienation, to the extent that there is one, can be seen as an aspect of over-demandingness. In this section

I will consider a different connection between the two problems: what I have said to defend the optimizing principle of beneficence from the charge of alienation might point the way to a partial defense against the charge of over-demandingness.[43]

We saw that the optimizing principle of beneficence will, in favorable circumstances, permit agents to have and act on partial motives.[44] On occasion, however, these partial motives will cause agents to choose actions that are less beneficial than some other possible action. I might out of love for my brother benefit him at the expense of some stranger, even though the stranger's need is much greater. If it would be better in the long run for me to keep my love for my brother than to lose it, it would be wrong for me to try to lose it. And even if we imagine a case where the benefit I could now bring the stranger is great enough to outweigh the long-term bad effects of my losing my partial motive, we could assume that until now it *would have been* worse, in terms of expected benefits, for me to try to lose the motive than to keep it; moreover, I cannot now suddenly rid myself of my motive. If it should be insisted that on any particular occasion I could act *against* my partial motive and do what I am required to do, it nevertheless remains true that my having this motive makes it much harder for me to act as required. These points show that the optimizing principle of beneficence must do more than assess my act as wrong, as if this kind of case were no different from ordinary acts of wrongdoing; the fact that I acted from a motive it would have been wrong for me to try to lose must surely affect the assessment of my act. On the other hand, however, since the evaluative scope of the optimizing principle of beneficence is not restricted to the motives people have,[45] it must condemn as wrong any action of mine that is less beneficial than some available alternative. Parfit's suggestion is that cases like this are instances of "blameless wrongdoing." The notion of blameless wrongdoing provides a principle that evaluates actions *and* motives with a way of responding to the apparent conflicts this generality can generate.

The notion of blameless wrongdoing is a supplement to utilitarianism, which does not offer an account of blameworthiness. Sidgwick held that for a utilitarian, praiseworthiness or blameworthiness was simply a matter of the expedience of praising or blaming in particular cases.[46] But this is to deny that there is any separate issue of when people are, in fact, praiseworthy or blameworthy. Cases of blameless wrongdoing, in Parfit's sense, are not cases where blaming the agent would make things worse; rather, they are cases where blame would be illegitimate or unwarranted, because of the special nature of the motives involved.

Now the relevance of this to the over-demandingness objection is due to the possibility that many failures to comply with the optimizing principle of beneficence are caused by partial motives it would be wrong for agents to try to lose, and thus that these actions count as instances of blameless wrongdoing. This would not affect our conclusion that the optimizing principle of beneficence is extremely demanding. But it could be claimed that extreme demands are *less objectionable* to the extent that failing to live up to them would count merely as blameless wrongdoing.[47] This very plausible claim could be developed as follows. We could see blameless wrongdoing as lying between wrong action and failing to act supererogatorily—which is not wrong at all. There could be no objection to a moral theory's granting its mere approval to beneficial actions that bring great loss to agents: that it includes an extensive realm of the supererogatory is no grounds for objection to commonsense morality.* The objection is to theories that condemn failures to sustain great losses. And the condemnation involved in verdicts of blameless wrongdoing is much weaker than that involved in simple cases of wrongdoing. To that extent, then, the force of the over-demandingness objection is weakened.

The problem with the suggestion we are considering is that the scope of its application is very narrow—for reasons that are by now familiar.[48] Failures to live up to the extreme demands of the optimizing principle of beneficence will count as blameless wrongdoing only in circumstances far removed from our own. I have already noted that while it would not make the outcome best if we all were to become pure do-gooders, it may—in our circumstances of minimal compliance—be best for some of us to become pure do-gooders. And the extent to which it would be best for agents to retain their partial motives does not just depend on the level of compliance. If we imagine a sudden turn to (nonoptimal) full compliance, it is still not clear, in current conditions, that it would not be best for at least some of us to be pure do-gooders. In any case, the possibility of required pure do-gooding is actually not the central issue here. Even if we suppose that no one is ever required to be a pure do-gooder, it is clear that in any situation short of optimal full compliance the optimizing principle of beneficence requires us to keep our partial motives sufficiently roped in for us to be able to perform acts of impartial beneficence without great difficulty. And, indeed, it is clearly possible to combine commitment to spouses and friends with very great personal sacrifice in the name of making things in general go better.[49]

Perhaps in a situation of optimal full compliance most failures to comply with stringent demands from the optimizing principle would count as blameless wrongdoing. Here it is plausible to think that an optimal set of motives would have as its most prominent members various strong

---

*Following Sidgwick, I use the expression "commonsense morality" to refer to what we could call the normative status quo; "ordinary morality" (Kagan's term) or "bourgeois morality" would do just as well. My use of "commonsense morality" should not be taken to imply that all people, or even all members of the Western bourgeoisie, share anything like a complete moral conception. For example, as emphasized in chapter 1, there is enormous disagreement about the shape of required beneficence.

partial motives, including self-directed motives, coupled with some standing dispositions to support certain institutions, to respond in rescue situations, to refrain from violence, and so forth. In the rare case where ordinary impartial beneficence is required, it may be difficult for agents with these ideal motives to comply, and if they do not it may count as blameless wrongdoing. This provides another reason to think that the optimizing principle of beneficence may raise no problem of over-demandingness under conditions of optimal full compliance.[50] But under nonoptimal full compliance, or in our own situation of minimal compliance, few failures to act as required by the optimizing principle of beneficence would count as blameless wrongdoing. And, as was said once before, we cannot solve the problem of over-demandingness by stipulating a situation of optimal full compliance.

VII. Confinement

Suppose that I live in Germany. On my walk to work each day I can take either of two routes, one of which crosses a patch of grass. The route with the grass is on the whole less pleasant than the other and is also slightly longer. Out of the blue one day, after years of taking the superior route, I have a whim to try the other—until I remember that walking on grass is most strictly forbidden. This kind of case might suggest that not all of the costs of compliance with a moral theory can be understood in terms of diminished well-being. Of course there are trivial losses in well-being here; after all, the frustration of my whim is presumably irksome, and though the other route is inferior there might have been some pleasure in the variation. But even if we suppose that my well-being is not at all reduced in this case, the fact remains that an option has been cut off. Taking the other route is one less thing that I am permitted to do; this could seem to impose a cost on me quite apart from any effect on my well-being. Moreover, morality does not just permit or forbid acting on one's wants; it permits or forbids actions one has no concern about one way or another.[51] Perhaps it is plausible to think that the more one is permitted to do the better—regardless of what one wants to do and of anything else relevant to one's well-being.

Following Samuel Scheffler, we can say that a moral theory is confining to the extent that it narrows the range of permissible options for action.[52] Scheffler lists confinement as one of two factors that determine the degree of a moral theory's demandingness, the other factor being the costs sustained by complying agents.[53] But I will continue to construe the problem of over-demandingness strictly in terms of losses of well-being. Thus for us the question is whether there is a distinct problem of confinement.

If there is a problem of confinement, it is easiest to illustrate with utilitarianism and other theories that include the optimizing principle of beneficence, for it is easy to see that such theories are potentially extremely confining. The optimizing principle of beneficence ranks all possible actions not otherwise morally spoken for, and in some circumstances this ranking will leave only a very few options tied for first place: the principle will require us to perform some one action, or one of some very few actions, out of all those that are available.

However, it is important to remember that there are also circumstances in which the optimizing principle of beneficence will not be nearly so confining, as the ranking of available actions will leave very many options tied for first place. To illustrate this variation, think of the range of career options available to a complying agent in current circumstances.[54] It is plausible to say that for most people the only permissible option is the one that will bring in the most money—so that most of that money can be redistributed—and also plausible to say that this rules out all but a few safe routes to riches. A successful college student in the United States who is choosing between law school and trying an acting career (or heading for the surf and waitressing for money, or pursuing graduate work in philosophy, or architecture . . .) should certainly choose law school, and once graduated should work for the highest paying law firm she can; later she should aim to "make partner," or perhaps move on to a job at an investment bank if that pays better, but not even think, for example, of taking up a teaching position. But in better circumstances, indeed even in circumstances of far-from-optimal full compliance, there might be dozens of career paths that are roughly equally beneficial from which our student could therefore permissibly choose. With everyone contributing, it would no longer be true that each complying agent must focus on helping to meet the world's most urgent needs, thus concluding that she should simply raise as much money as possible; in thinking of what career would be most beneficial, agents could consider the full range of goods associated with different options. And thus they would have a far wider range of options, since so many different careers are valuable either in themselves or instrumentally. Of course some careers are ruled out; someone who has always wanted to be a pirate will not be permitted to try this out. But this degree of confinement is imposed by any plausible moral view.

It might be thought that my example is misleading. Even if under favorable circumstances the optimizing principle will permit a variety of different careers, will it not still be terribly confining on a day-to-day basis? When our complying agent gets up in the morning to go off to work as an architect or whatever, will she not face a series of practical decisions that will be resolved by the optimizing principle into one or at most a few options for action? Perhaps in the work context there are often but a few "right" answers to the stream of practical questions faced. But it is hard to see that this kind of confinement is objectionable, since ordinary standards of responsibility on the job confine to the same degree. And when our agent comes home from work, her principle of beneficence will not give her a specific answer to the question of what to do for entertainment that night.

So it is not the case that the optimizing principle of beneficence is *essentially* extremely confining. But it nevertheless is very confining in some circumstances, such as those that now obtain; and of course we cannot solve the problem of confinement by stipulating favorable circumstances.

Now although the optimizing principle gives us our clearest case, it would be wrong to think that no other moral principle can be extremely confining. Most ordinary deontological principles can in some circumstances confine agents just as severely. If I am the American parent of a chronically and severely sick child and have no health insurance, a special obligation to care for my child might leave me with no option but to do whatever will bring in the most money so I can spend it on the medical bills; this situation could persist for very many years. But it would also be wrong to think that extreme confinement was a feature just of positive requirements, such as special obligations or beneficence. If I am told to cooperate with a murderous regime, with the likely result that others will be betrayed and killed, ordinary negative deontological principles may well leave me with but one or two permissible options—presumably flight or acceptance of my own demise.[55] Moral confinement of this kind is not now common in the industrial West, but for various places at various times the story is of course not in the least fanciful.

So there are possible circumstances in which the mostly negative prescriptions of standard deontological accounts will be extremely confining—just like the optimizing principle of beneficence. The difference is that the circumstances that result in extreme confinement are more widespread for the optimizing principle of beneficence than for standard deontological accounts. At least, this is the case now and for the foreseeable future; it may not have been the case prior to the technological developments that so greatly increased the ability of ordinary people to promote the well-being of others. And it bears repeating that for very many people in some parts of the world deontological constraints are even now likely to confine choices much more than the optimizing principle of beneficence.

Why might the potential for extreme confinement raise a problem for moral theories? We can begin our answer by investigating how much of the alleged problem of confinement might be accounted for within the problem of over-demandingness. To do this, we need to determine the extent to which a concern about confinement can after all be understood as a concern about effects on the well-being of complying agents.

Confinement reduces an agent's well-being in a direct way whenever the agent would have been better off pursuing impermissible rather than permissible options. So we might think that what is so objectionable about the restriction on career choice described earlier is just that the person would have been so much better off as an actress, say, than slaving away in an extremely well-paid job she could do but hated. I am inclined to think that this is indeed a big part of what seems so objectionable in that story. But the problem of confinement turns on the very fact that options are cut off, not with what is lost when particular options are cut off.

I can think of three ways in which a reduction in options might in itself affect an agent's well-being. The least important possibility is that a highly confining theory could give agents an irksome *feeling* of being confined. This seems hardly likely to be all that is going on here, and we can leave it aside. The other two possibilities are potentially more important, but they are also more controversial. Consider again restrictions on career choice. We might think that the option of choosing a career that I do not presently want to choose, or have reason to choose, nevertheless has value for me.[56] The fact that someone is permitted to quit her job as a corporate lawyer and head off to Tahiti to "do a Gauguin" in itself increases her level of well-being, even though she has no desire at all to do this and no reason to think she would benefit from doing it. This suggestion is immediately plausible if we see the added value of nondesired options to consist in a resultant greater commitment to and thus flourishing in the chosen career—for reasons akin to some of Mill's arguments in "On Liberty." So on this suggestion the benefits that come from more extensive options for permissible action are similar to the benefits that can flow instrumentally form ordinary political liberty.

This leads us to the third and most important possibility: lack of confinement brings an *intrinsic* benefit of greater autonomy.[57] The relevant kind of autonomy would consist in the moral permissibility of choosing among a variety of possible actions; Michael Slote calls this "moral autonomy."[58] And the suggestion is that moral autonomy as defined is analogous in content and importance to political autonomy. Now some will reject the very idea of moral autonomy. After all, morality does not coerce in the way that governments and people do.[59] Moreover, there is irony in the suggestion that morality's constraint on our deliberations, much celebrated as the ground for the possibility of human autonomy, should instead be seen as its enemy. These points could be summed up intuitively: we should not see morality as an alien system, restricting our self-expression, but rather as just the opposite. On the other hand, it is true that if something is required or prohibited by morality it is required or prohibited by something; and the fact that it is only me (or my superego)[60] that can do any compelling does not entirely remove the point of talking in terms of compulsion, and thus reduction of autonomy. If this way of seeing the connection between moral requirements and autonomy is plausible, there is content to the assertion that the greater our moral autonomy, the better for us.

Leaving aside instrumental benefits, ordinary political autonomy can be understood in two importantly different ways: as a substantive good for a person (an aspect of individual well-being), or as a right—on some account of rights that does not reduce rights themselves to aspects of well-being. It is the first view that is relevant to our present discussion of ways that moral confinement could reduce an agent's well-being. Should we accept that moral autonomy is a part of individual well-being, and thus that agents are worse off to the extent that moral theories narrow the range of their morally acceptable options?

I doubt that we should accept this, but as with the other ways that moral confinement might be thought to reduce well-being, I do not aim to settle the question here. We have seen that there are a variety of ways in which a highly confining moral theory might make life worse for complying agents. Thus if highly confining moral theories are intuitively problematic, the problem of over-demandingness can provide part of the explanation.[61]

What might be objectionable about a highly confining theory other than that it might make agents worse off? It would obviously be empty to assert that agents have a *right* to do what they like with their lives and that highly confining theories infringe that right; this would be to argue against, say, utilitarianism, by pointing out that it conflicts with some other moral conception. We might do better by returning to the notion of moral autonomy. I said earlier that ordinary political autonomy can be understood in two ways: as an aspect of well-being, and as grounded in a right. On the second view, interferences with political autonomy are, simply, wrong, whatever impact they have on well-being. Is there a plausible view of moral autonomy analogous to this second view? This seems very doubtful. It is one thing to accept the idea that morality can in some sense exert a compulsive force on agents, but quite another to accept that a moral theory could, in some non-question-begging way, wrong us or do wrong.

But perhaps we are taking the phrase "moral autonomy" too literally. What is at stake need not be exactly analogous to any more familiar value. So let us approach the problem of confinement directly. An extremely confining moral theory conflicts with a certain ideal of the moral agent. It is simply morally unappealing, it could be said, to think that moral agents have their lives fully mapped out for them by the dictates of morality. Much more appealing is a picture of moral agents as having broad space for individual decision within limited constraints.[62] Now utilitarians are likely to find this line of thought question-begging as well, for the ideal just described matches so closely the actual life of an agent complying with standard deontological conceptions in favorable conditions. But it is hard to deny, I think, that the image of a utilitarian agent being guided in her every deliberation by a principle that always provides an answer, and that constrains her to a very narrow path through the space of possible options, is very unappealing. In certain moods the idea that all my decisions are in this sense already made for me can seem preposterous. It not only seems a poor way to live but also can seem to rob us of some kind of dignity that has ethical significance.

A closely related line of thought could be presented in Nagel's framework: we could say that for utilitarian agents the impersonal point of view takes up all the morally legitimate deliberative space, leaving no room for the personal point of view. Given that we are agents capable of both points of view, this swallowing up of the personal is objectionable; a better understanding of the impersonal point of view would show that it is not the exclusive source of our reasons for action.[63]

Having presented these two arguments, however, we need to remind ourselves that no moral theory, utilitarian or otherwise, is *necessarily* extremely confining and that, on the other hand, all familiar theories are *potentially* extremely confining. So the picture of the utilitarian agent employed in the arguments just given is misleading: the most we can say is that a utilitarian agent is more likely to have all her decisions made for her than are agents embracing some other moral conception. But when we acknowledge this, the power of the problem seems to be weakened. If no familiar theory can guarantee plenty of options for us to deliberate over, or an extensive practical role for the personal point of view, the most we can say is that we prefer theories that are less likely to be very confining. And having retreated to this, it is no longer persuasive to say that what is at stake is the very nature of moral agency. That would be a plausible conclusion if some familiar moral conceptions were essentially confining and others essentially not. But with all theories potentially confining and confinement a matter of degree and dependent on circumstances, it is hard to see that the nature or the ethical status of the moral agent is implicated at all. It is not as if we think that an agent following some standard deontological account who finds himself with only one permissible option for action somehow loses dignity as an agent, or has failed to recognize the reason-giving force of the personal point of view.

What I have just said depends crucially on my claim that there is no principled difference in the confinement that might come from the optimizing principle of beneficence and the confinement that might come from ordinary deontological moral conceptions. This claim could be challenged. It might be said that even though at the level of actual agents' options for action any theory is potentially extremely confining, there is a more abstract level of reflection from which we can see that the optimizing principle of beneficence is uniquely objectionable for what it implies about moral agency. If so, the importance of the problem of confinement would be established after all.

One thought along these lines is that it is only because of the epistemological limits of human agents that the optimizing principle is not always very confining. If agents had perfect knowledge, it could be said, there would hardly ever be two or more options tied for first place. And so the optimizing principle is indeed confining in its very nature: it is only in the practice of actual agents that a choice between actions emerges. There are two things to say here.

First, on any conception of well-being a principle of beneficence employs, there will be many ties even with perfect information. For it is very implausible to believe that comparisons of well-being, especially interpersonal comparisons, are in principle precise. This means that there will be many ties where we say, not that two possible actions are equally good, but that neither is better than the other.[64] The second point is that the epistemological limits in question are themselves limits in principle. It is not as if we can hope for the day when our information-gathering abilities are such that we can predict with anything approaching certainty the different levels of benefit that would be produced by the various careers open to a twenty-year-old in favorable circumstances. Apart from predicting her own future successes and failures, we would need information about the future activities of everyone else, since that too greatly affects the benefits that would flow from different careers. When we reflect on the intractable uncertainties involved here, it becomes clear that our current situation—where, due to the three facts of extraordinary levels of need, the ability of the well-off to combat this, and minimal expected compliance, it *is* plausible to say that we know what it would be best for people to do with their lives—is exceptional rather than the reverse. If the claim is that the optimizing principle of beneficence would always be very confining if, per impossibile, we had perfect information about all possible futures, then of course my remarks are not to the point. But neither it is clear what relevance this claim could have to the nature or status of moral agents.

Another possible higher-level objection might be to the fact that the optimizing principle of beneficence "has something to say" about any possible situation.[65] On one interpretation, this objection depends on the implausible claim that there are some situations that are in principle not subject to moral assessment—that morality is not, as Scheffler puts it, pervasive.[66] On a different interpretation, the problem is that the optimizing principle of beneficence always assesses the available options, whereas a deontological principle will often simply not apply. But this seems a false distinction. The optimizing principle assesses all options for expected benefits; a prohibition on harming assesses all options for the presence of any harming actions. It would be arbitrary and misleading to say that the prohibition has nothing to say about options that involve no harming. It is true that a principle of beneficence might distinguish between two actions that a prohibition on harming treats as morally equivalent. But then that will be because there is a difference between the two actions that the principle deems relevant. In the same way a prohibition on harming would distinguish between two actions that are equally beneficial, and thus morally equivalent from the point of view of beneficence, if one of these actions but not the other would involve harming someone.

There may be other ways of motivating a problem of confinement that does not reduce to concerns about agents' well-being. But from what has been said so far, the case for regarding the problem of confinement as just an aspect of the problem of over-demandingness seems fairly strong. Confinement can reduce well-being indirectly, in that options that would be good for an agent are cut off. More interestingly, the very fact of having fewer options might reduce well-being, either because of certain instrumental bad effects that would flow, or because of a reduction in moral autonomy, where this is conceived of as an intrinsic good. Though I cannot claim to have established this, it is my sense that these effects on well-being are all there is to the problem of confinement.

3

DOUBTS ABOUT
OVER-DEMANDINGNESS

Of the three problems that might be raised about moral demands so far considered, over-demandingness has emerged as the problem to reckon with. What we will now see is that this problem, apparently so natural and so compelling, runs into severe difficulties of its own. These difficulties have already been alluded to in passing: a close investigation of the notion of a moral demand leaves it very unclear just what claim we make when we say that a moral theory is too demanding.

I. The Problem of the Baseline

What we know so far about moral demands is that a moral principle is demanding to the extent that compliance with it imposes a loss on the agent, where losses are understood as reductions in well-being (on whatever is the best general account of well-being). But to measure a loss we need to know not only how well-off a complying agent is, but also how well-off she would be if she did not comply. In other words, we need a baseline for assessments of loss. This is where things start to become very murky for the problem of over-demandingness. And the difficulties do not only afflict the version of the problem that is concerned with losses; as we will see in section VII, analogous difficulties also afflict the version that is concerned with agents falling below a certain minimally acceptable level of well-being.[1]

The problem of the baseline is not merely technical. Different possible baselines represent different possible normative perspectives from which the problem of excessive moral demands might be thought to arise, and thus different possible interpretations of the problem of over-demandingness. That there should be these different possible interpreta-

34

tions is not surprising. Over-demandingness is, after all, an unusual moral problem: a problem not for people but for moral theories. And so the question immediately arises, Where in normative space do we stand when we raise such a problem? To approach an answer to this question, we have to investigate various possibilities.

The easiest way to proceed is to begin with what I think is the best available answer and work back from there. My conclusion will be that demands, the losses that would be sustained by a complying agent, should be measured against a baseline of the factual status quo: how things are now and can be expected to be in the future.[2] This is hardly exciting, and it might seem to be obviously right at face value. As we will see, however, the adoption of the baseline of the factual status quo forces us to reconsider our understanding of the problem of over-demandingness.

The baseline of the factual status quo counts all the losses agents would in fact be expected to incur as a result of complying with a moral theory in prevailing circumstances. Thus, if I am required to give up goods that I have under my control and can in the circumstances expect to keep under my control, a demand is made on me; but no demand is made if the goods will be taken from me in any case. Being required to devote my life to famine relief counts as a demand so long as I can expect to do other things with my life if I so choose. Similarly, a constraint against killing imposes a demand to the extent that I would gain if I killed, so long as I can expect to be able to carry out the killing if I try. We can say that according to the baseline of the factual status quo a moral theory makes demands on an agent to the extent of any losses he does or would suffer *just because* of his compliance with the moral theory.*

The baseline of the factual status quo implies that the less powerful one is, and the more brutish one's neighbors, the lower the demands one faces from certain moral principles. This might seem to be unacceptable. But on reflection it is obvious that the demands agents face are affected by their natural abilities and social circumstances. If I can never hang on to anything for long before someone takes it away, then the loss to me that flows from being required to give it away is less than the loss that would flow if I could secure my possessions. And, to take the opposite case, the demands made by some moral principles on those who are very rich and powerful are much greater than for the rest of us. People who have more money under their control have more to lose from a principle of beneficence, and people who have the resources required for spectacular acts of theft face greater demands from a constraint prohibiting theft.**

---

*The effect on an agent of the complying behavior of *others* is discussed in section III and following sections.

**Greater, at least, than those faced by us ordinarily well-off people; once you get to be poor, the demands of constraints against theft rise again.

However, there are further and deeper grounds for objecting to our baseline. The requirement that a thief return stolen goods to their owner imposes a cost on a complying thief, but there appears to be a significant difference between such a cost and the cost of, say, giving one's money away for development aid. When thinking about cases like this, it is immediately tempting to think that we should assess demands not from the baseline of the factual status quo but rather from some normative baseline. Perhaps we should say that a moral requirement imposes demands to the extent that complying agents will lose something they are *entitled* to. Since the thief is not entitled to the goods in the first place, no demand is made when she is required to return them.

Pursuing this idea for the moment, what notion of entitlement might be appropriate? One possibility is that in the assessment of the demands of a given theory we should count agents as entitled to whatever that very theory counts them as entitled to. So, for example, if we are assessing the extent of the demands made by utilitarianism in respect of agents' possessions, we should use utilitarianism's account of possessory entitlement as our baseline. On that account I am entitled to only those of my possessions of which it is true that transferring them to someone else would not make the outcome better. As Godwin puts it, "Every shilling in my pocket has received its destination from the dictates of reason."[3] But if we use this principle of entitlement to fix our baseline for assessing demands, utilitarianism never makes any demands in respect of possessions—for agents never are entitled to those goods they are required to give away. Indeed, it is easy to see that this line of thought leads to the defining away of all demands. Since my moral theory morally governs my life, if it requires me to do something, I am not morally entitled to do anything else; so what I lose when I act as required is not something I am entitled to, and no demand is made.

We defined away all moral demands because we looked for the appropriate notion of entitlement "inside" the theories whose demands we wanted to assess. Perhaps we will do better with an *external* notion of entitlement. To find an appropriate external notion of entitlement we would have to fall back on our intuitive judgments of when a demand is made and when it is not. Standing outside given moral conceptions, that is all we have to go on. Let us return, then, to the intuitive point that no demand is made when a thief is required to return stolen goods. We seem to discount, in our assessment of demands, losses stemming from ill-gotten gains. Thus we might also believe that if a rich minority whose riches stem from exploitation is required to redistribute its riches among those it exploited, no demands are made.[4] These cases could suggest that we should measure demands from a baseline of what we are entitled to by what might be called "minimal morality."[5] This standard would have implications beyond the cases of ill-gotten gains. For example, even if people lose by not being morally permitted to murder, the constraint against murder imposes no demands, since under minimal morality the option to murder is presumably not something they are entitled to.

Now the suggestion that we should measure demands against a baseline of what we are entitled to by "minimal morality" is pretty clearly unacceptable, at least in this simple form. The over-demandingness objection forms part of a discussion of what the best moral theory might be. If we say that demands are made only to the extent that losses go beyond the losses involved in "minimal morality," we will in effect be using a conception of entitlement that is *internal* to some one moral conception in assessing the demands of all moral conceptions. This would undermine the force of objecting to any particular theory on the ground that it is too demanding.

The superficial appeal of the "minimal morality" baseline is easy to explain: it is the baseline of the normative status quo. The status quo moral conception in developed countries includes, centrally, constraints against violence and interference with property. Requirements of beneficence are typically considered to be over and above this "minimal" set of moral rules. The "minimal morality" baseline thus defines away the demands of the various supposedly minimal deontological principles, but counts the demands of beneficence. It defines away demands that, for those of us who are fairly well-off in current circumstances, are typically not that great, and counts as demanding only those principles we do not currently follow. So-called commonsense morality comes out imposing no demands at all, whereas, say, utilitarianism imposes extreme demands.

It might help here if I give some examples of the extreme demands that, intuitively, can come from parts of morality other than beneficence—for they are typically neglected.[6] An obvious case is the starving person who must steal or assault to get food, thus violating deontological constraints. Of course it might be said that a constraint against theft gives way in the face of dire need. But we can consider more serious constraints. Fifth-century Athenians would have suffered enormous losses from the abolition of slavery.[7] Much worse is the case, already mentioned, of victims of violent dictatorships who face the choice of betraying their associates or being tortured.[8] And the demands of deontology also fall heavily on those for whom a life on the straight and narrow offers so little that, for example, drug dealing with its associated violence offers substantial relative benefits. Certain so-called special obligations can also impose extreme demands. One example is that of a fairly poor person who must provide care for a very sick or very retarded family member.*

---

*Extreme demands from special obligations can fall on people who are otherwise very well-off as well, so it may seem that we could not put neglect of this kind of demand down to the complacency of the better-off. But the point in the text is the negative one that the demands of beneficence stand out as problematic for the better-off because these are demands it is almost certain that almost all of them face.

Demands such as these would presumably not count as such under the minimal morality baseline. That depends, of course, on what the content of minimal morality is taken to be; but this just points to a further problem with the minimal morality baseline—there is no uncontroversial account of the content of minimal morality. Of particular importance here is disagreement about a person's moral rights to property. The minimal morality baseline manages to disguise this disagreement only by tacitly treating legal rights as moral rights.

Now, in response to this last point, a more sophisticated entitlement baseline could be offered. Rather than claiming that there is some complete minimal moral conception available for us to appeal to, we could point to a set of considered moral judgments that form the background for discussions of those aspects of morality, such as beneficence, that remain controversial. In moral theory as in other areas of inquiry, it might be said, we must approach what is controversial from the standpoint of what is currently uncontroversial. In particular, it is appropriate to use as our baseline for the over-demandingness objection precisely those considered moral judgments that have not seemed to raise any problem of demands.[9]

A baseline of considered judgments, or what we might think of as interim normative conclusions, does avoid the crudeness of the idea of a fixed minimal morality and, more important, comes with the plausible rationale just laid out. However, the main problems that faced the minimal morality baseline remain. In the absence of agreement over property entitlement, the suggested baseline would have very little content; it would not move us far beyond the baseline of the factual status quo. Second, this more sophisticated suggestion does not alter the fact that if our baseline for the assessment of demands has the effect of defining away the demands of certain moral principles, we cannot point to extreme demands assessed in this way as posing an intrinsic problem for other moral principles; we cannot say that it is demands, *as such*, that we are talking about.

Now these last remarks might be thought to show that I have misunderstood the over-demandingness problem: the aim never was to come up with some assessment of demands that was neutral as between all moral conceptions; there is no need to do that. What is objectionable about utilitarianism is not that it is capable of imposing huge demands *as such*, but that it would impose huge demands on *decent people*.[10] On this interpretation, our considered moral judgments form a core of requirements that the minimally decent person will comply with, and we measure the demands of other requirements against a baseline of that core.

But if this is the right way to understand demands, their significance becomes obscure. To see this, we need to focus on what is in the core that captures minimal decency, and why. Suppose that a given theorist's

considered judgments do not support the optimizing principle of beneficence. In reflecting on whether such a principle is nevertheless plausible,
the theorist, according to the current suggestion, will take into account
the principle's extreme demands as measured against the core. But she
will only be able to do this at all because she has made a (provisional)
negative judgment about the optimizing principle of beneficence *prior* to
consideration of the question of demands. Whatever the merits of that
judgment, the upshot of this approach is that an objection to the demands of a moral principle is parasitic on some different and unrelated
ground for questioning it.[11]

Moreover, this account makes the very idea of a moral demand una-
vailable for those who believe either that the core of minimal decency
does include the optimizing principle of beneficence,[12] or that it would
do so but for the single problem of its apparent extreme demands. Of
course, if these people's initial convictions about what is decent and what
is not could be shaken, on grounds having nothing to do with demands,
a conversation about extreme demands would in turn start to make sense.
But that is a rather roundabout way of approaching what we thought
was an intuitively compelling problem.

It is obviously much more sensible to stick with the baseline of the
factual status quo and accept that all moral principles make demands.
Whether extreme demands made by different kinds of principle are objectionable can then be left for debate. The thoughts that led us to experiment with entitlement baselines are thus better understood as
thoughts about the significance of demands, not their existence.

This may seem to resolve all our difficulties. But in fact we have here
been led to the first important reason to doubt the force of the problem
of over-demandingness. For either extreme demands are objectionable as
such, or they are not. If they are, we must regard extreme demands as
objectionable whatever moral principle is involved. If they are not, we
cannot object to the optimizing principle of beneficence on the simple
ground that it is too demanding. Philosophers have not been rushing to
defend the idea that constraints against killing should be rejected or in
some way weakened because of the potential for extreme demands.[13] And
it seems likewise unlikely that many would argue that it is too demanding
to expect a group of robber barons to redistribute their riches among
those they have exploited. It seems, then, that we cannot object to the
optimizing principle of beneficence on the ground of extreme demands
either.

This conclusion is too quick. For it could be argued that while extreme
demands are indeed objectionable as such, it is only in the realm of
beneficence that the objection is conclusive. In all other parts of morality,
though extreme demands are objectionable in themselves, they are nevertheless acceptable all things considered.[14] Now it is very important to
see that this is a radical change in the objection to the optimizing prin-

ciple. We can no longer say, as I did in the previous chapter, that the problem of over-demandingness responds to a simple belief in a limit to the legitimate demands of morality; rather, we must say that it responds to a belief in a limit to the legitimate demands of beneficence.[15] But now, of course, we need to know much more. Why is it, exactly, that extreme demands, while not generally sufficient grounds for rejecting a moral principle, are sufficient grounds in the case of principles of beneficence?* Opponents of utilitarianism commonly point to the fact of extreme demands as the explanation and justification of their rejection of the theory. But it is clear that it is no such thing. We await an account of what it is about beneficence, *apart from the potential for extreme demands*, that makes the fact of extreme demands so problematic in this particular case.[16]

What is required is some kind of ranking that would allow us to say that principles of beneficence, being less central or important, cannot be extremely demanding, while all other moral principles, by contrast, are weighty enough to justify the imposition of extreme demands. I do not know what such an account would look like. It is true that it is widely held that deontological constraints trump beneficence in a conflict: I must not kill one to save five. But the mere fact that one kind of moral principle takes precedence over another in a conflict does not establish that the trumped principle is unimportant.[17] If rights are not absolute, they may still be extremely important; so, too, could be a trumpable principle of beneficence. Also familiar, and more to the point, is the thought that positive duties are generally less serious or important than negative duties; discussion of this issue typically focuses on the distinction between killing and letting die.[18] But this line of thought is not obviously helpful either because our focus is not on the difference between positive and negative duties. As we have seen, commonsense morality tolerates very high demands from certain positive special obligations, such as the obligation to care for a sick child.[19] Our task is to explain why it is only the demands of *beneficence* that must not be extreme. And it is noteworthy, moreover, that philosophers who discuss the relative stringency of positive and negative duties often provide an account that is the reverse of what we need—appealing to our tolerance of greater demands from neg-

---

*There is an additional problem that should be mentioned here: it is actually not the case that commonsense morality excuses "decent people" from extreme demands of beneficence altogether. Where one person is able to rescue another in an emergency situation, commonsense morality can impose very heavy demands, at least of a financial kind. So to save the problem of over-demandingness, we would also have to show that a requirement that one rescue a person in an emergency is not a requirement of beneficence, or that high demands from this requirement are for some other reason not problematic. I discuss rescue cases in detail in chapter 7, section 4.

ative duties as evidence of their greater weight,[20] or arguing that we had better accept that positive duties have lesser weight than negative duties, lest we be saddled with the absurd demands of the optimizing principle of beneficence.[21]

We cannot rule out the possibility of an account of the lesser importance of beneficence that explains why extreme demands from just this part of morality are unacceptable. (Though to save the problem of over-demandingness it must not prove too much: if beneficence is rejected wholesale, we once again lose the issue of demands.)[22] But it is striking that the debate about over-demandingness has scarcely even acknowledged the existence of extreme demands from elsewhere than beneficence, let alone the fact that they are objectionable. It seems that most philosophers do not, in fact, feel that the importance of deontological constraints is sufficient to overcome the objection stemming from high demands—but rather that the objection simply has no force at all in that context.

In any event, my own view is that we have already seen enough to undermine what seemed to be the powerful intuitive force of the problem of over-demandingness. Our excursion into entitlement baselines was, in effect, an attempt to save the problem by defining away the demands of moral principles other than those of beneficence. But once we see that this cannot be done without simply begging the question, we confront the fact that our objection to the optimizing principle of beneficence cannot after all be the simple one that it demands too much. Until we know why we should not tolerate extreme demands from principles of beneficence in particular, we have little reason to be confident that it is indeed the potential for extreme demands that makes the optimizing principle of beneficence seem absurd. Thus it may be that the problem with the optimizing principle is not over-demandingness but something else altogether.

I explore my own alternative account of what is wrong with the optimizing principle of beneficence in chapter 5. But, in the meantime, I want to put to one side the doubt about the problem of over-demandingness just raised. For that doubt is not in itself sufficient ground to dismiss the problem of over-demandingness as illusory; and there are further, more intricate difficulties yet to be considered.

II. Assessing Demands against the Status Quo

Before we can explain those further difficulties, we need to examine the baseline of the factual status quo in some more detail.

The Baseline Life

Note first that though the baseline of the factual status quo takes background circumstances as given, it cannot do the same for the behavior of the agent. Actual people's lives are at least imperfectly in compliance with various moral theories, and that fact must evidently be taken into account in our assessment. We cannot say that a moral theory makes no demands on a person who, in his actual life, will always follow that moral theory.

To settle on some terminology, we can say that an agent complies with some moral theory to the extent that he acts in the way that the theory requires.* Thus an agent who "always complies," or "perfectly complies," always acts as required, and an agent who "never complies" never acts as required. I use "imperfect compliance" to describe the middle category of agents who sometimes but not always act as required by the moral theory. In a world of partial compliance with some moral theory, there could be people in each of these three categories. It should be noted that the notion of compliance does not implicate in any way an agent's reasons or motives for acting as required or failing so to do.[23]

How, then, should we understand the baseline life of an agent in an assessment of demands? A possible first thought is that in her baseline life she never complies: we measure the demands of a moral theory by comparing the agent's expected well-being in a perfectly complying life with her expected well-being in a never-complying life. But such a measure would not capture what we seek to capture, which is the cost to the agent of complying with the moral theory. Since imperfect compliance with some moral theory might be better for an agent than never complying, we would distort our assessment if we used the never-complying life as the baseline. The appropriate measure of the demands of a moral theory is thus the difference between the agent's expected well-being as a perfect complier and her expected well-being in an optimally prudent life. This does capture the extent to which compliance makes life worse for the agent than (in the factual status quo) it could otherwise be.

This method of assessment has an interesting consequence. For two reasons, we can see that commonsense morality is less demanding on actual people than it would be if it did not occupy the normative status quo. In the first place, existing legal systems in most places attach penalties to various actions that are also prohibited by commonsense morality, with the result that the expected payoff from failing to act as required is less than it otherwise would be. Thus some of the potentially demanding requirements of commonsense morality that I have mentioned, such as, for very poor people, those prohibiting theft and violence,

---

*Acting as a theory requires can include trying to shape one's motivations.

are much less demanding than they would be in the absence of legal sanctions; in some cases, the requirements will impose no demands at all. By contrast, no legal penalties attach to failures to redistribute one's money to the extent required by the optimizing principle of beneficence. So we can see that existing legal systems do much to reduce the gap between an ordinary person's expected well-being as a perfect complier with commonsense morality and her expected well-being in an optimally prudent life.

The second way that commonsense morality benefits from its occupation of the normative status quo is due to the fact, noted in chapter 2, that a person who at some level accepts a certain set of moral principles will naturally structure his life, and have had it structured for him, so that the conflict between his own good and the requirements of these principles is reduced.[24] And so even without considering legal sanctions, it seems likely that for many people a hypothetical optimally prudent life would not be all that different, at least in the short run, from a life of perfect compliance.*

Now it may seem that these two sources of bias in favor of the normative status quo are as pernicious as the bias inherent in the entitlement baselines considered in the previous section. In the case of the second source of bias, that flowing from our tendency to reduce the gap between our own self-interest and the moral view we accept, this is not so. If our aim is to assess actual demands on actual people, we have no reason to want to try to avoid this kind of bias; still, it is instructive that we have here reached the limit of our ability to assess demands in a way that is fully neutral between all moral conceptions. The case is different, however, for the first source of bias. Even though existing legal systems can reduce the gap between a person's well-being as a complier and her well-being in an optimally prudent life, so that there is a sense in which it is true to say that the demands of the moral theory are lower as a result, there is also clearly another sense in which demands are made on such a person by the very legal system that alters the payoffs of her various choices. I return to this other way in which demands can be made in the next section.

Expected or Actual Costs?

Demands must be assessed "ex ante" rather than "ex post."[25] An ex ante assessment looks to the expected costs of compliance; an ex post assess-

---

*The life of perfect compliance could be *better* than the optimally prudent life if acting for the sake of duty (a motive that is compatible with, but not implied by, the account of compliance I am using) brings its own reward. In what follows I ignore the possibility of this kind of benefit from compliance.

ment would attempt to look to the actual costs of compliance. But such ex post assessments of demands are not possible. An assessment of demands compares two different extended courses of action—two different "lives"—for the agent. If we attempted an ex post assessment of the demands made on an actual complying person, we would compare her actual well-being over her perfectly complying life to her expected well-being in a baseline life of optimal prudence. This comparison would not give us an accurate measure of demands; it would not identify the losses the agent suffered just because of compliance.

To see why this is so, suppose that we are assessing the demands of utilitarianism on a complying agent who was required to move to a different part of the city to take up a job that brought in more money; in an optimally prudent life, she would certainly not have moved. Her actual level of well-being has turned out to be fairly high in her new life, as, to her surprise, she has found the new job satisfying. What has not been so good is that she has been mugged at gunpoint several times on her way home. Her new neighbors tell her she has been very unlucky. Do we count these muggings as part the costs of compliance? Even if we suppose that the ex ante probability of being mugged in her old neighborhood was close to zero, it would still not be appropriate to count the muggings as part of the costs of compliance. For our agent was unlucky to be mugged that many times in her new neighborhood, and it would be inappropriate to count her bad luck as a cost of compliance. What matters for an assessment of those costs is the difference her move made to her *chances* of being mugged, not how many times she was in fact mugged. If the ex ante odds of being mugged were equal in both neighborhoods, we should not count any of our agent's actual muggings as a cost of compliance.

The most accurate measure of the costs of compliance is thus the measure of the difference compliance makes to a person's expected well-being from some point onward. Now there will of course be special cases where the ex post perspective is adequate. Thus, if someone turns to compliance with utilitarianism and redistributes all his millions, we can fairly say, ex post, that the loss of money was a cost of compliance. But this is a case where the ex ante assessments approach certainty: ex ante, the probability that the agent would keep his millions is close to one for the baseline life, and the probability that he would lose his millions is close to one for the life of perfect compliance. With probabilities close to one, the ex ante and ex post perspectives roughly coincide. So this kind of case is not an exception to the rule that we assess demands ex ante. Moreover, this kind of case is likely to be comparatively uninteresting. To assess the demands on this agent, we want to know more than that he has lost his money; we want to know how this will affect his well-being over time. Once we move to the assessment that we are actually interested in, our ex ante assessments will no longer approach certainty.

We are close to very difficult issues here, but let me just add that the reason that we must assess demands ex ante is not that we have some concern to assess demands at some canonical point with fixed epistemic resources; rather, it is simply that we need to factor out luck in the assessment of demands. When our first agent discovers that she likes her new job, we can go back and revise our original ex ante assessment of her expected well-being in the complying life in light of this further information. We can do this because we believe that we have discovered something about her that was true all along. By contrast, we do not revise our assessment of the contribution muggings make to the costs of compliance just because she turns out to be unlucky with muggings; we revise only if we learn that the chances of being mugged were different than we thought they were.

Time

Having seen why we must always assess demands ex ante, we need now to discuss the question of the time period for the assessment of demands. The time period I will adopt, and from now assume unless I indicate otherwise, is the rest of an agent's life from some point onward. This is a natural choice, but it is not inevitable or uncontroversial. Given the way actual losses flow, it is clear that we could not sensibly talk of minute-by-minute demands, but periods shorter than the rest of an agent's life may be plausible. And the choice is not without consequence. Just as the promotion of long-term self-interest may bring short-term losses, a moral principle may be more or less demanding when the demands are assessed over periods shorter than the rest of an agent's life. However, this is probably only rarely the case; so even if assessing demands over the rest of an agent's life is ultimately not defensible, it seems unlikely that it would greatly distort the discussion of over-demandingness. This is fortunate, because the choice of time period may depend in part upon the criteria of personal identity—an issue I obviously cannot try to discuss here.[26]

What does seem likely to make a difference, however, is the particular time in an agent's life we choose as the starting point for our assessment. In the previous chapter I argued that contemporary ordinarily well-off and able-bodied adults face extreme demands from the optimizing principle of beneficence. But it is a salient fact about most such people that they have at best imperfectly complied with the optimizing principle in their lives thus far. If they had perfectly complied thus far, the demands from now on would doubtless be much less severe. A lifelong perfect complier at age forty would, we can assume, have far fewer resources to lose than a lifelong imperfect complier or never complier at the same age; the lost opportunities for consumption would thus be less for the perfect complier. The lifelong perfect complier would also probably have interests and wants that are more cheaply satisfied than those of the imperfect complier—who, even if she could now successfully mold her interests to her new constraints, would suffer at least great transitional losses.[27]

Assuming that this is so, the following thought arises. If a moral principle makes extreme demands, from now, on only those people who have not perfectly complied in the past, those extreme demands are not objectionable. For why should it be objectionable that demands build up after a lifetime of wrongdoing? There is only an objection if people who perfectly comply throughout their lives face extreme demands.[28] If this is right, the relevant point in an agent's life for the assessment of demands would seem to be the very first point at which she is morally responsible; only then would we be able to make sure that we do not take into account demands that an agent would not have faced if she had perfectly complied throughout her life.

If we are pushed to the first point in an agent's (morally responsible) life as the only appropriate point for the assessment of demands, however, the difference between the demands on our two agents disappears. For if the agents are in all other respects similar, they faced the same demands from the start of life.

Now there is an obvious epistemological problem facing assessments of demands from the start of life: since we do not know any people who have perfectly complied with the optimizing principle of beneficence throughout their lives, any claim about the extent of the demands faced at the start of a life of perfect compliance with the optimizing principle would be far more speculative than the claims about demands on contemporary adults that I made in the previous chapter. How serious a problem this is depends on how accurate an assessment of demands we need, a question that, in turn, depends on our purposes in assessing demands. If we need even a rough quantitative measure of demands faced by actual people, as we would to implement the kind of limited principle of beneficence discussed in the next chapter, it would seem to be very serious. Fortunately, our aim so far has been the more modest one of identifying cases where a moral principle can plausibly be said to impose extreme demands on someone. This aim requires no specification of the actual quantum of demands; and though the claim that a life of perfect compliance with the optimizing principle of beneficence—as assessed from the start of life—is extremely demanding is indeed speculative, it seems to me very hard to deny. Likewise, various deontological constraints can fairly clearly impose extreme demands from the start of responsible life. One example would be that of a very badly off person in a society, such as, perhaps, post-Soviet Russia, where criminal enforcement is lax and the potential benefits from criminal activity are very high, especially relative to the alternatives. Another might be that of a young person who finds that she must, upon the death of her parents, immediately set out to make as much money as possible, for the foreseeable future, in order to provide for her severely retarded younger brother.

Now, it would obviously be preferable if we could avoid the epistemological complications involved in a start-of-life point of assessment. But to do this, we would have to establish the irrelevance of history in the assessment of demands. Perhaps this could be done. Even if a person would not face extreme demands from now on if he had perfectly complied in the past, it could be said, it is still objectionable that he does in fact face them now—whatever is the case about the demands he faced from the start of life. For the over-demandingness problem treats bygones as bygones; what matters is not what demands would be faced by lifetime perfect compliers, but what demands can be faced by people as they actually are. This approach does not seem entirely implausible, but I will not discuss it further here. Both the normative issue of the relevance of history and the epistemological problem that turns on it would repay extensive discussion, but in the context of this chapter's skeptical stance, it is appropriate to move on.

Combining various points, then, we can say that according to the baseline of the factual status quo, a moral theory makes demands on an agent at a particular time to the extent of the expected losses, over the rest of his life from that point on, that fall to him just because he will always comply from then on; and that for the purposes of the over-demandingness problem, the appropriate point from which to assess demands appears to be the start of an agent's responsible life.*

III. Active and Passive Demands

We have seen that the baseline of the factual status quo does not assess a demand when the loss in question would have been forced upon the agent in any case. It is time to consider in detail a very important class of such forcings: those that are morally required by the theory in question. On most moral theories, the state is morally required to criminalize theft. And the result of moderately effective enforcement of the criminal law against theft, as I have already noted, is that most people who are neither very poor nor unusually powerful in some relevant way are more likely to lose than to gain from most acts of theft that they could carry out. Thus, for typical people the demands of the moral requirement that they not steal are low or nonexistent. Or consider the case of taxation. I

---

*In what follows I will typically not explicitly present claims about various kinds of demands in the framework of the start-of-life perspective, but all my claims could, more cumbrously, be recast in that framework.

am required to pay my taxes, but that amounts to a demand on me only to the extent that I can in my circumstances rationally expect to gain by not paying them. Under a taxation system with fully effective enforcement, the requirement that I pay my taxes would impose no demands at all.

The upshot of using the baseline of the factual status quo is that a moral scheme that is perfectly enforced through law can impose no demands. This seems absurd. But rather than reconsidering entitlement baselines, our response should be to distinguish two different kinds of demands. The demands I have been discussing thus far are those made on our voluntary behavior. Following F. M. Kamm, we can call them *active demands*. But also intuitively important are the demands that morality imposes on us, not through our own compliance, but through the compliance of others. We can call these *passive demands*.[29] In all areas of commonsense morality we can face passive demands, but the normative domain where passive demands are most significant is that of political justice.[30] Passive demands imposed by legal institutions will only sometimes take the form of actual physical compulsion; but influencing behavior by attaching prices to various options is just as clearly a way of imposing a demand.

We can now see that the over-demandingness problem is more complex than has so far been indicated. There are two kinds of demands, the active and the passive, and it is important that we take both into account when determining how demanding a theory is. For if we ignored the burdens flowing to our target agent from other agents complying with a given theory, we would end up with an artificially low assessment of overall demands.

As soon as we acknowledge this, moreover, it becomes clear that it is also true that we would end up with an artificially *high* assessment of overall demands if we ignored the *benefits* that flow to our target agent from other people complying with the theory. There is surely no reason to be interested in the measure of how other people complying with a theory will burden our agent without also being interested in how this will benefit him. What we are interested in, in fact, is the *net effect* the compliance of others with a moral theory has on our agent's well-being. This *net passive effect* may be either a burden or a benefit, and in either case it should be considered alongside the measure of active demands when determining the overall demands of a moral theory.

The recognition of the distinction between active and passive demands is progress in our understanding of over-demandingness, but it is progress that will generate further serious ground for doubt. For we shall see that there seems to be no suitable way to assess passive effects under partial compliance; this effectively undermines our ability to raise the objection of over-demandingness against the optimizing principle of beneficence. But even leaving aside problems of assessment, we will also see that a proper understanding of the passive effects of plausible moral theories forces us to adopt a quite different understanding of what it is to charge a moral theory with being too demanding. The only way to make sense of passive effects, it turns out, is to change the subject.

But before pursuing this skeptical argument, we need to pay some attention to the salient difference between active and passive demands— which is that the former, but not the latter, must engage the will. For it may be thought that the problem of over-demandingness is precisely about extreme demands on the will, and thus that passive effects can be ignored, or at least treated very differently. Some remarks of Thomas Nagel are relevant here:

> Sometimes it is proper to force people to do something even though it is not true that they should do it without being forced. It is acceptable to compel people to contribute to the support of the indigent by automatic taxation, but unreasonable to insist that in the absence of such a system they ought to contribute voluntarily. The latter is an excessively demanding moral position because it requires voluntary contributions that are quite difficult to make. Most people will tolerate a universal system of compulsory taxation without feeling entitled to complain, whereas they would feel justified in refusing an appeal that they contribute the same amount voluntarily. This is partly due to lack of assurance that others would do likewise and fear of relative disadvantage; but it is also a sensible rejection of excessive demands on the will, which can be more irksome than automatic demands on the purse.[31]

Now, in pointing to the additional *irksomeness* of demands on the will, Nagel does not suggest that the two kinds of demand have fundamentally different statuses. Nagel is rather pointing out that voluntarily giving up a certain amount of money may occasion a greater real loss than does the automatic removal of the same amount of money from one's pay. So he does not suggest that where the real losses are identical a demand on the will has a significance fundamentally different from that of a passive demand.

Nagel's observations could in fact be used to support the opposite view. It could be said that any temptation to think that extreme active demands are more objectionable than extreme passive demands stems from our failure to see that a kind of surcharge is sometimes added to losses that proceed via engagement of the will. Once we get right the measure of the real losses involved, we will see that the two kinds of demands are not relevantly different. This seems plausible.

A further argument to the same effect would be that if we regard extreme active demands as more objectionable than extreme passive demands, we may be being misled by the fact that in certain dramatic cases of losses proceeding via engagement of the will, any agent who in fact complies would display a highly unusual character. For example, it may seem clearly more objectionable that an agent is required to impose severe physical injury on himself than it is that a third person is required to impose the same injury on him. But on reflection we see that this is not so. In such "heroism" cases (discussed further in chapter 5), it would indeed be clearly objectionable to blame the agent for failing to do what hardly any of us would be able to do; as we know from the discussion of blameless wrongdoing in the previous chapter, however, his failure might nevertheless still be regarded as wrong. Once we focus our attention on the question of whether the demands as such are objectionable, prescinding from issues of blameworthiness, the apparent difference in the status of active and passive demands once more disappears.

In any case, if we approach the question of extreme passive demands directly, it is very implausible to see them as exempt from the charge of over-demandingness. I said earlier that it seems absurd to say that a perfectly enforced moral scheme can impose no demands. It would be hardly less absurd to say that a perfectly enforced moral scheme, though it indeed imposed (passive) demands, could never raise a problem of over-demandingness. By way of example, imagine a perfectly and legitimately enforced taxation scheme in, say, Norway. A new government, guided by the optimizing principle of beneficence, imposes a progressive "foreign development tax" on its people. Middle-class Norwegians might find that 75 percent of their income goes in taxes, with a resultant very significant loss of well-being. It would clearly be very odd to think that the optimizing principle of beneficence would be unacceptable if it directly required Norwegians to give up 75 percent of their income, but that the same losses raise no problem at all if they take the form of passive demands.

IV. Assessing Passive Effects: Full Compliance

So we can leave aside doubts about the relevance for us of passive effects and turn to the question of how they might be assessed. This turns out to be a very complicated matter indeed.

Like active demands, passive effects must be assessed ex ante. But whereas the relevant time for the assessment of active demands is the start of an agent's responsible life, the relevant time for the assessment of passive effects would seem to be the start of life—the time of the agent's birth. This, however, is not the most important difference between the two assessments. For the notion of a passive effect, unlike that of an active demand, requires us to think about the compliance behavior of more than one agent—we need to know what benefits and burdens will flow to the target agent from many *other* agents following the theory. This greatly complicates the picture, especially because the level of net passive effect on a person's well-being will vary with the degree of compliance with the theory or principle by others. It is therefore easiest to begin by restricting our attention to situations of full compliance with some theory.

What baseline might be used?[32] It must be grounded in the factual status quo, but we cannot simply look to the world as we actually expect it to go on. For of course that is a world of people behaving as they do in part because of various implicit or explicit moral commitments or because they are constrained by legal institutions that are themselves partly determined by moral and political commitments. Obviously enough, it would be pointless to measure the passive effects of common-sense morality against a baseline of the actual world. The question here is the same as that of the appropriate baseline life for an agent in the assessment of active demands. The answer, however, must be different. In the case of active demands, we ask what the agent's own compliance with the moral theory costs her, and it is appropriate to use as a baseline the best life she could otherwise lead. In the case of passive effects, it is not appropriate to use as a baseline the pattern of behavior by others that would be best for the agent. An agent can relevantly say that but for her own compliance, she could be living the optimally prudent life. She cannot relevantly say that but for their compliance, all other people could be devoting their lives to her well-being. Of course they could be doing that, but there are a lot of other things they could be doing, too.

Should we then imagine that in the baseline world all people lead an optimally prudent life? This, too, would be unmotivated. Optimal prudence is the relevant baseline life for the agent in the assessment of active demands just because our question is how much better off the agent could be if she were not a complier. When we assess the effects of compliance by others on a person's well-being, there is simply no reason to look to a baseline world where those others are optimally prudent. What we want to measure is the difference perfect compliance with the theory by others makes to a person's well-being, and it seems that the only appropriate baseline is the simple one of a world in which no others ever comply with the theory.

The trouble with this baseline, however, is that it is so indeterminate; there are an infinite number of very different ways not to act as required by a moral theory.[33] The extent of this indeterminacy would appear to make the notion of passive effects pretty much useless as an aid to moral theorizing. To assess passive effects under full compliance, we need to measure the difference between two assessments of expected well-being: A's expected well-being in a world where all others perfectly comply with theory T, and A's expected well-being in a world of total noncompliance with T. In the case of active demands we can say with reasonable confidence, applying the baseline of the factual status quo, that the demands on me if I complied with utilitarianism from now on would be extreme, while those that would be imposed by commonsense morality would not be. But applying the baseline just announced for passive effects, we cannot make even remotely confident similar claims about the different levels of passive effect that should be attributed to different theories—for there are an infinite number of possible baseline worlds, and, furthermore, we do not have the remotest idea what any of them would be like. The general problem here is familiar from discussions of a certain kind of contractualist moral theory that requires us to identify the varying extents to which different people benefit from social cooperation.[34]

Now this problem can actually be sidestepped. Given the substantial overlap in the requirements made by plausible moral theories, a world of total noncompliance with any particular theory (where no one ever acts as required by the theory) will resemble a Hobbesian state of nature. And on a sensible understanding of what the "war of all against all" is like, we can just assume that in our baseline world the expected well-being of everyone is very low, and roughly equally so.[35] So it would be possible simply to ignore the baseline level of well-being, letting it drop out as a constant, and to directly compare how well-off we think people would be under full compliance with various different theories.

This does seem to be the right way to assess passive effects. But we can now see just how significant a difference the incorporation of passive effects makes to the problem of over-demandingness. For it is clear that at least insofar as we restrict our attention to situations of full compliance, no (plausible) moral theory ever imposes a net passive burden. Indeed, we can surely say more: the sum of passive effects and active demands, which we can call the *compliance effect*, will always be a net benefit. The basis of this claim is simply the idea, familiar at least since the time of the Sophists, that a person's prospects are always going to be better if everyone, including her, follows one of the moral conceptions we take seriously.

Some might think that this is a reductio ad absurdum of our discussion of passive effects, on the grounds that it is quite obvious that our Norwegians face extreme demands. But we may now say that the sense that a demand is made in that case is due to our tendency to assess passive effects against the baseline of the normative status quo. Of course middle-class Norwegians take a loss compared with today's actual Norwegians, and even more of a loss compared with members of the middle class in most other Western countries. But that is not what we have been interested in. We wanted to investigate the losses that might flow just because of perfect compliance by all others with a moral theory, not what losses would flow if there were a change to the moral status quo. And what we have discovered is that the compliance effect, the sum of active demands and passive effects, properly assessed, is always a net benefit. The consequence of this is not just that our Norwegians face no demands; what we have found is that if the problem of over-demandingness must take into account passive effects, there is no problem of over-demandingness.

In response, it might be said that all we have seen is that those theories we regard as extremely demanding are, it turns out, those whose compliance effects on agents are not beneficial enough. And though this way of understanding extreme demands is very different from the one we started with, perhaps it does not matter if we condemn a moral theory for not giving enough rather than for taking away too much. To help bring this point out, we can consider again a baseline for the assessment of passive effects which we rejected earlier—the baseline where everyone acts optimally in promotion of the target agent's well-being. Assuming that all people's potential for well-being is roughly the same, the baseline of full compliance with a "me-theory" sets everyone's baseline well-being at roughly the same (high) level. Thus the baseline level of well-being once again drops out as a constant, and we can look directly at people's levels of well-being under full compliance with the theory the demands of which we are assessing. With the me-theory baseline, all plausible moral theories burden everyone, since everyone is better off under their own me-theory. But the person who is burdened the most by a particular theory is just the person who is worst off under that theory. This is the mirror image of the result we get with our preferred baseline of the Hobbesian war of all against all. Under the Hobbesian baseline, the person who is benefited the least is also just the person who is worst off under full compliance with the theory. With each of these approaches we end up focusing our attention simply on the level of well-being of the worst-off person, even though one approach is about burdens and the other is about benefits.

However, rather than rehabilitating the problem of over-demandingness, these reflections indicate a deeper difficulty. If the imposition of extreme demands turns out to be simply a matter of leaving someone too badly off under full compliance, it is hard to see that any independent concern with the *extent of demands* remains. People's absolute levels of well-being under full compliance with a moral theory are obviously facts we are traditionally interested in when assessing the plausibility of the theory, but our interest is direct—we are simply concerned about people's well-being. Perhaps some story could be told that would explain why absolute levels of well-being under full compliance raise not just one issue but two importantly distinct issues—not just how well-off people would be but also how burdensome or beneficial the theory is. But I do not know what that story might be; in its absence, we once again seem to have lost the problem of over-demandingness altogether.

Perhaps a bolder recasting of the problem of over-demandingness can prevent our skeptical conclusion: the problem is not that in absolute terms some theories benefit us too little or burden us too much; rather, some theories are objectionable for leaving us less well-off than another plausible theory would, and a highly demanding theory is just one with a much less beneficial compliance effect than some plausible alternative. This certainly makes sense, and in Nagel's book *Equality and Partiality* the issue of demands is approached in just this way. In the context of Nagel's contractualist methodology, a proposed theory of justice counts as demanding to the extent that it leaves someone worse off than he would be under some feasible alternative theory.[36] "Feasible" here does not mean any theory that we imagine might possibly be complied with; as Nagel makes clear at one point in the book, I cannot assess demands relative to a me-theory.[37] For our purposes, we can simply say that demands are assessed relative to some plausible moral theory.

Now of course Nagel's concerns are quite different from ours, and the notion of moral demands he offers is intended to be used within a very specific contractualist structure of moral argument. Thus I cannot hope to do justice to Nagel's discussion here. Rather than try to do that, I want to use his approach as a model for a possible construal of the problem of over-demandingness.

So the idea we are considering is that a moral theory counts as demanding to the extent that its full-compliance effect is less beneficial for a person than some plausible alternative theory; let us call this the comparative conception of demands. Applying this conception to the problem of over-demandingness, utilitarianism might be said to be excessively demanding on a person of very high earning capacity in virtue of the fact that she would do so much better under some laissez-faire version of commonsense morality. This sounds plausible; the intuitive thought would be that utilitarianism faces a very strong prima facie objection for leaving this person so much worse off than do other theories that are, after all, plausible. And the point here is *not* simply that, all else being equal, we prefer a theory that leaves a person with higher well-being— just because higher well-being is always welcome. Our target agent in this case can object to the high demands of utilitarianism independently of any direct objection to her lower level of well-being under it. There is a clear independent issue of demands here because not everyone with the same level of well-being under full compliance with utilitarianism can claim that they would be so much better-off under plausible alternatives: our target agent can claim this demand because of her relatively high earning capacity.*

But the striking feature of the comparative conception of demands is that it allows a person of very low earning capacity to raise exactly the

---

*There are differences in people's earning capacities, relevant to how well a person fares under some plausible theory, that remain even in an assessment of passive effects from the start of life. These differences need not be natural; on the baseline of the factual status quo, we do not imagine away socially caused differences in earning capacities.

same objection to commonsense morality, only with the terms inverted: commonsense morality is very demanding on him in virtue of the fact that he would do so much better under utilitarianism. If the problem of over-demandingness is to be interpreted in these comparative terms, it seems that it will backfire: we must reject not only radical revisionist utilitarianism but good old commonsense morality as well.[38]

This is the second time we have reached the conclusion that the problem of over-demandingness applies more broadly than its followers typically suppose. But the route followed here is very different from that which led us to say that if extreme active demands are a problem for the optimizing principle of beneficence, they must be a problem for all other kinds of moral principle as well. Furthermore, the conclusion here is in fact stronger than the earlier one: on the comparative conception of demands, commonsense morality comes out as very demanding not just on odd occasions but, at least for the very poor, all the time. So it is immediately clear that most people who level the charge of excessive demands against utilitarianism would not be happy with the results of adopting a comparative conception of demands.

But the effect of moving to the comparative conception appears to be worse still for the problem of over-demandingness. For it might turn out that *every* plausible moral theory is just as demanding on *someone* as utilitarianism is on people of very high earning capacity, and thus that all "plausible" theories must be condemned. We know that a person of very high earning capacity can point to a very large gap between his well-being under utilitarianism and his well-being under some laissez-faire version of commonsense morality. It is likewise fairly clear that a person of very low earning capacity would prefer utilitarianism to the laissez-faire theory by roughly the same extent. What is less obvious, but which seems nevertheless plausible, is that a person of very low earning capacity can also reject "intermediate" theories, such as moderately egalitarian versions of commonsense morality, for leaving him so much worse off than he would be under some egalitarian version of utilitarianism; the person of very high earning capacity could also presumably reject the moderately egalitarian commonsense theory for being too demanding relative to some libertarian view. Thus the problem of over-demandingness could be fatal for all the moral theories we currently think plausible. Now Nagel in fact embraces a conclusion similar to this—at least, he does so for the special domain of international distributive justice.[39] But since we are considering the problem of over-demandingness as a general problem applicable to all domains of morality, this would appear to be an unacceptable result.

It might be thought that yet another reinterpretation of the problem of over-demandingness can help here. If all plausible moral theories count as very demanding on some group or other, perhaps we should stop thinking of a charge of excessive demands as fatal objection to a moral theory, and instead see our task as finding, from among plausible theories, that theory which is least demanding on the person on whom it is most demanding.[40] But by now we have wandered very far indeed from the problem of over-demandingness as originally presented. We are still using the term "demands," but that is about all that the two discussions have in common. The problem of over-demandingness arose as a special objection to utilitarianism: that theory seemed absurd, we said, and it was very plausible to conclude that this was because its demands were absurdly extreme. We now think that the problem of over-demandingness is actually a problem for all plausible moral theories, and that, giving up on finding a theory that is very demanding on no one, our task is to find a theory that is least demanding on the person on whom it is most demanding. Needless to say, this is not an idea directly pressed upon us by our first intuitive reflections on rival moral conceptions. Equally clearly, it may nevertheless be an important idea for moral theory: that would depend on the plausibility of the argumentative structure that we might be able to create for it. But in pursuing that idea we could not say that we were delving deeper into the very strong intuitive belief that the optimizing principle of beneficence simply demands too much. It would appear that in attempting to make sense of that belief we have managed to change the subject. Since I continue to believe that there *is* something especially troubling about the optimizing principle of beneficence, I do not yet want to do that.

V. Assessing Passive Effects: Partial Compliance

In any case, this last interpretation of the problem of over-demandingness suffers from a further fatal flaw. The comparative conception of demands depends on an assumption of full compliance that, as we will now see, it cannot do without. For it appears that there is no meaningful way to assess the passive effects of a moral theory under partial compliance. As we know, if we cannot discuss partial compliance, we are no longer talking about the problem of over-demandingness.

It initially seems easy enough to adapt the method used for full-compliance cases and say that the passive effect on A of a prevailing level of (partial) compliance with theory T in a world W is assessed by comparing A's expected well-being in W with her expected well-being in a baseline world of zero compliance with T. If we follow this procedure through, we get apparently strange results. Remember that in a world of zero compliance with T, no person ever acts as T requires. As I have recently noted, this suggests, given the substantial overlap between the requirements of plausible moral theories, that for any plausible T the world of zero compliance with T is Hobbes's war of all against all. The upshot is that whatever pattern of compliance with T there may be in W, T gets all the credit for the difference between A's nasty and brutish baseline level of well-being and her well-being in W. Moreover, it follows that all the other theories that are to some degree complied with in W must get all the credit as well.

So it seems that we cannot separate out, from within a world of various different degrees of compliance with various different moral conceptions, the passive effect of compliance with just one moral conception. But perhaps we have made a mistake. Perhaps the baseline world should not be one where no people comply with T, but rather one where those people who *do* comply with T *in W*, do not comply with T. Couldn't we in that way separate out just the passive effect of compliance with T? This suggestion depends on a misunderstanding of partial compliance. We need to remember that the notion of full compliance is doubly ideal: *all* people *perfectly* comply. When we turn to partial compliance, both ideals can fail—a world of partial compliance is not necessarily a world where different people are perfectly complying with different moral conceptions. Indeed, our actual world, and thus any hypothetical world that we should be interested in, is a world of *imperfect* compliance with a range of moral conceptions that overlap considerably. But the misunderstanding goes further. For even in a world divided into groups of people who always comply with some particular theory, a different one for each group, it would be artificial to say that the passive effect of, say, utilitarianism, was due to the impact of the complying behavior of just the people who perfectly comply with utilitarianism. Since various theories overlap, all the people complying with other theories are *also* complying, though imperfectly, with utilitarianism. Where moral theories overlap in their requirements, any assignment of the effects of compliance to one theory rather than another would be arbitrary. It is thus actually not correct to say that our method for assessing passive effects does not separate out, from a world of various different degrees of compliance with various different moral conceptions, the passive effect of compliance with just one moral conception. Our baseline of zero compliance with theory T will "take away" from W precisely what we want it to—all compliance with T. And where T is a plausible view, the result will resemble the war of all against all. The results of following through our procedure for assessing passive effects under partial compliance turn out not to be strange after all.

Now it follows from these last points that even under full compliance with a certain theory, it is true to say that there is also imperfect compliance with various other theories. So the passive effect of full compliance with T is also the passive effect of various degrees of compliance with various other theories. But two things are special about a world of full compliance with some theory. First, it represents theory T's ideal, and so the salient passive effect in that world is the passive effect that flows from full compliance with T; this explains our tendency to think that other moral theories are simply not represented in that world. More important, it is easy to *describe* full compliance with some theory. This is not the case for any particular situation of partial compliance; and herein lies the problem for the assessment of passive effects under partial compliance.

It is of course possible to ask the following kind of question: What would the passive effect be in a world where 30 percent of the population perfectly complies with utilitarianism and no other people ever comply with any other moral theory? But as soon as we think about any relevant partial-compliance situation, such as that of the actual world, where pretty much everyone is at least imperfectly complying with pretty much every plausible theory, we are at a loss to say "how much" or "what level" of compliance there is with any given theory. We know that in our actual world any plausible theory can be credited with a passive effect on me equivalent to the difference between my expected well-being now and my expected well-being in a world of zero compliance with the theory. Since the baseline world is one where everyone would have the same very low level of expected well-being, we can give as a rough measure of that passive effect my actual level of expected well-being from now. But this information is of little use, since we have no idea how we might specify the extent of compliance there is with the theory in our actual world.

Without some sense of what levels of compliance we are talking about, we are in no position to say that one theory has a more or less beneficial passive effect than another. All plausible moral theories impose the same passive effect on me in the actual world, but since there are obviously (in some sense) different levels of compliance with the different theories, we cannot conclude from this that "under partial compliance" all theories have the same passive effect. And since we know nothing about the different levels of compliance prevailing in the actual world, there is nothing else we can conclude either. Similarly, though we might try to *describe*, in appropriately complex detail, various hypothetical patterns of compliance, and somehow rank these patterns in terms of degrees of compliance, this would also be to no avail because we would not have any idea what, in concrete terms, a hypothetical world with pattern P of compliance with theory T would be like—let alone what levels of expected well-being particular people would have in that world.

It might be thought that the impossibility of assessing passive effects under partial compliance is no threat to our understanding of the problem of over-demandingness. For all we need to know is whether some theories are extremely demanding, and we can answer that question without being able to specify the extent of compliance with the relevant theory. But in fact we already know that in any world even remotely likely to be actual, the passive effect of any of the theories partially complied with will be a net benefit. Take any plausible mixture of different degrees of compliance with different theories, and assess the passive effect of compliance with any one of them against a baseline of zero compliance with that theory, and the result will be a net benefit. Of course we also know that the problem of over-demandingness can be reinterpreted in the face of this result: we can adopt the comparative conception of demands. But to apply the comparative conception of demands to situations of partial compliance we *do* need to know what the passive effects of different theories are for specified levels of compliance. Under the comparative approach, we would presumably understand a theory's demands under partial compliance as the extent to which the theory leaves a person worse off than some other plausible theory does *at the same level of compliance*.

Our inability to assess the passive effect of particular degrees of partial compliance with a particular moral theory provides further independent ground for skepticism about the problem of over-demandingness. For we have here not just an inability to provide precise measurements to back up intuitive rough guesses. On the contrary, we have seen in this section and the last that the assessment of passive demands is not at all what we initially thought it might be. This being the case, the conclusion that we cannot offer even the roughest assessments of passive effects under particular levels of compliance short of full compliance leaves us with no data: we are in no position to begin to think about what the normative significance of passive effects under partial compliance might be.

This whole problem can of course be avoided by restricting discussion of passive effects to situations of full compliance. But that would be disastrous for the over-demandingness problem. As I have noted more than once, the over-demandingness problem is not about a theory's active and passive demands under the idealizing assumption that everyone, or at least everyone in some one society, is perfectly complying with the theory. If it were, the force of the traditional objection against utilitarianism would be immeasurably weaker.

VI. The State of the Problem

In any case, whether or not we restrict our discussion of passive effects to situations of full compliance, the conclusion remains the same: if the problem of over-demandingness must take into account passive effects, we lose our intuitive grip on the problem. Using the comparative conception of demands, we were able to understand passive effects under full compliance in a way that enabled us to at least make rough guesses about the differing passive effects of different theories. But this came at the cost of changing the topic; whatever the significance of the project of finding the moral theory that is least demanding, comparatively speaking, on the person for whom it is most demanding (or something similar) might be, it cannot be based on the simple and compelling intuitive idea that there must be limits to the legitimate demands of morality. Taking into account passive demands under partial compliance only makes a very bad situation worse.

At a general level, this discussion of passive effects has illustrated the difficulty of thinking about the impact of morality on our lives. Our individual and social lives are so thoroughly structured by moral and political concerns that we apparently lack any independent perspective from which to examine the impact of those concerns on what they structure.[41]

This does put the point a little too strongly; what we should say is that the extent to which we can take such an external perspective appears to be very limited. For there is a way to salvage the original problem of over-demandingness: we can restrict it to the problem of extreme active demands. To justify this restriction we would have to establish what I earlier said was implausible. The fact that active demands engage the will could be the basis of an argument to show that passive effects are simply in a different normative category from active demands, and that it is entirely appropriate to focus on active demands alone. We should remember the implications of this line of thought. We cannot object to our Norwegian foreign development tax on the grounds of extreme demands, but we can use those very grounds to object to a principle that requires Norwegians to give up the same amount voluntarily. And when assessing theory T's active demands for the purposes of determining whether they are extreme, we should entirely ignore any benefits that have flown to the agent from others following T. These implications are hard to accept. Nevertheless, I do not think we can rule out the possibility that by building on the undoubtedly significant fact that only active demands engage the will we could mount a case for a version of the problem of over-demandingness objection that applies to them alone.

But of course we must not forget, in the midst of the dark problems facing passive demands, the grounds for doubt that I introduced in section I. The conception of (what we now call) active demands that I developed there represents the extent to which we *are* able to stand back from morality to assess its impact on us. But in developing such a conception, a conception of active demands that provides us with a non-question-begging objection to the demands of particular theories, we at the same time undermined the prima face intuitive force of such an objection. In the absence of further explanation, we can object to the extreme active demands of a principle of beneficence only if we also object to extreme active demands from deontological constraints, special obligations, and indeed any other kind of moral principle one can think of.

The state of the problem is thus bleak. But I will nevertheless continue, in the next chapter, to take seriously the idea that extreme demands—or at least extreme active demands as assessed against the baseline of the factual status quo—are objectionable per se. For I want to consider the plausibility of responding to that idea, at least so far as beneficence is concerned, by offering a principle with limited demands.

VII. The Absolute-Level Version of the Problem

Our skeptical argument against the problem of over-demandingness is not, however, quite complete: we have not yet shown that the argument applies equally to the absolute-level version of the problem. In this version, it will be recalled, the objection to extremely demanding theories is not that they impose unacceptably large losses on complying agents, but that they bring complying agents down below a minimally acceptable level.

Compare three people, each of whom has fallen below the level of expected well-being identified as the limit below which the requirements of morality cannot legitimately take a person. Person A is where he is because he is a perfectly complying utilitarian. Person B is where she is because after decades of swindling the poorest members of her community, she has decided that she ought to pay back her ill-gotten gains; even her total ruin, however, has not yielded enough money to compensate her victims fully, so she must continue, in the years to come, to work to pay off this moral debt, keeping only enough for herself to enable her to keep working. Person C lives in desperate poverty; he knows a way out of his situation, but it would involve injuring and possibly killing someone—something he refuses to do because he believes it would be wrong. Now some may balk at putting B and C in the same normative boat as A. The demands made on A are objectionable because he has given up what he is entitled to; but B was never entitled to her riches to begin with, and C is certainly not entitled to kill or injure for personal gain. But we know where this line of thought leads. Either there is a general objection to the very fact that compliance with a moral theory brings an agent below a certain minimal level of well-being, or there is not. If there is, we must face the conclusion that it is objectionable that the compliance of B and C has left them below the minimal level; this will not be easy. If there is not, then we are owed an account of just what is objectionable about A's situation in particular.

So the absolute-level version of the problem faces the same difficulties we identified for active demands understood as losses measured against the baseline of the factual status quo. And unless it can be shown why an active ruin of my life is objectionable but a passive ruin is not, this version also faces analogues of the problems associated with passive effects. If we are to object when the compliance of others brings someone below the specified lower limit, we need to be able to identify when this happens; that is, we need to know when it is the compliance of others that is responsible rather than, say, some natural disaster. This, in turn, requires a way of determining how well-off the agent would have been if the others had not complied. But we know that the answer to this question will almost always be that the person would have been even worse off. Moving, then, to the comparative conception of demands, we will ask whether the person would have been left below the lower limit if the others had instead followed some other theory. We can answer this question only for situations of full compliance, which means that we have no hope of doing justice to the problem of over-demandingness; but we have no hope of that anyway, for this comparative question, though it might be interesting and important, is simply not what the problem of over-demandingness is about.

4

MODERATE BENEFICENCE?

If the problem of over-demandingness is to retain its force, we will need arguments that explain why extreme active demands are objectionable while what appear to be extreme passive demands are not, and why extreme active demands are objectionable only when they come from a principle of beneficence. I do not know what plausible arguments of either kind might look like, but neither do I think it obvious that such arguments are impossible. So it is appropriate to discuss further difficulties that emerge even for a version of the problem of over-demandingness that concerns just the active demands of beneficence.

But my aim in this chapter is not just to continue to chase difficulties for the problem of over-demandingness. Philosophers who have concluded that the optimizing principle of beneficence is unacceptably demanding have, naturally, defended principles of beneficence with moderate demands. Given our interest in the possibilities for a plausible principle of beneficence, these are clearly suggestions we need to examine. I will do that in this chapter, and further reasons for skepticism about the problem of over-demandingness will emerge along the way.

Before I begin, it should be recalled from chapter 1 that I understand a principle of beneficence to be one that at least sometimes makes requirements of us, in the sense that if we are required to do something, it is wrong not to do it. Charity, as traditionally understood, can never impose extreme demands just because it never requires us to do anything; charity is always supererogatory. So charity cannot give us our moderate principle of beneficence because it is no principle of beneficence at all.

I. A Limited Principle

The active demands of the optimizing principle of beneficence have no limit.* As a result, they can be extreme in certain circumstances. An obvious candidate for a moderate principle of beneficence is one that sets a limit to its own demands: it requires sacrifice only up to a certain point. Different ways of formulating a limit to the demands of beneficence will result in different principles of beneficence. We call any principle of beneficence that makes only limited demands a "limited principle of beneficence." Such a principle would not prohibit agents from promoting the best outcome, but neither would it always require them to do so. Thus a limited principle of beneficence is structurally the same as the optimizing principle of beneficence coupled with what Scheffler calls an "agent-centered prerogative" to favor oneself.[1] But it is somewhat misleading, I think, to talk of two principles—one that makes extreme demands and another that permits us not to meet those demands. What we are in fact investigating is a principle of beneficence that "starts out" making limited demands. The other way of talking may suggest a certain priority, normative or justificatory, to the optimizing principle, with deviations from that principle requiring special justification.

Having made this clarification, it would seem natural to begin a discussion of possible limited principles of beneficence by turning to Scheffler's well-known suggestion for an agent-centered prerogative. In fact, however, Scheffler's prerogative as formulated does not set a limit to the demands of beneficence at all. It operates by allowing agents, in assessing what they are required to do, to give their own interests greater weight than they give the interests of others; they can multiply the value of their own interests by some fixed factor.[2] It is true that for given circumstances a limited principle of beneficence that incorporates a multiplying factor will be more or less demanding depending on the size of the factor. But no such principle will actually set a limit to demands—a level of sacrifice beyond which agents are not required to go. For whatever demands flow from a principle using a given multiplying factor in given circumstances, changes in circumstances could increase the amount of good to be done, and thus the demands, without limit.

That Scheffler's prerogative does not respond to the problem of over-demandingness is not surprising, since it is offered as a response to Williams's "integrity objection" to utilitarianism as Scheffler interprets it. People do not typically adopt the impersonal perspective, this objection runs, but rather value their own interests out of proportion to the weight they receive in an impersonal assessment. Scheffler's response, which he calls the "liberation strategy," is that a moral theory should reflect this

---

*In the remainder of this chapter I will use "demands" to mean "active demands."

fact by allowing agents to promote their own interests out of proportion with their impersonal value.[3] Clearly, Scheffler's prerogative serves exactly this purpose.

However, I am inclined to think that the liberation strategy must also be partly motivated by a concern with agents' well-being; in any event, Scheffler certainly raises the issue of over-demandingness directly on a number of occasions.[4] So it is worth asking whether a revised prerogative could set a limit to demands.

Since the use of an appropriate multiplying factor does limit demands in given circumstances, we could index the multiplying factor so that it increases with the amount of good to be done, thus keeping demands down to whatever seems to be an acceptable level. This would not be the only indexing required, however. As we have seen, the demands of a principle of beneficence are greater under partial compliance than under full compliance. In our current situation of minimal compliance and great need, an enormously large multiplying factor would be required to make a dent in the demands of the optimizing principle of beneficence. But a multiplying factor large enough to do anything about over-demandingness in this situation would be too large under full compliance: even under full compliance a great amount of benefiting might remain to be done, but agents would nevertheless find that their own heavily weighted interests almost always outweighed the interests of others, and that they were hardly required to benefit others at all. So to avoid a principle of beneficence that would be either too demanding in our current situation or too minimal under full compliance, we would need to index the multiplying factor to levels of compliance as well.

Clearly, for our purposes it would be more straightforward just to determine a level of sacrifice beyond which agents are not required to go. We would have reason to adopt the doubly indexed multiplying factor only if we were concerned both to respond to over-demandingness and to implement Scheffler's liberation strategy. As we have just the former concern, we should turn our attention to limited principles of beneficence that simply set a limit to required sacrifice.

It is time to look more closely at how we might decide what level of demands is the highest that can acceptably or reasonably be made of agents. In chapter 2 we granted the initial intuitive force of the belief that there is a limit to the legitimate demands of beneficence. But we have considered this belief only as a reaction to the extreme demands of the optimizing principle of beneficence. What remains to be seen is whether it retains its plausibility when we try to fix on any particular account of the limit.

If there is a limit to the acceptable demands of beneficence, it would emerge from some picture of the appropriate place of beneficence in people's lives—of the extent to which this part of morality can impinge on a person's well-being. Here again we can turn to Scheffler for the most developed account. His book *Human Morality* is in large part a defense of "moderate" morality, and apart from the fact that our focus has now narrowed to beneficence alone, this account seems to present the kind of picture we need.[5] This is what Scheffler says about moderate morality:

> Although there are many versions of this view, with significant differences among them, they all agree on two important points. The first is that, under favorable conditions, morality permits people to do as they please within certain broad limits, and that it therefore lacks stringency. The second point is that morality does nevertheless make demands and impose constraints: it prohibits some things, requires others, and imposes costs—sometimes very great costs—on agents. The view that morality is moderate is therefore intermediate between the minimalist position that morality imposes no independent constraints and no net costs on agents, and the maximalist position that it is stringent.[6]

"Stringency" is defined as "the property of being very demanding."[7] On the moderate view, as Scheffler says elsewhere, the conflict between self-interest and morality "is neither ubiquitous nor in general stark"; "moral norms should be capable of being integrated in a coherent and attractive way into the life of the individual agent."[8]

Note that a careful reading of Scheffler's account of the moderate position shows it to be allied to the losses version of the problem of over-demandingness rather than the absolute-level version. Thus Scheffler's picture of the role of morality in human life is not a picture of a life of at least some minimum level of well-being, but a picture of a life with a certain maximum degree of potential conflict between morality and self-interest. So Scheffler's account of moderate morality suits our focus on losses; we can look to it for help in finding a limit to the extent of the losses legitimately imposed by a principle of beneficence.*

Despite its promise, I do not think that an acceptable limit emerges from Scheffler's picture of moderate morality. Suppose we believe that a principle of beneficence could not be so demanding as to radically disrupt our life plans. We thus see a limit to the demands of beneficence such that my expected well-being as a perfect complier can never be very much less than my expected well-being in my optimally prudent life in the factual status quo. This might imply that I am required to, say, contribute a regular modest amount to OXFAM and to provide direct emergency assistance to various people from time to time, but I am not required to devote most of my resources and energies to promoting human well-being. But now suppose that the amount of good there is to be done in

---

*I will describe a limit to demands that operates by setting a minimum acceptable level of well-being shortly.

the world increases dramatically. Catastrophe on an unprecedented scale hits some part of the world, and many millions will die unless *all* of us in the industrial West give up a great deal of money over a period of years. Are we content to say that once the upper limit to demands is set at the level suggested by our picture of the role of morality in human life, no change in the circumstances, no amount of increase in the amount of good to be done, can increase the demands of beneficence? That this should have no impact on the question of what level of demands is reasonable or acceptable is, on reflection, very hard to believe.

It might seem that the words "under favorable conditions" in Scheffler's description of the moderate view could help us here. Our picture could then be understood as contemplating an increase in demands, even to the point of stringency, under conditions such as those I have just described. The problem with this suggestion is that we have no warrant for believing our *current* conditions to be favorable, rather than, indeed, sufficiently bad to generate very high demands. The current circumstance of enormous need for beneficence from the better-off could be considered favorable only if we adjusted what counted as favorable to ensure that demands on us were always, apart from occasional hiccups, moderate. And if we did that, the reference to favorable conditions could no longer allow us to accommodate greater demands when circumstances change.

There is perhaps one plausible fixed limit to the demands of beneficence. An absolute-level limit could be set at a very low level of well-being, so that, say, agents are not required to sacrifice their lives, or their well-being until their lives are not worth living; it is somewhat plausible to say that no change in circumstances would justify demands even greater than *these*. The explanation for this, I think, is that it might be thought that at the edge of the agent's life, as it were, beneficence, if not any other part of morality, loses its grip, no matter what is at stake.[9] Even if such a very high limit to the demands of beneficence is plausible, however, it will give us a limited principle of beneficence that is almost as demanding as the optimizing principle.

It seems that we face a dilemma. As we have just seen, it is difficult to embrace any picture of morality that keeps the demands of beneficence fixed at a certain level whatever the changes in circumstances. If there is a limit to demands, it will have to be more flexible than that. On the other hand, as we saw in the discussion of multiplying factors, the relevant kind of flexibility will produce a limit that keeps getting raised as there is more good to be done—and that is no limit at all. The simple belief in a limit to the demands of beneficence is starting to look very unstable.

But perhaps we have not been considering the right kind of flexibility in our limit. One could propose a limit that is indexed to circumstances, but in a nonlinear fashion.[10] The idea would be that demands are limited to a certain level for given circumstances; when circumstances worsen, the demands increase, but the rate at which they increase declines as the total level of demands increases. Different ways of fleshing out this idea will seem plausible depending on which horn of our dilemma is regarded as the more serious. Thus, if responsiveness of the requirements of beneficence to increased need is the most important concern, we could opt for a limit that slows the approach to extreme demands but never stops it. More plausible as a response to the problem of over-demandingness would be a principle that allows demands to approach a nonextreme upper limit asymptotically. Such a principle could of course still be faulted on the ground that there will be cases in which radical changes in circumstances increase required beneficence only slightly. But the principle could nevertheless perhaps display sufficient flexibility to blunt the force of this kind of complaint.

A lot evidently turns here on the precise form of the proposed principle, but I want to leave these details aside for now. For there is a more fundamental objection to be considered at this point. Perhaps we can find a flexible limit that serves as a compromise between the two horns of the dilemma. My concern is with what gives content to the compromise. What are our *criteria* for setting the right balance between demands and the amount of good to be done?[11] Following Scheffler, we have appealed to a picture of the role of morality in human life. But it is my contention that we in fact lack even the roughest such general picture: what we might think of as a picture of the appropriate role of morality in human life will just reflect our preexisting sense of the shape of a morally decent life.

In the previous chapter we concluded that an attack on extreme demands threatens to collapse into an affirmation of commonsense morality; we found no independent issue that related to the extent of demands as such. What I am now claiming serves as confirmation and elaboration of that conclusion: when—forgetting our earlier doubts—we ask what an acceptable level of demands would be, all we can say is that the demands made by the morality we are committed to are reasonable. Once again, an independent concern with the extent of demands drops out.

A good way of testing my rather strong claim is this. Can we imagine any remotely plausible general picture of the role of morality in human life that does not approximate our commonsense picture of the life of a decent ordinary person, or a least our picture of a life of compliance with some familiar moral theory? We are familiar with views that reject the very question of what is an acceptable degree of conflict between self-interest and moral requirements. Thus there are various versions of the view that morality and self-interest, properly understood, cannot conflict.[12] And the opposite view that the well-being of complying agents is in principle irrelevant to the content of morality is, if not so familiar, easily grasped.[13] But suppose someone proposed that on the correct view of the role of morality in human life a far higher level of demands is acceptable than is tolerated by the moderate view—or imposed on ordinary well-off people by commonsense morality. Our reaction to such a proposal, considered in the abstract, is likely to be puzzlement.

There are limits to legitimate demands, the claim would be, but they are far higher than the demands that normally fall on well-off people complying with commonsense morality. Why would we believe this? The only reason would be that we were committed to a certain set of substantive moral principles that might impose demands up to the proposed limit. Our convictions about an acceptable level of demands always reduce to our convictions about what, on reflection, we believe we are required to do. It is true, as Scheffler says, that the view that morality is moderate imposes "a significant constraint on the content of morality."[14] But the constraint operates merely to rule out the claim that morality and self-interest necessarily coincide and the claim that agents' well-being is never relevant in the determination of moral requirements. The rejection of these abstract propositions does not require a judgment about the *appropriate degree* of potential conflict between self-interest and morality. And it is my claim that when we try to make such a judgment, we have nothing to say. We simply do not have any concrete intuitions on the matter; any conclusions we reach will reflect our prior beliefs—prior, that is, to reflection on the issue of demands—about how we ought, morally, to live.[15]

It could be objected here that I am missing the point: the view that morality is moderate just is the view that the well-being of the complying agent is a relevant factor in determining how it is we ought to live. So if we find some principle of beneficence plausible, that will be in part because of the way that it impacts on the life of the agent. But my point is that if this were really so, we would be able to make an independent judgment about the appropriateness of the degree of conflict between self-interest and compliance with the principle. This is what we cannot do. Why *that* (rough) level of potential conflict, and not much less, or much more? Any such independent judgment, I believe, will either seem entirely arbitrary or simply reflect the shape of the demands of one's prior beliefs about the decent life.

The problem of over-demandingness is now in an even worse state than it was at the end of chapter 3. One of the two main problems we were left with there was that it seemed that extreme demands were objectionable only if they came from a principle of beneficence, but we had no explanation of why this should be so. We now have further reason to think that the optimizing principle of beneficence, if objectionable, is not so on account of its extreme demands. For if extreme demands are not acceptable, we ought to have some sense of what level of demands *would* be acceptable. There is no need for anything like precision, of course—that is not the issue. The problem is that we seem to lack any convictions at all, however vague and imprecise, about what reasonable demands of beneficence would be. We can of course describe the demands made by commonsense morality on us decent folk, or describe the demands of utilitarianism, or of some other theory, but that is not the same thing. If we have no views at all about what acceptable demands might be like, this gives us further reason to doubt what was granted as uncontroversial in chapter 2—that the apparent absurdity of the optimizing principle of beneficence is due to the extent of its demands.

II. No Problem

This concludes my attempt to dissolve the problem of over-demand-ingness. The argument just made is of a piece with those made in the previous chapter. To give content to the problem of over-demandingness, we would have to be able to abstract from our beliefs about how we ought to live and produce an independent normative assessment of the impli-cations for agents' well-being of those very moral beliefs. That this in-dependent assessment is not possible has been brought home to us in three different ways. First, if what appear to be passive demands are taken into account, and as an intuitive matter it is hard to see how they could not be, we find that our original problem of over-demandingness disap-pears altogether. We also saw in the previous chapter that the problem of over-demandingness cannot really be a problem about the extent of demands as such, but must rather be a problem about the extent of the demands of beneficence. But since it is entirely unclear why just the demands of beneficence should be problematic, the problem of over-demandingness appears to reduce to a reaffirmation of commonsense beliefs about how we ought to live. Finally, we have seen in this chapter that even if we ignore these first two problems and pretend that there is a special problem about the extent of the active demands of beneficence, we find that we lack any sense of what an appropriate level of demands would be. When we abstract from our beliefs about how we ought to live, we have no thoughts about the extent of legitimate demands, and any thoughts we *seem* to have about the extent of demands will simply reflect prior ideas about how we ought to live.

III. Scalar Wrongness

This dissolution of the problem of over-demandingness does not eradicate the intuitive sense that the optimizing principle of beneficence is absurd, nor that its absurdity has something to do with its demands. In the next chapter I begin to offer a different possible explanation of the apparent absurdity of the principle. Before turning to that, however, we should return to the sophisticated limited principles of beneficence introduced earlier. For even though we have concluded that limited principles of beneficence will not be shaped by independent judgments about the appropriate degree of conflict between self-interest and morality, the discussion may have pointed the way to a plausible principle of beneficence nevertheless.

I described a principle of beneficence that allows demands to approach an upper limit asymptotically: for a given amount of possible benefit to others, the principle requires beneficence only up to a certain level of sacrifice; as the amount of good to be done increases, so, too, does the amount of required sacrifice, but the increase in required sacrifice is less for a given increase in good to be done, the greater the absolute level of the sacrifice. I then argued that we have no criteria with which to set the various variables that are involved in such a principle. Now if there were consensus about what the requirements of beneficence were, we could pick out values for the variables such that the resulting principle conformed in its requirements to that consensus. Lacking independent judgments about levels of acceptable demands, let alone judgments about acceptable levels of demands in given circumstances, we would not have any satisfactory *explanation* for the shape of the principle; but we would at least have a generalized representation of the commonsense requirements of beneficence. But of course there is no such consensus to appeal to: as we saw in chapter 1, most people are quite unsure just what a decent level of beneficence in different circumstances might be. So we have not found a plausible principle of beneficence, but rather only the *form* of one.

However, at this point it could be thought that my standards for a plausible principle of beneficence are too strict. In particular, it could be thought that the best that can be done in this part of morality is precisely to outline the form of a principle—by listing various relevant variables or factors. We should not expect to be able to find (rough) weightings for the relevant factors such that we can always say, in a given case, (roughly) what degree of beneficence is required. This, indeed, could be thought to be precisely the lesson of section I: whatever is the case for other kinds of moral principle, beneficence does not admit of a line, even a rough one, between what is required, and thus wrong not to do, and what is morally optional.

A suggestion along these lines is that of Michael Slote. On his account of "scalar beneficence," agents never act wrongly in respect of beneficence, but rather understand that the more good they do, the better.[16] The problem with this view is simply that it is equivalent to the charity view rejected in chapter 1; we are interested in principles of beneficence understood precisely as accounts of when people act wrongly in respect of beneficence.[17] (Also roughly equivalent to the charity view is Kant's "imperfect duty of beneficence." This duty applies to "maxims" of ends, not actions; it forbids us to adopt a maxim of indifference to the welfare of others. Someone who never actually did anything to benefit other people may be suspected of having adopted the forbidden maxim, but a few minor acts of beneficence from time to time would seem to be enough to reestablish her good name. Kant's imperfect duty, at least as standardly understood, also fails to qualify as a principle of beneficence in my terms.)[18]

However, there is a way of recasting the scalar approach that makes it more promising for our purposes. Instead of saying that failing to act beneficently is never wrong, one might believe that it is always wrong, but that such failures will fall on a scale of degrees of wrongness.[19] Just how wrong a particular failure in beneficence is would be determined by appeal to any factors identified as relevant, including those discussed for a limited principle of beneficence.[20]

This suggestion is promising. It is familiar from commonsense morality that some acts, while wrong, are only trivially so, while others are very seriously wrong. It is very wrong to kill someone, rather trivially wrong to negligently bump into people while negotiating a crowded street. So the idea of "scalar wrongness" is not in itself revisionary. The novelty here is to take the agent's degree of sacrifice into account in the determination of how wrong a failure in beneficence is. So the claim is that just as it is more wrong to fail to be beneficent the more good a particular beneficent act will do (and, perhaps, the more good there is to be done generally), it is *less* wrong to fail to be beneficent the greater the sacrifice required of the agent. Thus, for example, it is very wrong to fail to convey a great benefit at trivial cost, and hardly wrong at all to fail to sustain great sacrifice for a very small net benefit. Of course the relevant exculpatory factor would be total sacrifice, not the amount of sacrifice from case to case: otherwise it would still be very wrong for a person who has given away a very great deal to fail to send one more ten-dollar check to OXFAM.[21]

To evaluate this suggestion, note first that using agents' sacrifice as an exculpatory factor is most plausible in the domain of beneficence, and then only when beneficence is not taken to be the whole of morality. Commonsense morality and the criminal law recognize various excuses for the crime of murder. But the range of excuses does not include high cost to the agent for not killing—certainly not high *monetary* cost. And the same point could be made about many other deontological constraints; this is in effect just the same point as that made in chapter 3 about our differing attitudes to the demands of beneficence and the demands of other parts of morality.[22] So a scalar-wrongness view of beneficence might be plausible as part of a pluralist moral theory containing traditional deontological principles, but not otherwise: a scalar-wrongness version of utilitarianism is not plausible.[23]

The scalar-wrongness view can seem appealing precisely because it sidesteps the problems confronted by limited principles of beneficence, and does so without collapsing into the charity view. When we tried to give even a rough account of how much beneficence we are required to deliver, we found that we lacked the moral judgments about appropriate demands necessary to do this. One response would be to conclude that "the more beneficence, the better" is the best we can say, and leave it at that. And the scalar-wrongness view takes beneficence more seriously than the charity view. For on the scalar-wrongness view we do not regard beneficence as morally optional. So doesn't this give us everything we need for a plausible principle of beneficence?

I do not think that it does. As I said in chapter 1, everyone who takes beneficence seriously must confront the fact that our views about this part of morality are very unsettled. Many people believe that they should "do more" but have no idea what an appropriate amount of beneficence would be. Unfortunately, the scalar-wrongness view does not help us with this problem. For if we are told that we should in principle always comply with the optimizing principle of beneficence, but that failures to do so are often only mildly wrong, we naturally want to know which failures to comply are more than mildly wrong. After all, trivial moral wrongs do not matter that much; it is in fact a vice (called "moralism") to be too concerned about them. What matters is serious wrongdoing. But a scalar-wrongness view of beneficence cannot identify serious wrongdoing for us; it can at best provide us with a list of relevant factors and their interaction. It cannot give us an answer to the question that matters to us for the same reason that the limited principle of beneficence failed: we lack independent conviction about the weight of the various factors involved.

Now it may be that no answer to the question of which failures in beneficence are seriously wrong is available. If so, the scalar-wrongness view of beneficence is likely to be the best we can do in the way of a principled account of this part of morality. But the attempt to provide an alternative account of what is objectionable about the optimizing principle of beneficence that begins in the next chapter will also generate a different suggestion for a principle of beneficence, one that does delineate what is required and what is not. We should decide whether the collective principle of beneficence is plausible before admitting defeat and adopting the scalar-wrongness view.

5

RESPONSIBILITY IN NONIDEAL THEORY

The Compliance Condition

The optimizing principle of beneficence appeared to be absurd for the simple reason that it is too demanding. But the problem of over-demandingness turned out to be far from simple, and our efforts to give it content led us to conclude that it is no problem at all. I do not see how the problem can be rehabilitated, though of course I do not take myself to have shown that it cannot. My concern in the rest of this book is to explore a different diagnosis of the apparent absurdity of the optimizing principle of beneficence. This diagnosis, and the suggested principle of beneficence that it generates, are by no means free of their own difficulties; but they are, I believe, more plausible than the alternatives.

I. Something Special about Beneficence

A principal theme of my skeptical discussion of over-demandingness was that it could not be extreme demands as such that we were objecting to because it was intuitively plausible to object to extreme demands only when they came from beneficence. A rebuttal would need to take the form of an account of what is special about beneficence such that its extreme demands matter more, and, as I said, it is doubtful that there is any such account. But the fact that it is so natural to think that a principle of beneficence and *only* a principle of beneficence is objectionable on account of its demands should not simply be forgotten. It suggests, indeed, that an alternative diagnosis of the apparent absurdity of the optimizing principle of beneficence will be more plausible if it is a diagnosis that applies only to principles of beneficence. For then we would have some warrant for saying that it was the alternative problem, and not extreme demands, that concerned us all along.* It is encouraging, then, that the problem of unfair demands under partial compliance can best be introduced precisely by pointing to a feature of principles of beneficence that they share with no other familiar kind of moral principle.

Of all the principles that might find their way into a pluralistic moral theory, only principles of beneficence take an *agent-neutral* form, in the sense that they give us all the same aim. Deontological constraints and typical special obligations are, by contrast, *agent-relative*, in that they give each agent a different aim, directing her that *she* do or not do so and so.** The intuitive contrast can be brought out by noting that whereas a constraint against killing prohibits me from killing an innocent person even if this will prevent others carrying out several killings, a principle of beneficence tells me *not* to try to benefit someone myself in a situation where this will prevent others conveying greater benefits. In the former case my aim is that I not kill, not that killings be minimized. In the latter case we all have the one aim that people be benefited as much as possible, not individual aims that each of us benefit people. It is easy to see, indeed, that an agent-relative principle of beneficence would be very implausible. Where strangers are concerned, it would be pure self-indulgence to insist that I convey some benefit myself when I know that this will lead to people being benefited less overall.[1]

We could say, somewhat tendentiously, that a principle of beneficence is directed to agents as a group, whereas other moral principles are directed to agents individually. So long as the group as a whole is acting optimally to promote well-being, an individual has discharged her duty of beneficence: it does not matter to her, morally speaking, if the benefits flow much more through the agency of others than through her own agency. For agent-relative principles, by contrast, it is essential that "not killing," or "caring for their children," and so forth, be properties of the agency of each person.

Now there are two questions that naturally arise for a principle directed to people as a group that do not arise for principles directed to each person individually. It can be asked, first, how responsibility for promoting the common aim should be distributed among the members of the group and, second, how an agent's responsibility is affected when another member of the group shirks her responsibility. In other words, when a group pursues a common aim, there are questions about the distribution of responsibility and about the responsibility of complying agents in situations of partial compliance. The optimizing principle of

---

*For more on our warrant for claiming this, see section VIII.
**Some special obligations might be seen as giving a common aim to some group smaller than the whole of humanity; I discuss such principles briefly in section VII.

beneficence seems absurd, I will propose, because it gives the wrong answer to the second of these questions: what is wrong with the principle is that its demands under partial compliance are unfair. Thus the problem with the optimizing principle of beneficence consists in its giving the wrong answer to a question that does not arise for other kinds of moral principle.* If this is right, it is not surprising that concern about moral demands has focused almost exclusively on principles of beneficence.

II. The Compliance Condition

Consider the position of someone who tries to act in accordance with the optimizing principle of beneficence today. She will be aware that she must go on promoting well-being until her own level of well-being is very low indeed, and aware that she is one of very few people headed in that direction. Moreover, she will know that one main *reason* that her compliance with the optimizing principle of beneficence will result in such great sacrifice is just this fact that she is one of very few people complying. She knows that if everyone always acted according to the optimizing principle, much less would be required of her. In the face of this she may well ask: "Why should I have to do more just because others won't do what they ought to do? Why should I have to take up the slack caused by their wrongdoing? Surely I should only have to do my own fair share?"[2]

Our agent may be unmoved by the reply that indeed she "should" only have to do her own fair share, but that unfortunately the wrongdoing of others makes this impossible. She may deny that the only targets for complaint are the noncomplying agents, and insist that the principle that demands that she make up for their noncompliance is itself objectionable.

The over-demandingness problem focuses only on the demands faced by individual agents, considered alone. When each agent thinks about the demands the optimizing principle of beneficence makes on her, it is natural for her to form the belief that there is a limit to the demands of beneficence. But if we take a wider perspective, and think about the way that demands on particular agents are affected by the behavior of other agents with the same moral aim, another thought is also natural: that it would be objectionable to expect agents to take up the slack caused by the noncompliance of others. We may come to believe that though we are required do our fair share, which can amount to a great sacrifice in certain circumstances, we cannot be required to do other people's shares

---

*This claim is defended in section VII.

as well as our own; that would be, in the terms of the previous section, an inappropriate imposition of responsibility under partial compliance.

Let us then suggest a *compliance condition*:

> An agent-neutral moral principle should not increase its demands on agents as expected compliance with the principle by other agents decreases. Demands on an agent under partial compliance should not exceed what they would be (all other aspects of her situation remaining the same) under full compliance from now on.

The words "all other aspects of her situation remaining the same" make clear that the concern is with a difference in demands that is due *just* to the level of compliance. I will typically omit these words in what follows. The words "from now on" make it clear that the compliance condition is not concerned with higher demands that all people may face because of noncompliance in the past. The issue of past noncompliance will be largely bracketed in this chapter, as the next chapter provides the more appropriate context for its discussion. Note finally that this is a condition on *principles*: the right level of analysis for this issue is the agent-neutral principle considered alone, not, as was the case for the issue of over-demandingness, whole moral theories.[3] The reason for this is clear: the suggestion being explored is that agent-neutral moral principles, in giving a particular aim to all people, must impose requirements in line with a certain condition. That condition does not apply to agent-relative principles, and thus also not to a pluralistic theory that contains agent-relative principles. Of course, if an agent-neutral principle does take its place in a wider theory, "full compliance from now on" must mean full compliance with that wider theory.

The compliance condition gives expression to the idea that an agent should not be required to "take up the slack left by the noncompliance of others." It also gives expression to the idea that agents should not be required to do "more than their fair share," so long as we assume that the demands made of a person under full compliance are always fair. If a full-compliance share is a fair share, then to be required to do more than one's full-compliance share just is to be required to do more than one's fair share. For now it will be helpful to retain this assumption without further explanation; I will return to it in section VI.

I believe that the compliance condition has a good deal of plausibility. But before I discuss what deeper motivation for it that there may be, I must improve the formulation just offered. As so far stated, the compliance condition makes use of our old vague intuitive notion of demands; it is necessary to develop a formulation that takes account of the discussion of the notion of moral demands in chapter 3.

It will be recalled from chapter 3 that a measure of the active demands of a principle on a person is a measure of the difference the person's own compliance makes to his well-being in the prevailing circumstances, while a measure of the passive demands of a principle on a person is a measure of the difference the compliance of others makes to his well-being in the prevailing circumstances. Now the compliance condition cannot plausibly concern just active demands. For suppose that Norway's institutional arrangements for development aid at first extract from Norwegians just the amount of money that would be optimal if all the world's countries were providing an optimal amount of development aid. The utilitarian Norwegian government notices, however, that what would be optimal under full compliance is not optimal in the actual world where hardly any country comes close to providing its full-compliance share; so the government increases foreign-development tax rates to the levels that are in fact optimal in the actual world. If utilitarianism is unfair in respect of its active demands on people under partial compliance, then this utilitarian tax scheme is surely likewise unfair; the fact that active demands engage the will seems unlikely to be significant in the context of a concern about doing more than one's share.[4] Instead, we should conclude that the compliance condition applies to the *combination* of active and passive demands that people face under partial and full compliance.

Now we also saw in chapter 3 that if passive demands are to be considered, so, too, must benefits that flow from others' compliance; once more, there seems to be no reason not to apply this point to the compliance condition. Thus, rather than active and passive demands, we are in fact interested in active demands and passive effects. Indeed, because the compliance condition must look to the combination of active demands and passive effects on a person, we can say that the real focus is simply on net *compliance effects*. A net compliance effect is the passive effect of the prevailing level of compliance with the relevant theory in the factual status quo less any loss that flows to the agent from his own compliance in the status quo. Because this net compliance effect could be positive or negative, it emerges that the compliance condition is not, strictly, about demands at all. It is about agent-neutral principles whose compliance effect on complying agents *worsens* as expected compliance by others decreases. A more accurate (and simplified) formulation of the compliance condition would thus seem to be:

> The compliance effect on a complying agent under partial compliance should not be worse than it would be if her situation were one of full compliance.

However, while it is a step in the right direction, this statement of the compliance condition remains inaccurate in fundamental ways.

To see this, consider a complier the active demands upon whom are zero; only passive effects are relevant in his case. These passive effects comprise both benefits and burdens; most moral principles, moreover, will yield net passive benefits. Typically, then, a complier who faces no active demands will enjoy a worse compliance effect under partial compliance than under full compliance just because of lost passive benefits. But that is hardly the "fault" of the principle. There is nothing a moral principle can do about this result: the noncompliers are supposed to comply, but they do not. A moral principle can have an impact on actual compliance effects only through the content of the requirements it makes of agents; it cannot control the rate of compliance.

One way a moral principle can affect the compliance effect on a complying agent is by making or withholding requirements that make the compliance effect worse for him; making or withholding requirements, in other words, that impose active demands on him. The other way a moral principle can affect the compliance effect on a complying agent is through the shape of the requirements that it makes on *other* compliers. It will be easier to deal with these two cases separately, calling them the first- and third-person dimensions of the compliance condition, respectively. For the sake of easier exposition, I will focus exclusively on the first-person dimension in this section; the third-person dimension of the compliance condition will be discussed separately in section IV.

In the first-person dimension, a moral principle can affect the compliance effect on a complying agent by making or withholding active demands. As we have seen, this does not make it possible for a moral principle to ensure that the compliance effect on a complying agent will be the same under partial as under full compliance. A moral principle can do nothing about lost benefits due to the noncompliance of others; it can affect compliance effects by reducing active demands, but that does not mean that it can in this way recoup all the lost benefits of others' compliance. So in this first-person dimension of the compliance condition, the most we can require of a moral principle is that under partial compliance its active demands on a complying agent neither reduce the compliance effect on him *so that* it is worse than it would be under full compliance, nor, where this is already the case, make the compliance effect even *worse* for the agent.

To impose an active demand on a person is to make a requirement compliance with which makes the agent worse-off; in other words, it is to require a *sacrifice* from the agent as measured against the optimally prudent life in the factual status quo. Note that a required *act* can constitute a sacrifice, in this sense, if in itself it makes the agent worse-off in the status quo, even if the *overall* compliance effect is a net benefit. For of course my compliance with a principle can bring a loss to me that is smaller than the passive benefit to me flowing from compliance by others. This confirms that the compliance condition can be violated even where the net compliance effect on a complying agent under partial compliance is a benefit; the compliance condition is violated in such a case because under full compliance the compliance effect on our agent would be even better.

I can now present the official formulation of the first-person dimension of compliance condition:

> Agent-neutral principles should not under partial compliance require sacrifice of an agent where the total compliance effect on her, taking that sacrifice into account, would be worse than it would be (all other aspects of her situation remaining the same) under full compliance from now on.

Our compliance condition is by now rather opaque. Because this is due mostly to the unfamiliarity of the notion of compliance effects, it may help somewhat to spell out its application to our most familiar case. Consider us rich people who, our persons and property now protected by a high level of compliance with deontological constraints, would certainly all be worse-off under full compliance with the optimizing principle of beneficence. Under both full and partial compliance, then, the total compliance effect on us when we comply with this principle would be worse than that of the normative status quo. But the *relevant* point is that under partial compliance each of us is required to make sacrifices even though these sacrifices would make it the case that the overall compliance effect on us of the principle is a good deal worse than it would be under full compliance. The optimizing principle of beneficence violates the compliance condition.

The illustration just given would perhaps be more intuitively compelling if cast in the language of demands. But, to repeat, this is due mostly to the unfamiliarity of the notion of a compliance effect. That is, I do not believe that the initial intuitive plausibility of our first formulation of the compliance condition depended on ambiguities in the ordinary vague notion of a moral demand. The initial complaints about "taking up the slack" and "doing more than one's fair share" are not as accurate once we move beyond the realm of active demands and into that of compliance effects, but this inaccuracy consists only in incompleteness. We have seen that it would be hard to defend a concern about the way the optimizing principle of beneficence imposes active demands under partial compliance other than as a special case of a more general concern about the imposition of compliance effects under partial compliance. This more general concern, roughly expressed, is that a person's fulfillment of the responsibility she has under partial compliance for promoting a moral aim shared with others should not leave her with a worse compliance effect than she would enjoy if she fulfilled her responsibility under full compliance.

III. Assessment

There is an obvious objection to our reformulation of the compliance condition in terms of compliance effects. In chapter 3 I was able to describe an effective and non-question-begging way to assess active demands, or sacrifice. Taking the factual status quo as our backdrop, we assess the difference between the agent's expected well-being as a perfect complier and her expected well-being in an optimally prudent life.[5] But we found no similarly plausible method of assessment for passive effects, at least not under partial compliance. This problem obviously carries over to the assessment of compliance effects, and thus it seems that we will never be able to tell whether a moral principle satisfies the compliance condition or not.

But we must remember that the problem with the assessment of passive effects under partial compliance lay not so much with the assessment of the effect of compliance on well-being as with the specification of the *level* of compliance the effect of which we were assessing. And it is clear that the compliance condition does not require us to be able to identify compliance effects for particular degrees of partial compliance. All we need to know is whether the compliance effect is different under full compliance from what it is under any level of partial compliance.

Furthermore, the compliance condition actually does not require absolute measures of compliance effects at all; thus we can avoid having to make assumptions about people's well-being in a world of zero compliance with some theory. To find out whether the compliance effect on an agent is worse under partial compliance than it would be under full compliance, we need only compare the agent's levels of expected well-being in the two situations. A measure of a compliance effect is just a measure of the impact of compliance, by the agent and others, on expected well-being, and so we know that the compliance effects under partial and full compliance are equal if, all other aspects of his situation remaining the same, the complying agent's level of expected well-being would be the same under full as under partial compliance. So when assessing compliance effects as required by the compliance condition, we can say that if a change solely in the level of expected compliance with a moral principle—from partial to full compliance—would not affect an agent's level of expected well-being, or would affect it only for the worse, then the compliance effect under partial compliance is not worse than it would be under full compliance. The difficulty of assessing passive effects creates trouble for the problem of over-demandingness because that problem requires a (rough) assessment of the *actual* demands made by a moral theory. The compliance condition requires no such assessment, and thus avoids the trouble entirely.

As a final point, note that we do not look to any one moment in an agent's life when we evaluate whether the compliance effects of a particular principle violate the compliance condition. In chapter 3 I noted that for the purposes of the over-demandingness problem, active demands should be assessed from the start of responsible life and passive effects from the start of life.[6] Since the compliance condition is not concerned with the extent of actual compliance effects across a person's life, but rather with the difference between compliance effects under partial and full compliance from now on, it does not make use of canonical moments in an agent's life.

IV. The Third-Person Dimension

I have discussed the compliance condition's strictures about the impact a person's own compliance with a moral principle can make on the total compliance effect on her of that principle; this was the first-person dimension of the compliance condition. But of course our highly taxed Norwegians have cause to be concerned about the contribution to the total compliance effect they enjoy that is due to the complying behavior of *other people*. The Norwegians may contribute nothing to development aid voluntarily, but, because of the structure of their economic institutions, still be contributing more than they would have to under full compliance. In such a case the optimizing principle of beneficence may have breached the compliance condition in virtue of the impact of the complying behavior of members of the government on the total compliance effect enjoyed by the citizens.

If we approach the third-person dimension of the compliance condition directly, we come up with this:

> Agent-neutral moral principles should not under partial compliance require an agent to act such that a loss is imposed on some other person where the total compliance effect on that other person, taking this loss into account, would be worse than it would be (all other aspects of her situation remaining the same) under full compliance from now on.

The clause "such that a loss is imposed" is the third-person analogue to the first-person dimension's "require a sacrifice." As we have seen, all we can demand of a moral principle is that under partial compliance its requirements neither reduce the compliance effect on a person *so that* it is worse than it would be under full compliance, nor, where this is already the case, make the compliance effect even *worse* for that person. To illustrate, consider again our Norwegians, contributing more to development aid under their taxation scheme than they would need to under worldwide full compliance. So long as we assume that if the government were not to comply with the optimizing principle of beneficence it would institute a taxation scheme more beneficial to Norwegians, this case shows the optimizing principle of beneficence in violation of the compliance condition.

It is clear that violation of the compliance condition is highly contingent on the nature or character of the particular agent or agency. For what counts as a sacrifice or loss for the purposes of the compliance condition depends on what the agent would be expected to do as a noncomplier. This contingency may seem to be objectionable in the third-person case. Thus suppose that I am able take some of your money— more than you would be required to give away under full compliance. There are two reasons that I might do this: because I am required to by the optimizing principle of beneficence for the purposes of redistribution, and because I want the money for myself. If we suppose that if I were not to comply with the optimizing principle I would surely take the money for my own use, then compliance with the principle brings no loss to you. In the first-person case it seems clearly right to say that I suffer no loss from acting as required if, as a noncomplier, I would do the same thing anyway. But in the third-person case it may seem that the relevant kind of loss still falls to *another person* even if the complying agent would have done the same thing in any case.

I think that this doubt is misplaced. The concern captured by the third-person dimension of the compliance condition is that my compliance with a moral principle imposes losses on you that leave you contributing more toward the principle's aim than you would need to do under full compliance. It is appropriate that the objection applies only when the loss in question is imposed in order to promote the relevant moral aim, and that it otherwise would not occur. If you can do nothing to keep me from taking your money, you need have no complaint against a moral principle that, in effect, tells me to apply that money to more appropriate ends than the improvement of my own life.

This reply might seem to be inadequate. However, the reason for continued resistance may well come from beyond the confines of the compliance condition. The structure of the case I have been discussing is that the optimizing principle of beneficence requires me to impose a loss on you that, under full compliance, it would not require you to impose on yourself. If we accept the compliance condition, it will be accurate to say that I am here, in our real world of partial compliance, required by the optimizing principle to impose a loss on you that you are not rightly required to impose on yourself. But it is plausible to believe that any moral theory should include a constraint prohibiting agents from imposing sacrifices on others that those others are not required to sustain voluntarily; we can refer to this as a constraint against imposing unrequired sacrifice.[7] If this general position could be defended, we would not need to concern ourselves further with the third-person dimension of the compliance condition. Any moral principle that satisfied the first-person dimension of the condition would come accompanied by a constraint against imposing unrequired sacrifice, and thus the third-person dimension would be redundant. If people are not required to direct 50 percent of their income to development aid on a voluntary basis, it would be wrong to institute a taxation scheme that does this automatically, just because of the constraint that says it is always wrong to impose a sacrifice on a person that he is not required to impose on himself.

A constraint against imposing unrequired sacrifice has some dramatic implications. In the venerable trolley case it is typically held to be permissible to redirect a deadly trolley toward one innocent person and away from five; but trolley experts do not suppose that the one person is required to direct the trolley onto herself. A constraint against imposing unrequired sacrifice would make this combination of views impossible.[8] Notwithstanding such implications, I believe that a constraint against imposing unrequired sacrifice is quite plausible. But if there is such a constraint it must have general application, and thus a full discussion of the arguments for and against it would take us far afield.[9] So I will not rely on a constraint against imposing unrequired sacrifice in what follows, but rather defend the compliance condition in its first- and third-person dimensions.

V. The Collective Principle of Beneficence

It is one thing to state the compliance condition and to know how to decide when it is satisfied, but quite another to find or design a principle of beneficence that does satisfy it. (Recall from the previous chapter that a confident sense that some principles are too demanding does not guarantee that we can identify with confidence principles that would not be too demanding.) If we cannot describe a principle of beneficence that meets the compliance condition, we will not only have made no progress in our search for a plausible principle of beneficence; without such a principle to discuss and evaluate, we will also be in a much weaker position to make a judgment about whether the compliance condition does indeed capture what is wrong with the optimizing principle of beneficence. So as one last preliminary task before I discuss the motivation for the compliance condition in more depth, I should try to describe, at least in outline form, a principle of beneficence that satisfies it.

What we need is a principle of beneficence that meets the two parts of the compliance condition as set out in sections II and IV.* Recall from section III that we assess whether the compliance effect on a person is

---

*See pp. 80 and 82.

worse under partial compliance than it would be under full compliance by assessing whether that person's expected well-being under partial compliance is worse than it would be, all other aspects of the situation remaining the same, under full compliance. Taking this into account, we can say that a principle that meets the compliance condition will meet the following tests:

> First person: the principle does not require sacrifice of an agent under partial compliance where the agent's level of expected well-being, taking the sacrifice into account, would be less than her level of expected well-being would be (all other aspects of her situation remaining the same) under full compliance from now on.

> Third person: the principle never requires agents to act under partial compliance such that a loss is imposed on some other person where that other person's level of expected well-being, taking this loss into account, would be less than it would be (all other aspects of her situation remaining the same) under full compliance from now on.

Now it might seem that we do not need to *invent* a principle of beneficence that meets these tests, since we are already familiar with versions of utilitarianism that require agents always to do the very same thing under partial compliance as under full compliance, and it might be thought that such theories automatically pass the tests.

I have in mind what could be called *ideal collective* versions of utilitarianism, such as rule-utilitarianism (ideal collective act-utilitarianism and ideal collective motive-utilitarianism are also possible).[10] Any ideal collective version of utilitarianism determines the rightness of action by appeal to the consequences of *everybody* following a certain rule (or performing a certain action, or having a certain motive), even in circumstances where it is clear that not everyone *will* follow the rule (etc.). This idealization to full compliance ensures that under partial compliance each person is required to act in just the same way as she would be required to act under full compliance.

Now the idealization to full compliance in determining rightness of action is also responsible for a well-known objection to ideal collective versions of utilitarianism. Under partial compliance these theories can require us to act in a way that, since not enough others are also acting in that way, is entirely pointless, or perhaps makes the outcome worse— possibly very much worse. One possible way to avoid some aspects of this problem—available to rule- and motive-utilitarians—is to suggest an overriding rule or motive to prevent great harm.[11] But such a solution would bring the theory into obvious conflict with the compliance condition; indeed, it is hard to see how any solution to this objection could avoid conflict with the compliance condition.

But even without such a modification, it is actually not the case that ideal collective versions of utilitarianism satisfy the compliance condition. For the fact that a theory requires an agent to do the same thing under partial as under full compliance does not guarantee that the compliance condition is met. This would follow only if we believed that active demands were the only relevant kind of compliance effect.[12] We are instead interested in the total compliance effect on an agent, and when we remember the benefits that might come to an agent under full compliance, it is clear that one of the ideal collective theories could require sacrifice of an agent that leaves her with a compliance effect worse than she would enjoy under full compliance. To put the point in the terms of our first-person test: though I am required to do under partial compliance exactly what I would be required to do under full compliance, this does not ensure that under partial compliance I am never required to make a sacrifice that leaves me with a level of expected well-being lower than I would have under full compliance, where I enjoy the benefits flowing from the compliance of others.

But though ideal collective versions of utilitarianism cannot be models for the principle of beneficence we need, discussing them has pointed us in the right direction. Like those theories, a principle of beneficence that satisfies the compliance condition will clearly have to make use of an ideal of full compliance in some form. Having seen that we cannot use the ideal to determine rightness of action, the obvious possibility to consider next is that the ideal operates only at the level of compliance effects. When it comes to the question of what agents should do, the principle we are looking for should cease to idealize, and return to the actual, nonideal world. In this sense, what we need is a *nonideal* collective principle of beneficence—or the collective principle of beneficence, for short.

To describe the collective principle of beneficence, we can consider the two dimensions of the compliance condition in turn. The collective principle of beneficence holds that an agent should assess rightness of action in terms of the expected benefits she could produce in the actual circumstances she is in. So far the collective principle of beneficence is like the optimizing principle of beneficence and unlike the ideal collective theories. But the collective principle differs from the optimizing principle of beneficence in that it does not require agents always to promote the best outcome. For the extent to which the collective principle requires each person to promote well-being under partial compliance is determined in the following way: each agent is required to sacrifice only as much as will make it no longer true that his level of expected well-being is higher than it would be, all other aspects of his situation remaining the same, under full compliance (where, of course, he also complies).

In rough terms, then, the collective principle of beneficence holds that a person need never sacrifice so much that he would end up less well-off than he would be under full compliance from now on, but within that constraint he must do as much good as possible. More precisely, the main part of the collective principle can be stated as follows:

> Everyone is required to perform one of the actions that, of those available to her, is optimal in respect of expected aggregate weighted well-being, except in situations of partial compliance with this principle. In situations of partial compliance, a person's maximum level of required sacrifice is that which will reduce her level of expected well-being to the level it would be, all other aspects of her situation remaining the same, if there were to be full compliance from that point on. Under partial compliance a person is required to perform either an action—of those requiring no more than the maximum level of required sacrifice—that is optimal in respect of expected weighted aggregate well-being or any other action which is at least as good in respect of expected weighted aggregate well-being.[13]

Though this formulation is horribly cumbersome, the basic idea of the principle is simple enough. It is, to repeat, that a person need never sacrifice so much that he would end up less well-off than he would be under full compliance from now on, but within that constraint he must do as much good as possible. Not surprisingly, however, the practical operation of the collective principle is rather complicated. But since the purpose of this chapter is to explore the motivation for the compliance condition, I will postpone detailed discussion of the various complications until chapter 7. All that needs to be said in advance is that I do not imagine that the collective principle could or need be appealed to by agents on a case-by-case basis. As with the optimizing principle of beneficence, the main practical role of the collective principle would be to provide various rules of thumb for action and a test for the acceptability of possible patterns of motivation.

It is an obvious implication of the collective principle of beneficence that under partial compliance no sacrifice is required whenever a person's expected well-being as an optimally prudent agent in the factual status quo is not greater than it would be under full compliance. Since this describes the situation of many—perhaps most—people in our actual world, it may seem that the collective principle of beneficence can be rejected out of hand as implausibly weak. I postpone discussion of this issue to chapter 7 as well; but, to avoid misunderstanding, it should be noted that I do not believe that the collective principle of beneficence could plausibly stand alone as an account of the whole of morality.*

---

*In chapter 7, section 4, I will also discuss an apparent counterexample involving a rescue situation: if there are two potential rescuers, one a noncomplier, and two drowning children, does not the complying rescuer have to take up the slack left by the other person's noncompliance?

To complete our statement of the collective principle of beneficence we need a clause that will bring it into line with the third-person test. This seems straightforward:

> However, no one is required to act in a way that imposes a loss on some other person unless that other person's level of expected well-being after the loss would be at least as high as it would be, all other aspects of the situation remaining the same, under full compliance from that point on.

We can call this the "third-person rider" to the collective principle of beneficence. Once again, it is of course easier to state than to act upon; but I will leave that issue until chapter 7. Again, only one point needs to be emphasized here. It is no surprise that there is nothing in the first-person dimension of the principle to *prohibit* optimal action in situations of partial compliance; like the limited principles of beneficence discussed in chapter 4, the collective principle of beneficence merely sets a limit to *required* sacrifice. This is what we would expect, there being no case for prohibiting supererogatory action. But the equivalent point holds true of the third-person rider to the collective principle, and this may be more surprising. Our principle never requires agents to impose losses on others beyond what would bring their expected well-being down to the full-compliance level, but it does not prohibit agents from imposing greater losses than that. The collective principle of beneficence does not, in other words, come with a *constraint* attached; it has nothing to say about the moral legitimacy of imposing losses on people beyond what it requires of them. As a result, it remains a fully agent-neutral principle in the sense discussed in section I. If this seems wrong, that is likely to be because of a commitment to the constraint against imposing unrequired sacrifice, discussed in the previous section (and further in chapter 7).

VI. Compliance, Distribution, and Fairness

It is time at last to return to the motivation behind all these cumbersome formulations. As I said in section I, two special questions can arise for agent-neutral moral principles. That these questions *must* arise for an agent-neutral principle has not yet been argued, but let us continue to assume for the moment that they do. The questions are those of how responsibility for promoting the aim that all people are given in common is allocated among them, and of how the responsibility of a complying agent is affected when other people fall short in their responsibilities.

I developed the compliance condition as a generalization of some intuitive objections to the way the optimizing principle of beneficence imposes demands under partial compliance. But the compliance condition is at the same time an answer to the second of our two questions. It says, very roughly, that discharge of a person's responsibility under partial compliance should not leave her in a worse position than she would be in if she discharged her responsibility under full compliance. As formulated, the compliance condition offers no answer to the first of the two questions; it makes no mention of the allocation of responsibility under full compliance. But the case for the compliance condition is much stronger if it is understood as part of a general view that does offer answers to both our questions.

Someone who finds unpersuasive the intuitive objections to the optimizing principle of beneficence that led us to develop the compliance condition—that it appears to require agents to do more than their fair share and to take up the slack left by others' noncompliance—could point out that there is no automatic legitimacy to an agent's responsibility under full compliance. And, indeed, it is true that if we thought that a person's full-compliance responsibility was somehow objectionable or illegitimate, we would not be inclined to use it as the benchmark for responsibility under partial compliance. If, on the other hand, we are convinced on independent grounds that a person's responsibility under full compliance is the result of some appropriate allocation, or at least meets some appropriate normative standard, the case for taking it as the benchmark for responsibility under partial compliance is strong. An agent who knows the shape of his legitimate responsibility under full compliance knows what he is rightly responsible for and what *others* are rightly responsible for; knowing that, he can object to greater responsibility under partial compliance as in effect the assumption of duties that rightly belong to others.

Thus the compliance condition should be understood as the second of two answers that stand together. But this means that we need to address the first question. What can be said about the appropriateness of different allocations of agents' responsibility under full compliance? As a matter of logical possibility, this issue could be approached in a variety of ways. If there is a proper division of responsibility among agents, there must be some normative basis for that division, but it would be possible, on some views of morality, to hold agents responsible for promoting a moral aim according to their rank, or nationality, or whatever. In the realm of plausible views, however, the obvious normative guide in the division of responsibility is the notion of fairness: the proper way to distribute responsibility for the pursuit of a moral aim among agents is to distribute it fairly. It is no doubt the overwhelming plausibility of using fairness as the relevant normative guide in the division of responsibility that accounts for the natural affinity between our two initial intuitive objections to the demands of the optimizing principle of beneficence under partial compliance: it will seem objectionable that I have to take up the slack left by others' noncompliance just in case that means that I am doing more than my fair share.

Now a fair distribution of responsibility will not be determined by merely abstract considerations. If something needs to be fairly distributed among the members of a group, it will be because that thing affects the interests of the group members; if a fair distribution of responsibility were thought to consist, for example, in a fair distribution of opportunities to promote the relevant aim, we would quickly lose interest. What matters are the effects on people's well-being of compliance with the agent-neutral principle; this is what needs to be fairly distributed. If there are benefits to each from compliance by all, those benefits should be fairly distributed; and likewise for burdens. Thus a fair distribution of responsibility is a distribution of responsibility that affects the well-being of the members of the group fairly: what we look for, in fact, is the distribution of responsibility that yields a fair distribution of compliance effects.[14]

The next chapter is devoted to the question of what a fair distribution of the compliance effects of an agent-neutral principle would look like. The conclusion will be that any plausible agent-neutral principle automatically distributes compliance effects fairly under full compliance; at least, this is so if we employ a minimal notion of fairness. This conclusion is not self-evident, since, as we will see, the optimizing principle of beneficence distributes its compliance effects very unequally under full compliance, and this inequality might seem unfair. But it would complicate our discussion of the compliance condition too much to turn to that issue now; for the remainder of this chapter, we can simply continue to assume that the full-compliance distribution of compliance effects by agent-neutral moral principles is fair.

Now if the question of the appropriate distribution of responsibility by an agent-neutral principle under full compliance is answered by an appeal to the idea of fairness, is it right to say that the same normative concern shapes our answer to the question of the appropriate responsibility of agents under partial compliance?

I have said at various points that the optimizing principle of beneficence imposes demands unfairly under partial compliance. This is a defensible way of putting the matter, but it needs to be made clear that the kind of potential unfairness the compliance condition responds to is very different from the kind of unfairness a full-compliance distribution of compliance effects might display. For under partial compliance with the optimizing principle of beneficence, each agent is required to fulfill what would be his own fairly allocated responsibility under full compliance plus (speaking roughly) some of the responsibility that properly belongs to noncomplying agents. Since *each* agent faces exactly the same requirement—and in substance, not just in form—no standard issue of fairness can arise. It is true that noncomplying *agents* could be accused of *acting* unfairly, in that they know that complying agents will enjoy lower compliance effects because of their noncompliance. But the principle itself would be unfair, in the standard sense, only if, for example, some but not all people were required to make sacrifices that would leave them in a worse position than they would be in under full compliance. The idea of fairness, in its standard or central sense, is comparative or distributional; and so the optimizing principle of beneficence, since it treats all agents substantively the same way under partial compliance, cannot be said to impose responsibility under partial compliance in a way that is unfair in that central sense.[15]

Nevertheless, it is, as I say, defensible to describe the requirements of the optimizing principle of beneficence under partial compliance as unfair. There is nothing to be gained, and much to be lost, from using the notion of fairness to cover any normative issue whatsoever. But the question of responsibility under partial compliance is so closely connected to issues of fairness, in the central sense, that it would in fact be rather odd to say that the question did not bring up an issue of fairness at all. For if we conclude that a certain allocation of responsibility *is* fair, the further thought that one should not be required to do *more* than that fair share does not come from some different normative realm; rather, it fills out the content of that initial conclusion. Here is L. Jonathan Cohen on the matter: "Burdens, like benefits, ought to be fairly distributed, and *ceteris paribus* no-one is morally required to take on more than his fair share of a burden because someone else defects, any more than he is morally permitted to receive more than his fair share of a benefit just because someone else does not take up a share."[16] Now Cohen could perhaps be read as suggesting that it simply follows from the fact of a fair distribution that one is not required to take on more than one's fair share. If that is the right way to read the passage, I would disagree with it; for one *could* hold that it would be appropriate for compliers to be required to take up, in addition to their own fairly allocated shares, the shares of noncompliers. But what I do want to insist is that both views are appropriately understood as part of one's broader view about the normative acceptability of different possible distributions of responsibility. So even if the compliance condition is not in itself strictly a condition *of* fairness, fairness is the normative idea that gives rise to it.

My point here really just follows from what I earlier said strengthened the case for the compliance condition. I said that the compliance condition is most plausible if seen as part of a general view that answers both of our two questions about responsibility imposed by agent-neutral principles. There is no magic in the idea of full compliance as such; rather, the idea is that *if* it is the case that fairness determines the legitimate division of what I am responsible for and what you are responsible for, the further normative idea that I am not responsible for what you are responsible for seems highly compelling. All I have now added to this is the claim that it is more natural than not to describe that further idea as itself an idea about fairness.

Having said this, however, it is important to emphasize the specific and limited notion of unfairness being invoked here. I say that the optimizing principle is unfair under partial compliance for requiring complying agents to take on more than their fair share of the responsibility for promoting overall well-being. It could be objected that the collective principle of beneficence is even more unfair because it lets the costs of noncompliance fall on the people who should have been benefited by the noncompliers. Those "victims" of noncompliance are likely to be worse off than the compliers whom the optimizing principle requires to take up the slack, and we would normally think it fairer to let some cost fall on the better-off of two people.[17] But this objection assimilates a concern with the fairness of the way a principle of beneficence imposes responsibility on agents to a general concern about the fairness of the distribution of well-being.[18] A principle of beneficence is not a principle of fairness in the latter sense; it simply requires people to promote overall well-being. And though the victims of noncompliance with the optimizing principle are worse-off than they would be under full compliance, this is not unfair to them in the sense of fairness embodied in the compliance condition. The compliance effect on them is worse than it would be under full compliance because of people's noncompliance, not because of the requirements the optimizing principle makes of people under partial compliance—not because of a sacrifice the victims are required to make or because a loss has been imposed on them by others complying with the optimizing principle. Similarly, though the collective principle of beneficence leaves the victims of noncompliance worse-off than they would be if the compliers took up (some of) the slack, it cannot be said that the victims have been required to take on (either actively or passively) responsibilities that rightly belong to others.[19]

A further connection between the compliance condition and the standard notion of fairness is worth mentioning. If a person fails to act as morally required, we say that she has acted wrongly. It could be thought that another secondary kind of unfairness inherent in the optimizing principle of beneficence lies in the attributions of wrongdoing it generates. Thus suppose that I have not fulfilled my full-compliance responsibility and that while you have fulfilled yours, you balk at taking on mine as well. In this case, we are both wrongdoers according to the optimizing principle of beneficence. You may complain that this is unfair: we are held to have acted equally wrongly, but our cases are very different. Now it seems easy enough to say in rebuttal that while we are indeed both wrongdoers, I am a worse wrongdoer than you. But it is notable that the optimizing principle of beneficence lacks the resources to make this discrimination in the relevant way. Let us stipulate that both of us have failed to save many lives at little cost: Why, according to the optimizing principle, is my failure more seriously wrong than yours? In any case, I do not think that an appeal to degrees of wrongness is sufficient to silence your concern here. You might insist that fairness requires a categorical distinction between your case—where you have, after all, done all you would have been required to do if only I had done what I was required to do—and mine. In not allowing for such a distinction, it might be said that the optimizing principle of beneficence treats you unfairly.[20] If this is plausible, it provides further support for saying that the compliance condition responds to considerations of fairness.

Having defended the propriety of my statement that the optimizing principle of beneficence imposes responsibility unfairly under partial compliance, I should add that I do not believe that much turns on the issue. The argument in favor of the compliance condition that I have presented connects at important points with the idea of a fairness, and this is what really matters. So let me conclude this section with a summary of that rather roundabout argument.

Our compliance condition is the generalization of an intuitive objection to the way the optimizing principle of beneficence imposes requirements under partial compliance. The initial objection to "taking up the slack left by others' noncompliance" became an insistence that a person's fulfillment of the responsibility she has under partial compliance for promoting a shared moral aim should not leave her with a worse compliance effect than she would enjoy if she fulfilled her responsibility under full compliance. As a generalization of an intuitively powerful response to the demands of the optimizing principle of beneficence, the compliance condition is supported, in one direction, by just that intuitively powerful response. But the case for the compliance condition is much stronger if we see it as part of an answer to a pair of questions that can arise for agent-neutral principles. If we take it that agent-neutral principles should be held to a standard of fairness in the distribution of responsibility under full compliance, and that in fact they meet such a standard, the compliance condition can be understood as a very natural answer to the question of the proper responsibility of agents under partial compliance. If there is such a thing as a fair allocation of responsibility, it is natural to think that it is unfair, or at least inappropriate, to require agents, under partial compliance, to exceed that fairly allocated responsibility.

VII. Collective Beneficence

Two aspects of the case that can be made for the compliance condition on its own terms remain incomplete. I have put off until the next chapter defense of the claim that agent-neutral principles do meet a standard of fairness in the distribution of responsibility under full compliance. Let me now turn to the other gap in the argument: while it is not controversial to assert that the two questions about responsibility can arise for agent-neutral principles, it is controversial to say that they *do*; we need some reason to believe this claim.

When I introduced the two questions about responsibility under agent-neutral principles in section I, the main point was that these were questions that could not arise for agent-relative principles. Let me first say a little more about this claim.

There is very little plausibility to the idea that the compliance effects of deontological constraints should be fairly distributed under full compliance. It follows from the very structure of agent-relative principles that an agent is not concerned, at a fundamental level, with others' compliance. As Nagel puts it, "It seems that you shouldn't break a promise or tell a lie for the sake of some benefit, even though you would not be required to forgo a comparable benefit in order to prevent someone else from breaking a promise or telling a lie."[21] Any moral concern you have with others' lies would be via some *other* moral principle; for example, as a beneficent agent you would be concerned about any bad effects of those lies. Since deontological constraints give people no concern or aim in common, the distribution of the compliance effects of these constraints has no normative significance. Deontology is individualistic; we are not in it together, but each on our own. To say that the compliance effects of a constraint against killing should be fairly distributed among all agents would be like saying that the children of two families that have no contact with each other should all be treated fairly by the four parents.

Now, some so-called special obligations can be seen as giving a group of people a common aim; for example, the citizens of a nation might be thought to have an obligation to promote the nation's well-being that foreigners lack. Such restricted principles of beneficence could be characterized as group-relative but agent-neutral principles—within the group, they are agent-neutral. Here it clearly is appropriate to inquire about the fairness of the distribution of full-compliance responsibility among the members of the group. Other special obligations, by contrast, are genuinely agent-relative in that they give a particular person an aim that is not shared with any other person, and to such principles the question of the fairness of the distribution of responsibility does not apply.

It is equally clear, I think, that without a common aim the issue of people's responsibility under partial compliance simply does not arise. A constraint against killing may become more demanding on an agent if many others violate that same constraint, but if the agent is indeed committed to a deontological constraint against killing, she is not likely to think that a continued prohibition becomes inappropriate or unfair. Since she has no aim in common with the noncompliers, the worsening of the compliance effect on her that is due to their noncompliance is of no special significance—it is no more or less significant than a worsening due to natural causes would be.

But now it should be noted that both our questions might arise for agent-relative moral principles if such principles were believed to be themselves not fundamental, but rather the deliverances of some more general kind of moral reasoning. Contractualist views could be said to show agent-relative moral principles as valid only in virtue of the availability of a contractualist justification for them. And if the contractualist justification in question is one that appeals to substantive aims that all people have in common, distributive questions and questions about responsibility under partial compliance will naturally arise.[22] Moreover, there are versions of contractualism that could be said to be *all about* a fair distribution of compliance effects. I have in mind theories that suppose people to have essentially two practical aims: to promote their self-interest, and, insofar as co-operation with others is beneficial to them, to cooperate on terms that are fair. Gibbard labels this second kind of view "justice as fair reciprocity."[23] I do not find views of either variety especially plausible, but this is not the place to discuss them. The range of contractualist views that have been defended is so wide, and the differences between the views so significant, that it would be impossible to do them justice here. Fortunately, we can justifiably set such views aside, as the fact that our questions about responsibility become relevant for apparently agent-relative principles if those principles are explained and justified in terms of some commonly held aim, or directly in terms of a fair distribution of compliance effects, does not contradict the point I am making.

Nevertheless, the existence of these contractualist accounts does show that my claim that the two questions about responsibility can arise only for principles of beneficence is not strictly accurate. A more accurate claim—expressing the underlying point I was trying to make—would be that the problem of over-demandingness appears to arise where and only where the two questions may be appropriate. But this claim might now also seem to be false, since contractualist moral accounts are not typically subjected to charges of over-demandingness. However, contractualist theorizing usually proceeds on an assumption of full compliance and is silent about what might be required of people under partial compliance; it is fair to say, therefore, that such theories have not properly been put to the test in this respect.

In any case, the most we have so far shown is that our two questions do not plausibly arise for moral principles that, in a fundamental way, give different aims to different agents. We need now to turn to the missing piece in our case for the compliance condition and offer reasons for believing not just that these questions can arise for agent-neutral principles but that they do. Since a decision on this issue for any particular agent-neutral principle will depend upon our understanding of the moral concern in question, this means that we need to reflect on our understanding of beneficence as a moral requirement.

I mentioned in section I that agent-neutral principles apply to agents *as a group*. This was tendentious because it is one thing for people to have the same aim, another for them to have it as a group. Beneficence could, in other words, be understood either as an aim people have *as* individuals, and just happen to share with all other individuals, or as an aim people have together with others in the stronger sense that each person views his beneficent activities as part of a collective undertaking.

If beneficence is understood in the first sense—as an individually held aim—people have no moral interest in whether others are also complying. Individual beneficent agents trying to promote well-being in their circumstances must of course take into account the predictable behavior of other people as a causally important part of those circumstances, but it makes no difference whether this predictable behavior is *complying* behavior or not. Indeed, any kind of behavior by other people has exactly the same instrumental significance for a beneficent agent as do changes in natural circumstances.

If, by contrast, beneficence is a collective aim, beneficent agents do not just happen to share an aim with everyone else, they see themselves as *working together with others* to promote human well-being. If beneficence is a collective undertaking in this sense, the question of the fairness of the distribution of the effects of participation naturally arises. If we promote well-being as a group working together, we will naturally want to do that on fair terms. And the question about responsibility under partial compliance also naturally arises. Whether someone else complies or not is a fact of special significance if our aim is to promote well-being together with others: we will not treat increased need for beneficence due to natural circumstances, such as a drought, in just the same way that we treat increased need for beneficence that is due to others' failing to do their part.[24]

It is no surprise that I find the collective view of beneficence more plausible than the individualistic view. But I should emphasize that this does not mean that I deny that agents ever have, or should have, individually held concern for the welfare of others. When moved by the motive of benevolence, we typically have only instrumental concern with the beneficent actions of others; we simply want to benefit the object of our benevolence as much as we can. But this is consistent with viewing morally required beneficence in collective terms. In other words, I do not suggest that benevolent feelings or desires are in some sense mediated by thoughts about the possible actions of all other people. The claim is rather that insofar as we believe that beneficent action is morally required of people, it is natural to understand that as a collective requirement.[25] And it is simply a mistake, I believe, to hold that beneficence as a moral requirement must be somehow continuous with ordinary benevolent motives that people typically have. Hume was right to say that the benevolence of human beings is strictly limited, and any attempt to defend a robust principle of beneficence by appealing to natural benevolence will surely fail.[26] But it is just as true that a robust principle of beneficence need not depend on such a defense: in no sphere of morality does obligation simply track our ordinary feelings, desires, and dispositions. Benevolence and moral requirements of beneficence are closely related in various ways, but neither can be fully explained in terms of the other.

If it is more plausible to think of beneficence in terms of a collective aim than in terms of an aim agents have strictly as individuals, we have more reason to ask our two questions about responsibility, and we are thus on our way to the compliance condition and the collective principle of beneficence. But though I find the collective understanding of beneficence very plausible, I do not think of it as playing anything like a foundational role in this story. The conception of beneficence as a group project where each group member sees himself working together with others is, rather, just one more plausible idea to add to the set of mutually supporting considerations I have advanced in this chapter. The case for the compliance condition and the collective principle of beneficence depends on the overall plausibility of the whole set taken together.

It is even more important to note that the full case for the compliance condition and the collective principle depends on the *relative* overall plausibility of the set of ideas I have advanced. After my long and abstract discussion of the compliance condition, it is worth remembering that the background issues to which that set of ideas is offered as a response are not manufactured or marginal. Anyone interested in normative theory will want to be able to explain the apparent absurdity of the optimizing principle of beneficence, and anyone who takes beneficence seriously will want to be able to describe at least the rough shape of a plausible principle of beneficence. And so if the collective understanding of beneficence and indeed the compliance condition itself seem wrong, we are left with a choice between the optimizing principle of beneficence, its apparent absurdity unexplained and unmitigated, or some as yet undescribed and unmotivated limited principle of beneficence. It is in this spirit of a search for a relatively plausible view in a field with no overwhelmingly compelling contenders that I will continue to defend the compliance condition and the collective principle of beneficence. The next piece of the argument returns us to my central comparative claim.

VIII. The Compliance Condition and Over-demandingness

I have claimed that the compliance condition offers a plausible diagnosis of the apparent absurdity of the optimizing principle of beneficence. If I am right, our skeptical arguments against the problem of over-demandingness are greatly strengthened, for without some such alternative diagnosis it is very hard to accept the conclusion that there is no problem of over-demandingness—after all, the optimizing principle of beneficence still seems absurd. And of course the case in favor of the compliance condition is also greatly strengthened if it does indeed provide a convincing explanation of this rather vivid intuitive belief. But so far I have not said much in defense of this part of the case for the compliance condition. I have noted that while the complaint about excessive demands should apply to other parts of commonsense morality if it does to beneficence, the complaint about unfair demands plausibly applies only to principles of beneficence; and noted that this supports the claim that what those who say the optimizing principle of beneficence is too demanding are in fact responding to is its unfairness under partial compliance. But apart from this promising structural point, I have defended the plausibility of the compliance condition purely on its own terms. And whatever the success of that defense—and of my skeptical arguments about over-demandingness—it may still seem that insofar as we do continue to think that the optimizing principle of beneficence is *absurd*, we think it is absurd *for being too demanding*. Something more needs to be said about the relationship between the problem of over-demandingness and the problem of an unfair imposition of responsibility under partial compliance.

Because the problem of over-demandingness is compelling only in the context of active demands considered alone, this will be the focus of my discussion. For convenience I will use "demand" to mean active demand.

We need to start by noting that the relationship between the problems could cut two ways. It might be thought that far from offering an independent diagnosis of the optimizing principle of beneficence's problems, the collective principle of beneficence gains whatever plausibility it has from the fact that, as contingent matter, it is much less demanding (on us rich people) than the optimizing principle. That the demands of the collective principle are typically lower is clear: under full compliance the collective and optimizing principles of beneficence are extensionally equivalent, and, as we know, the optimizing principle of beneficence is typically very much more demanding under partial compliance than it is under full compliance, while the collective principle of beneficence is never more demanding than it is under full compliance. But it is not plausible to attribute the entire appeal of the collective principle of beneficence to this fact. If the ideas advanced in this chapter are not plausible on their own terms, the fact that we have stumbled on a less demanding principle of beneficence seems hardly sufficient to justify a principle shaped entirely by those ideas. Moreover, since the collective principle of beneficence *can* be very demanding, it would seem to be a poor option for someone whose sole concern was the extent of demands.

Nevertheless, I do not think that the extent of the demands of the optimizing principle of beneficence is totally irrelevant to the case for the compliance condition. A fair distribution of compliance effects and a fair imposition of responsibility under partial compliance will *matter more* the greater the difference unfairness of either kind can make to the compliance effects agents enjoy. If the differences in compliance effects were trivial, the choice between the unfair optimizing principle of beneficence and the fair collective principle of beneficence would probably not be sufficiently important to deserve our attention. To say this is not to weaken the claim that the real problem with the optimizing principle of beneficence is its unfair imposition of responsibility rather than the extent of its demands. As I have already said, fairness matters when it concerns people's interests; it is to be expected that fairness matters more the more people's interests are affected by unfairness.

Now to evaluate our claim that the compliance condition offers a plausible diagnosis of the apparent absurdity of the demands of the optimizing principle of beneficence, we need to consider whether very high demands that do not violate the compliance condition seem any less objectionable than those that do.

Consider first the truly extreme demands the collective principle (and the optimizing principle) could make in certain emergency situations. It is often said that morality cannot plausibly require people to be "heroes." But some well-known cases of "heroism," often presented as clear examples of sacrifice beyond the call of duty, do not involve great sacrifice at all. Think of the (actual) case of Captain Oates, a member of Scott's expedition to the Antarctic, who "sacrificed" himself for the sake of his companions; or the case of a soldier throwing himself on an exploding hand grenade to save those around him. In both of these cases the heroic person would have died anyway; what is impressive is thus not the size of their loss, but rather their extraordinary characters.[27] Most of us would not be able to do what they did, despite the fact that the personal loss was almost nil and the potential benefits to others very great. Discussion of "heroism" needs to keep the issues of agents' character and the amount of sacrifice distinct.

But there are, of course, possible cases where an emergency situation does call for a great sacrifice; moreover, we can think of cases where the issue of character is not so salient, since the harm involved to the agent is somewhat intangible and thus not so likely to trigger the survival instinct. Thus suppose you are the only person in a position to prevent a nuclear accident that would kill many thousands of people. If you do what is needed, however, you will receive a painless but eventually fatal dose of radiation. Do you escape in the helicopter, leaving many thousands to die, or do you, in effect, sacrifice your life? Under full compliance with the collective principle, it would be optimal for you to prevent the accident and sacrifice your life. Since you would die under full compliance, your maximum level of required sacrifice is the loss of your life. Thus, given how many lives are at stake, it seems that whatever the actual level of compliance, both the optimizing principle of beneficence and the collective principle hold that you act wrongly if you make your escape.* While many cases of extreme sacrifice involve actions that it would be motivationally very hard for most of us to bring ourselves to perform, I have here tried to describe a case where this is not necessarily so. Undistracted by the issue of motivational difficulty, I am inclined to think it is not implausible, much less absurd, to say that you are required to sacrifice your life in this case.

But cases involving sacrifice of the agent's life are actually not very important for present purposes. We saw in chapter 4 that there was one defensible limit to the active demands of beneficence, namely, an absolute-level limit set *very* high, such as at the level of loss of life. So if I am wrong about your sacrifice in this case, it would not be hard to add such a limit to our collective principle of beneficence. This would not compromise our alternative diagnosis, because the practical significance of this kind of case is minimal. People are hardly ever in the position to make things better by sacrificing their lives.[28] As we know, the practically relevant losses are those of pleasure, accomplishment, satisfaction, rest, comfort, and so forth; it is by giving up these things that, unfortunately for us, we can do so much good.

Let us now move directly to the hardest, but also the most important, kind of case for the collective principle of beneficence. Imagine a world where one small country is very well-off, and the rest of the world is very badly off. So that we can focus just on beneficence, assume also that this is the result of pure luck—there has, for example, been no exploitation of the worse-off by the better-off.[29] Both the optimizing and the collective principles of beneficence would impose extreme demands on all the residents of the lucky country.** The difference between this case and our actual case of world poverty is that the extreme demands are not in any part due to agents being required to take on more than their fair share of the demands of beneficence.

I do not find the demands on the lucky people absurd. Those who do may find it harder to disagree with a domestic version of the example. Instead of a lucky country, imagine a lucky class of people in a single country. Once again we can stipulate that the inequality is due just to luck; perhaps the lucky people are simply more talented. Is it absurd to

---

*As we will see in chapter 7, the application of the collective principle of beneficence to particular decisions is not so straightforward as this suggests.

**We shouldn't assume that a small country would be required to ruin itself entirely just for the sake of very slight increases in the well-being of everyone else. For thus ruining the culture and economy of the better-off country could well be worse for everyone in the long run.

expect all the members of the lucky class to accept a much lower standard of living in order to benefit their impoverished compatriots? Note that I am not asking whether it is obviously right to say that the better-off are required to give up a great deal for the sake of the worse-off; the question is whether such a requirement qualifies as absurd *for the reason that its demands are absurdly extreme*. For that is the test here. My contention is that while it would seem absurd, under partial compliance, to expect any given member of the lucky class to act as required by the optimizing principle of beneficence, it is not absurd to expect all of them to do so under full compliance. If I am right, this supports the claim that the problem with the optimizing principle of beneficence is that it imposes demands unfairly under partial compliance.

Now some philosophers would immediately object that this second case triggers our intuitions about *justice*, not beneficence. As explained in chapter 1, I reject the assumption behind such a response, but we can leave that aside here.[30] For if this is the response, it has already been conceded that extreme demands, as such, are not problematic; that the problem with the optimizing principle of beneficence must lie elsewhere. The purpose of the current discussion is simply to ask—*leaving aside* all of chapter 3's skeptical arguments about over-demandingness—whether extreme demands that come from the collective principle of beneficence are intuitively absurd in just the same way that the demands of the optimizing principle of beneficence in our actual world of enormous hardship and minimal compliance seem to be. For my own case the answer is no; fairly imposed extreme demands do not stimulate the same confident negative reaction that unfairly imposed extreme demands do. But of course, as with every aspect of the case for the compliance condition and the collective principle of beneficence, others will disagree.

6

THE DISTRIBUTION OF THE
EFFECTS OF COMPLIANCE

The compliance condition is most plausible, I have said, if it is understood as the second part of a joint answer to our two questions about agent-neutral principles and responsibility. The answer to the first question was that agent-neutral principles should distribute responsibility under full compliance in a fair manner. And a fair distribution of responsibility, I said, is one that yields a fair distribution of compliance effects. If we add to this first answer an assumption that plausible agent-neutral principles *do* distribute compliance effects fairly under full compliance, the compliance condition can be seen as a very plausible answer to our second question—that of how agent-neutral principles should impose responsibility on agents under partial compliance. For if an agent's responsibility under full compliance is allocated on some fair basis, it is natural to insist that her responsibility not increase to her detriment just because other people will fail to meet *their* fairly allocated responsibilities. Fulfillment of her partial-compliance responsibility should not leave her with a worse compliance effect than she would enjoy if she fulfilled her fairly allocated responsibility under full compliance.

In this chapter I will try to justify the crucial assumption that under full compliance plausible agent-neutral principles produce a fair distribution of compliance effects.

I. The Distribution of
Compliance Effects

Before we can think about what fairness might require in the distribution of compliance effects, we need to have some idea of the shape of this distribution for familiar agent-neutral principles. Naturally, we turn to the optimizing principle of beneficence, which under full compliance is extensionally equivalent to the collective principle of beneficence. Because we are concerned with the fairness of the distribution, the obvious first question to ask is whether the compliance effects of this principle are distributed equally among agents.

In chapter 2 I noted in passing that I believed that a plausible principle of beneficence will weight benefits to worse-off people more than benefits to better-off people.[1] That is one way in which the morality of well-being could take into account distributive concerns. Another way is that a principle of beneficence could be accompanied by some principle of equality, holding that equality of well-being matters in itself. For most of my discussion, this issue of distribution in the domain of principles' aims has not been important. But it may become important now that I turn to consider the issue of distribution in the domain of compliance effects. For ease of exposition, I will first discuss the distribution of the compliance effects of an optimizing principle of beneficence that is not sensitive to distribution in its aim—the traditional utilitarian principle can serve as our example.

It is quite clear that the compliance effects of the utilitarian principle can be unequally distributed under full compliance. I said in chapter 3 that the compliance effect on a person under full compliance is just the difference between the person's expected well-being in a world of full compliance and her expected well-being in a baseline world of zero compliance with the relevant moral principle. I also noted that the baseline level of well-being could, for practical purposes, drop out as a constant— it would be some very low level of well-being, roughly equal for all people. Thus a person's expected well-being in a world of full compliance with a moral principle can itself count as the measure of the compliance effect on her of that principle, at least for the purposes of determining whether compliance effects are unequally distributed.[2] Since there is no reason to think that the expected well-being of agents under full compliance with the utilitarian principle will always be equal, it follows that this principle could, and indeed typically would, distribute its compliance effects unequally under full compliance.

Now though equality of well-being is in no sense part of the aim of the utilitarian principle, it might be thought that, due to the fact of the diminishing marginal utility of money and other resources, full compliance with the utilitarian principle would over time lead to an equal distribution of expected well-being and thus an equal distribution of compliance effects.

One reason that this is not so is that the diminishing marginal utility of money does not entail that a given amount of money always brings relatively high marginal benefits to the worse-off; a very badly off severely handicapped person might be benefited only very slightly by the expense of a great deal of money.[3]

Further reasons emerge when we change the focus from beneficiary to beneficent agent, and consider that different people vary greatly in their ability to promote the well-being of others. Imagine a highly skilled utilitarian surgeon who has specialized in a particular operation the need for which has traditionally been rare. If we suppose that the need for the operation increases more quickly than other surgeons can acquire the specialist skill, then even under full compliance with utilitarianism our surgeon could end up very badly off, spending all her waking hours operating; the long hours are bad for her, but this burden is easily outweighed by the good of saving lives. If circumstances conspire in the right way, the situation could persist—we may suppose that the optimal division of labor under full compliance is one under which our surgeon remains the only specialist, working around the clock. The upshot is that she would enjoy a lower compliance effect under full compliance with utilitarianism than would most other people. And the reason for this is that she is so much more *efficient* in promoting well-being than others are: a given level of sacrifice produces much greater benefits when it comes from her than from the rest of us. This phenomenon of differing levels of efficiency at promoting well-being is quite general—it is found among teachers, entertainers, administrators, and so forth.[4]

In any case, establishing the long-term egalitarian tendencies of full compliance with the utilitarian principle would not settle anything. We are interested in the distribution of compliance effects in the short run as well. To use terminology introduced in chapter 2, we cannot ignore the distribution of compliance effects under nonoptimal full compliance and consider only the utopian situation of optimal full compliance (full compliance in a world optimally improved by generations of compliance). But since this is so, there can be no question but that an optimizing principle of beneficence that in its aim is not sensitive to the distribution of well-being can and will distribute compliance effects unequally under full compliance.

What is perhaps surprising is that this result does not change when we consider versions of consequentialism that in their aims *are* sensitive to the distribution of well-being: there is no distributive element that could be incorporated into the aim of a principle of beneficence or a supplementary principle of equality that would guarantee an equal distribution of compliance effects. It is clear enough that an "egalitarian" principle of beneficence of the sort that merely weights benefits according to the beneficiary's absolute level of well-being will not reliably produce equal levels of expected well-being under full compliance. But neither will the most egalitarian morality of beneficence that we could describe. Imagine a version of consequentialism—an extremely implausible one— that requires people, in lexical order, to achieve equality of well-being and to optimize the level of equal well-being. Full compliance with such a theory could not achieve equal levels of expected well-being overnight.

Indeed, it could not do it within one generation. Many of the advantages that the rich have, such as superior education, cannot simply be given to others, nor can they even be dumped into the sea.[5]

I can now make a claim about agent-neutral moral principles and theories generally. Even a principle that gives all people the sole aim of achieving equality of well-being in the world is not guaranteed to have an equal distribution of compliance effects under full compliance. Because this is so, we can be sure that there is no agent-neutral principle that, simply in virtue of the content of its aim, is guaranteed to produce an equal distribution of compliance effects.

II. Different Distributive Concerns

I have stressed the difference between distributive elements in the aim and the distribution of the effects of an agent-neutral moral theory because it is tempting—especially once we take levels of expected well-being as our measure of the compliance effects of a moral theory under full compliance—to think that any concern with the distribution of compliance effects can be met by including an appropriate distributive element in a theory's aims. My illustrations show that this is not so. But the main point here is that we are dealing with two different kinds of distributive concern. Whether distributional factors figure in people's moral aims will depend upon what matters in the determination of moral aims. Do benefits to worse-off people matter more? Does the degree of inequality—determined by the relative levels of well-being enjoyed by people—matter in itself? These questions are discussed in the same breath as the question of whether agents ought to promote well-being at all. The question of the distribution of the compliance effects of an agent-neutral principle is different. This is a question that arises *after* we know what moral aim people have. Once we have specified an aim that all people are plausibly thought to be responsible for, we can ask the question of how collective responsibility for the aim devolves into the responsibilities of individuals. It is at this stage that what we could call a second-level moral thought arises: responsibility should be allocated such that compliance effects are fairly distributed. Without trying to be too precise about it, we could distinguish between a concern with a fair distribution as in itself a moral aim, and a concern with a fair distribution as a (moral) condition on a group's pursuit of some other aim.

But there is a familiar normative concern that seems to occupy both sides of this distinction. As I said in the previous chapter, some contractualist theories present morality, or at least "justice," as the result of subjecting the terms of mutually beneficial cooperation to a requirement of fairness. According to such theories of "fair reciprocity," one cooperates with others (primarily by refraining from harming them and by recognizing property rights) for reasons of self-interest; the familiar and ancient idea is that each person prefers refraining from interfering with others for the sake of the benefit of not being interfered with. The additional element added by the fair-reciprocity view is that the terms of cooperation are to be set so as to ensure that the consequences of cooperation do not include, in addition to increases in individual well-being, new *inequalities* of well-being.[6] The striking feature of such a view for our purposes is that fair terms of cooperation are precisely those that secure a fair distribution of the effects of compliance with them.[7]

But we have here a very different moral idea than the one I have been exploring. According to morality as fair reciprocity, all people share the moral commitment that if we are to benefit from cooperation with each other, we must ensure that the benefits are fairly distributed. But the reason that each person cooperates in the first place is that *he* benefits from cooperation; if a person will not benefit from cooperating with others, he has no reason, prudential or moral, to do so. We can see, then, that according to morality as fair reciprocity, the primary aim agents have in cooperating with others is that of promoting their own well-being; morality enters in at the secondary stage where it is asked what constraints there may be on the distribution of the effects of such cooperation. In morality as fair reciprocity, a fair distribution of compliance effects is not a constraint on people's pursuit of some other moral aim; it is a constraint on people's pursuit of a nonmoral aim. This is the sense in which such theories, *as* theories of morality, are *all about* a fair distribution of compliance effects: the content of morality is to be derived from the idea of fair terms of cooperation, and fair terms of cooperation turn out to be those that ensure a fair distribution of the effects of compliance with the rules that govern the cooperative venture. The difference between this picture and the picture of a principle of beneficence providing people with a collective project is evident. The primary aim of a group of people following a principle of beneficence is the moral aim of promoting aggregate well-being. The concern that the compliance effects of pursuing the principle be fairly distributed is parasitic on that prior moral aim.

So having first drawn the distinction between a concern with a fair distribution as in itself a moral aim, and a concern with a fair distribution as a condition on a group's pursuit of an aim, we have now seen that there is a further distinction to be made between a concern with a fair distribution as a condition of a group's pursuit of a jointly held moral aim and a concern with a fair distribution as a condition of the terms under which people cooperate in the pursuit of their several nonmoral aims. As we will see, these differences affect what we might think fairness requires of the distribution of compliance effects.

III. Formal Fairness

Familiar agent-neutral principles at least sometimes distribute compliance effects unequally under full compliance. We now need to consider whether this is fair. That the idea of fairness has something to do with equality is clear enough.[8] Does fairness demand that otherwise plausible agent-neutral principles, such as the collective principle of beneficence, be modified so as to promote an equal distribution of compliance effects under full compliance?

We can start with a minimal conception of fairness. Let us say that *formal fairness* requires that a distribution be equal unless there are good grounds for departing from equality. Formal fairness seems to be an uncontroversial requirement on any distribution. Sidgwick says that in cases where different available actions produce the same "quantum of happiness," a utilitarian agent should choose according to the principle of "pure equality"; he justifies this by saying that "this principle [of distribution] seems the only one which does not need a special justification; for . . . it must be reasonable to treat any one man in the same way as any other, if there be no reason apparent for treating him differently."[9] Note that equality functions as a tiebreaker for Sidgwick not because his version of consequentialism gives people two goods to promote (in lexical order)—the optimization of happiness and the promotion of equality. Rather, the tiebreaker comes from general normative considerations that govern any distribution: "We have to supplement the principle of seeking the greatest happiness on the whole by some principle of Just or Right distribution of this happiness."*

I take Sidgwick to be advancing the following view. A question of justice or fairness can be raised about any distribution at all. And in all cases there is one view about what fairness requires that stands out as not requiring special justification, namely, that distributions should be equal unless there is good reason for departures from equality. Extending this idea, we can say that the more equal of two unequal distributions should be chosen unless there is good reason to the contrary.[10] Thus, though utilitarianism as a moral theory displays no concern with equality, an agent's compliance with utilitarianism does affect the distribution of well-being, and this distribution, like any other, must be evaluated by the independent moral idea of formal fairness. But when the "quantum

---

The Methods of Ethics, 416–17. This sentence is ambiguous between a concern with the distribution of the *benefits* that an agent's action yields and a concern with the distribution of well-being that obtains after those benefits have been conveyed. On the interpretation I have offered, Sidgwick means the latter. This does not fit so well with Sidgwick's words about treating people equally, but most of his language suggests that it is the distribution of happiness that matters. Moreover, the other view is implausibly fixated on particular actions.

of happiness" produced by some action is greater than that produced by another available action which leads to a more equal distribution of well-being, good reason for choosing the former action is easy to find—it produces a higher total increase in happiness.

Formal fairness is a minimal notion of fairness, but it is by no means empty. Unequal distributions that cannot be justified by some acceptable reason are unfair to those who do worse under the distribution, and should therefore be rejected. Unequal distributions are thus not justified when they are based on no reason at all (they are simply arbitrary) or where the reason for the unequal distribution is not morally acceptable.[11] An "acceptable" reason need not be a strong or important reason. All that is required is that the reason is generally acceptable as a basis for decision, all other things being equal; this would rule out, for example, various forms of prejudice as acceptable reasons. But formal fairness does tell us something, namely, that equal distributions matter, and that de-partures from equality require a reason that we can acknowledge as having weight. And so utilitarians—or indeed followers of the collective principle of beneficence—who acknowledge the importance of formal fairness cannot be indifferent between two actions that would produce the same amount of happiness if one of them leads to a more equal distribution of well-being than the other. Moreover, as Sidgwick noted, this is more important in practice than it may seem. It may seem that such ties for the amount of happiness produced would be very rare, and in an objective sense this may be so; but from the subjective perspective of an agent deliberating with imperfect information, such ties may be quite common.[12]

Now my suggestion is that the idea of formal fairness can be applied not only to people's decisions about what to do but also to agent-neutral moral principles as a criterion of plausibility; formal fairness can be used to evaluate the distribution of responsibility of agent-neutral principles.

This evaluation is easy to carry out. Imagine a theory of beneficence that distributes its compliance effects as equally as is possible; we can call it Theory E. The underlying moral aim in Theory E is the promotion of an optimal level of aggregate well-being, but, in order that its compliance effects be distributed as equally as possible, the theory also gives agents the lexically prior aim of promoting an equal distribution of expected well-being. As I noted earlier, there is no moral theory that can bring about equality of expected well-being instantly, and thus no theory that can, in its structure, ensure an equal distribution of compliance effects. But a theory that gives us the lexically prior aim of promoting equality of expected well-being will do as well as possible in this respect. Now from the point of view of formal fairness, if we have two agent-neutral moral theories with the same underlying moral aim, the theory that distributes compliance effects more equally is the more plausible of the two unless it is judged inferior for some other good reason. But a good reason to judge Theory E inferior is readily to hand: the optimizing principle much better achieves the aim of promoting people's well-being than does Theory E. This is a good reason, since the promotion of well-being is our underlying moral aim, and the concern with the distribution of compliance effects comes in only as a constraint on the distribution of responsibility for the promotion of that prior aim. So just as for Sidgwick the availability of an action that will produce a greater quantum of happiness justifies an agent's failing to perform an action that better promotes equality of well-being, the greater total benefits that flow from compliance with the optimizing principle justifies that principle relative to Theory E.

Formal fairness permits an unequal distribution of compliance effects from a principle of beneficence because acting on Theory E would promote aggregate well-being less well. And, in general, we can say that any agent-neutral principle that distributes its compliance effects less equally than it would only if it less well achieved the underlying aim of the principle passes the test of formal fairness. For better achievement of the aim of the principle is always going to count as a good reason for the purposes of formal fairness. Since no plausible agent-neutral principle will impose arbitrary requirements, or distribute responsibility along, say, racial lines, we can say that any plausible agent-neutral principle distributes its demands fairly under full compliance if we take formal fairness as our criterion.

There is one caveat to add to this conclusion. There are possible cases where under full compliance with the optimizing (or collective) principle two actions are available such that both will bring about the same total level of expected (weighted) benefit, but one of them yields a more equal distribution of compliance effects than the other does. Suppose A is better-off than B, and I can either benefit A somewhat, or B somewhat less, and the two actions are equally good from the point of view of weighted beneficence. The second of the two actions will achieve a more equal distribution of compliance effects, but the optimizing and collective principles are indifferent between them. We here see the need for a supplementary rule requiring agents to choose, where two acts are tied in this way, the act that has the more equal distribution of expected well-being associated with it. Now this is the very same supplementary rule that Sidgwick introduced, reached by a different route. In one route (Sidgwick's), we took the perspective of the agent and asked what distributive concerns fairness demanded of her. In the other route, we take the perspective of the principle governing a collective enterprise and ask what it would be for the principle to distribute compliance effects fairly.[13] In any event, the need for the supplementary rule does not threaten our conclusion that the optimizing and collective principles, as they stand, distribute their compliance effects fairly under full compliance, since they do not require us to choose the action that produces the less equal distribution of compliance effects, but merely fail to require us to choose the action that produces the more equal distribution.

The tie just illustrated was between two actions available to a single agent, and we assumed that each action was equally burdensome to the agent. The differing impact on the degree of equality in the distribution of compliance effects in this case is due to the different pattern of passive effects produced by the two actions. Similar ties in the realm of active effects, where the optimizing and collective principles would be indifferent between different distributions of sacrifice among agents, will be rare. This is because the well-being of the agent herself is always relevant to the determination of what should be done. Thus suppose that A and B are equally well-off, and that it would be optimal for them each to give $500 to C. C would be equally well served by a $1,000 check from A alone, but this would be suboptimal. In the first place, the diminishing marginal value of money makes it the case that $1,000 from A reduces the total level of well-being more than $500 from each of them would. Here we should remember that other resources, such as personal time, also display diminishing marginal value. And the second reason that action from A alone would be suboptimal is that the weighting contained in the principle of beneficence gives us reason to ask for sacrifice from better-off people first, which in this case means that after one unit of real sacrifice from A, it is B's turn, and so on.

Nonetheless, though rare, ties between two distributions of responsibility among agents are possible. One possible case would be where A and B are equally well-off, and each able to perform an action that would benefit C, but where the burden cannot be shared. Here the optimizing principle is indifferent between A acting and B acting (this tie, incidentally, would raise problems of coordination). But though what we have here are different distributions of responsibility that are equally optimal, neither distribution is superior from the point of view of equality of expected well-being and thus compliance effects.

IV. Substantive Fairness

We have established that according to the criterion of formal fairness the optimizing and collective principles of beneficence distribute their demands fairly under full compliance. But of course other notions of fairness might also be appropriate for the evaluation of the distribution of responsibility under full compliance. If some more substantive notion of fairness is plausible here, this would not lead us to reject formal fairness, but it would mean that satisfaction of the criterion of formal fairness was not sufficient.

Thus we need to investigate whether there is a substantive notion of fairness that displaces formal fairness as the criterion for the distribution of the compliance effects of agent-neutral principles under full compliance. The obvious criterion to consider is one that requires equality in distribution, or as near to it as possible, irrespective of the reasons there may be for departing from equality. If we used this notion of "fairness as equality" as our criterion, we would have to say that Theory E distributes its compliance effects fairly, and the optimizing and collective principles do not.

Is fairness as equality a plausible criterion to apply to the distribution of the compliance effects of a principle of beneficence? Thinking about the question abstractly, the answer seems to be yes. In general, a principle that distributes its compliance effects equally would be preferable on the ground that it is more fair to the cooperating agents. On the other hand, however, Theory E is an extremely implausible account of beneficence, very much less plausible than the collective principle of beneficence. The weight given by Theory E to equality of compliance effects is simply too great. It cannot be right that beneficent agents should aim first at achieving as great a degree of equality as possible and only secondarily at increasing overall levels of well-being. If we change focus from the narrow question of the criterion for the fairness of the distribution of responsibility under full compliance to the more general question of the overall plausibility of the rival accounts of the morality of beneficence—taking into account, of course, all the arguments on either side—Theory E rather clearly comes off second-best. Since this is how things look at the level of overall plausibility, we can in turn conclude that formal fairness is the more plausible criterion for the fairness of the distribution of responsibility by agent-neutral principles. There is an obvious circularity to this way of proceeding, but that is entirely appropriate. We are looking for a principle of beneficence that appears plausible and that can be defended by plausible arguments (which, we hope, in turn explain the gross implausibility of the optimizing principle of beneficence). The argument from the substantive criterion of fairness as equality to Theory E is initially plausible, but Theory E itself is not; this must cast doubt on the substantive criterion of fairness. Formal fairness, on the other hand, is both a plausible criterion for the distribution of responsibility, and results, as I hope the next chapter will confirm, in a plausible principle of beneficence.

Now the two criteria of fairness we have considered lie at extreme ends of a spectrum, the one presenting the presumption in favor of equality of compliance effects as easily rebuttable and the other presenting it as not rebuttable at all. It is natural to wonder whether there may be some substantive requirement of fairness of intermediate strength, for example requiring pursuit of equality of compliance effects except when there are strong or powerful reasons to the contrary. A strong reason to the contrary in the context of principles of beneficence would be the production of great benefits to people. Perhaps some such intermediate criterion is plausible, but it is hard to know in the abstract whether this is so. Much depends, as we have seen, on the overall plausibility of accounts of beneficence that meet the criterion. An appropriate theory would presumably weaken the ordering of the two aims in Theory E, allowing the promotion of a higher total level of well-being to trump the promotion of equality of compliance effects in some cases. I doubt that any such principle will be more plausible than the collective principle. But we do not in any case need to pursue this possibility further. If some moderate version of Theory E, or indeed even Theory E itself, turned out to be more plausible, all things considered, than the collective principle of beneficence, the structure of my main arguments would not be substantially affected. We would still have explained what was wrong with the optimizing principle of beneficence and come up with a relatively plausible principle of beneficence in its stead.

So we can move forward, taking the view that formal fairness is a plausible criterion to apply to the way principles of beneficence distribute responsibility under full compliance. It is plausible considered on its own, and other, more substantive criteria of fairness that would displace formal fairness appear to be less plausible. We can continue to believe, therefore, that the optimizing principle and the collective principle distribute responsibility fairly under full compliance.

As a final point in this section, it can be noted that in the context of morality as fair reciprocity, formal fairness and fairness as equality coincide. This is because the theory of morality as fair reciprocity draws on no aims other than that cooperation be on terms that yield a fair distribution of compliance effects. So there never are any good reasons to depart from an equal distribution of compliance effects. It is true that in the Rawlsian version of this view inequality that benefits everyone is tolerated, but this is best understood as an interpretation of the default requirement of equality itself: it is not unfair in the first place that I have less than someone else if I would have less still if we had equal amounts. At least, this must be the right interpretation so long as morality as fair reciprocity really does presuppose no jointly held moral aims other than that of cooperation in pursuit of self-interest on fair terms.

V. Past Noncompliance

In my discussion of the full-compliance distribution of responsibility under agent-neutral principles, I have used the temporal perspective of "from now on." But the compliance effects on some people of the optimizing or collective principles under full compliance from now on are certainly worse than they would have been if there had been more compliance in the past. Wouldn't fairness require some adjustment to take account of this fact?[14]

Obviously enough, responsibility cannot be shifted back onto past people, people now dead. But among people now alive, some will have complied more fully in the past than others. And it might be thought that past noncompliance is relevant to the fairness of the distribution of compliance effects under full compliance from now on in the following way. If A, a lifelong complier, enjoys under full compliance a certain level of compliance effect but would have enjoyed a better compliance effect if B, a past noncomplier, had complied in the past, it would be fair to require B to take on greater sacrifice so that A could enjoy a level of compliance effect closer to what it would have been if B had always complied. The concern here is not with equality of compliance effects under full compliance, or indeed with the way a moral principle in the first instance distributes responsibility at all. Rather, there is a distinct intuitive notion of fairness at play here, one concerning the assignment of responsibility for burdens that a person has imposed on others through failing to play her part in a collective undertaking. As such this new intuitive idea of fairness—which we can refer to as the idea of "fair rectification"—is, like the compliance condition, a piece of nonideal theory (its relationship to the compliance condition will be discussed in the next section).

Now it would seem that if we take a formal approach to the fairness of the distribution of compliance effects under full compliance, we should also take a formal approach to the issue of fair rectification. To see this, we must first note that rectification of worse compliance effects due to past noncompliance by others will typically lead to a suboptimal outcome. As we have seen, it will be rare that two different acts or assignments of responsibility will be tied in respect of expected weighted well-being while differing in the distribution of compliance effects. In most cases, then, rectification for past noncompliance would lead to less good being done.

A formal approach to fair rectification would have it that rectification is required unless there is good reason not to do it. Better achievement of the aim of the moral principle would surely count as a good reason here, just as it does in the case of the distribution of compliance effects under full compliance. In both cases we have a concern that can typically only be addressed at the expense of worse achievement of the aim of the principle. And there seems to be no reason that we should regard the demand for rectification as intrinsically of much greater weight than the demand for an equal initial distribution of compliance effects. There seems to be no reason, that is, to adopt a formal approach to the fair distribution of compliance effects but a substantive approach to fair rectification. It may seem more unfair to you if, for the sake of greater benefits, you have to sacrifice more than you would have had to if I had made sacrifices in the past, than it is unfair to you if, for the sake of greater benefits, you are required by an initial distribution of responsibility to sustain greater sacrifice than me. This thought may be based on some sense that I have been free-riding and should now make up for this.

But the trouble is that it is no more possible for me to make up for my past noncompliance than it is for people who are now dead—in the cases we are considering, any rearrangement of the assignment of responsibility will lead to less good being done. And if the greater achievement of the aim of promoting well-being justifies requiring more of you than me in the first instance, it would seem odd that the greater achievement of the same aim would not be more important morally than the rectification of my unfair behavior in the past.

Rectification does, however, seem appropriate in those cases where two actions or assignments of responsibility are tied in respect of expected weighted well-being but differ in respect of the distribution of compliance effects. We require another supplementary rule to deal with these cases. If the optimizing and collective principles are indifferent between A conveying a benefit to B or to C, but the compliance effect on C from now on is worse than it would have been if B had complied in the past, the benefit should go to C.[15] Likewise, if our principles of beneficence are indifferent between A or B transferring some indivisible benefit to C, but the compliance effect on A, even without the current demand, is less good than it would have been if B had complied in the past, then the sacrifice should come from B.

Now, as Sidgwick noted, the ties that give rise to the need for supplementary rules may not be all that uncommon, given imperfect information. Further, the supplementary rule he proposed—which, as we have seen, is the same rule as that required by fairness in the distribution of compliance effects under full compliance—is potentially of some practical significance for agents, for it is often not too hard to know which of two actions will better promote equality of well-being. The supplementary rule required by fair rectification, on the other hand, would seem to be of little practical significance, since it would be rare for a person to know enough about the past compliance of others, and the effects that noncompliance has had on current compliance effects, to know what adjustments should be made, if any.

VI. Past Noncompliance and the Compliance Condition

The compliance condition, it will be recalled, states for the first-person case that agent-neutral moral principles should not under partial compliance require sacrifice of an agent where the total-compliance effect on her, taking that sacrifice into account, would be worse than it would be (all other aspects of her situation remaining the same) under full compliance from now on. Thus the ideal of full compliance employed by the compliance condition is explicitly forward-looking. It might now be wondered whether this is justified. It is true that except where there are ties, a past noncomplier cannot make up for his past noncompliance—in most cases, the rearrangement of responsibility under full compliance from now on would lead to the collective aim being less well achieved. But the compliance condition countenances the lesser achievement of collective aims. It holds that compliers should not be required to take on the responsibilities of noncompliers; shouldn't it therefore hold that complying agents today should not be required to take on responsibilities that rightly belonged to people in the past? What justifies the compliance condition's exclusive focus on present and future noncompliance?

The compliance condition tells us that in a collective enterprise a person's fairly allocated responsibility, starting from now, is the proper measure of her responsibility even under partial compliance. One is not required to take on the fairly allocated responsibilities of others. The motivating point here is that the members of the collective undertaking are agents, not forces of nature. That I know that you will not do what you are supposed to do does not alter the fact that you are responsible for what you are responsible for, and I am responsible for what I am responsible for. This recognition that the members of the collective undertaking are responsible agents leads directly to the forward-looking orientation of the compliance condition, because the background idea is that starting from now the group of agents *could* achieve its collective aim. The compliance condition reflects a view about what my responsibility is when I know that you will not perform your responsibility; the view is that your responsibility remains your responsibility, it does not become mine. It *remains* your responsibility in the strict sense that you could fulfill it, if you chose to; it is because this is so that I do not have to take on your responsibility. But if the time for you to fulfill your responsibility is past, there is nothing you can now do about that. Once that point is reached, the collective faces a new practical problem: What can we all do from now on to best promote our aim? The compliance condition is about people doing only their fair shares in the sense that one person does not have to take on responsibilities that other people should, *and could*, take on.

Thus once the issue of past noncompliance has been given due attention in the fair allocation of responsibility to agents under full compliance from now on—the issue of fair rectification—it is of no further relevance to the compliance condition.

VII. A Formal Compliance Condition?

I have argued that formal notions of fairness are appropriate in the domain of the allocation of responsibility under full compliance from now on. Departures from equality in the distribution of compliance effects are fair so long as they are made for some good reason. The compliance condition, by contrast, imposes a strong substantive constraint. For of course the requirement by the optimizing principle of beneficence that complying agents in situations of partial compliance do more than their full compliance share is made for the same good reason that we approved of in the discussion of equality in the distribution of responsibility: it will do more good. Why is that good reason not enough to override the concerns behind the compliance condition, when it is enough to override the concern for an equal distribution of compliance effects under full compliance?

The answer has once more to do with the specific and distinctive underlying motivation of the compliance condition. The compliance condition does not concern the *allocation* of responsibility, but rather the attitude complying agents should take to noncomplying members of the collective enterprise. The compliance condition insists that we treat people who we believe will not comply as the agents they in fact are: people able to make the decision to comply. It insists that individuals are not required to take on the entire responsibility of a collective project, but only to do their part in it. If complying people did take on the entire responsibility, more good would be done, it is true. But this is only a "good reason" on the assumption that noncomplying agents will not do what they are required to do. There is even better reason for that state of affairs to change. Moral principles, of course, are not self-enforcing; they cannot make the noncompliers comply. But rather than "give up" on the noncompliers and increase the sacrifice required of complying agents, the appropriate response, I believe, is to leave the allocation of responsibility where it always was. It is the fact that decisions are open to noncomplying agents that would make the extra sacrifice from complying agents unnecessary that renders a formal approach to the compliance condition unappealing. Nothing comparable is the case when the issue is the allocation of responsibility under full compliance from now on.

We must also remember that significant support for the specific combination of views discussed in this chapter comes from the fact that they together generate what strikes me as a relatively plausible principle of beneficence—relative, that is, to the alternatives. The final part of my argument is therefore to show that the collective principle of beneficence is indeed a plausible principle of beneficence that can play its role in people's practical lives.

7

THE COLLECTIVE PRINCIPLE OF BENEFICENCE

I have said that the collective principle of beneficence is a plausible principle of beneficence, at least relative to the alternatives of the optimizing and limited principles of beneficence and no principle of beneficence at all (charity). This claim is important not just because one of our aims is precisely to find a plausible principle of beneficence, but also because its truth would lend significant support to our other main claim—that the apparent absurdity of the optimizing principle is due to its violation of the compliance condition. Having presented all I have to say about the plausibility of the compliance condition as a more or less abstract idea, I try in this chapter to make good the claim that the collective principle is a plausible concrete moral principle that could guide people's behavior.

This may seem to be a daunting task. For though the basic idea of the collective principle is simple enough—a person need never sacrifice so much that he would end up less well-off than he would be under full compliance from now on, but within that constraint he must do as much good as possible—the full formulation of the principle is terribly complex:

> Everyone is required to perform one of the actions that, of those available to her, is optimal in respect of expected aggregate weighted well-being, except in situations of partial compliance with this principle. In situations of partial compliance, a person's maximum level of required sacrifice is that which will reduce her level of expected well-being to the level it would be, all other aspects of her situation remaining the same, if there were to be full compliance from that point on. Under partial compliance a person is required to perform either an action, of those requiring no more than the maximum level of required sacrifice, that is optimal in respect of expected weighted aggregate well-being, or any other action which is at least as good in respect of expected weighted aggregate well-being.

However, no one is required to act in a way that imposes a loss on some other person unless that other person's level of expected well-being after the loss would be at least as high as it would be, all other aspects of the situation remaining the same, under full compliance from that point on.

(It should be recalled that "sacrifice" and "loss" are to be measured against the baseline of the factual status quo as explained in chapters 3 and 5.[1] An agent's sacrifice is the difference between her expected well-being as a perfect complier from now on and her expected well-being in an optimally prudent life in the factual status quo.)

It may fairly be asked how a monstrous principle like this could play a practical role in real agents' lives. To make discussion somewhat tractable, I will discuss the two paragraphs of the principle in turn, leaving the third-person rider for section II.

I. Motivations and Rules of Thumb

Despite what is sometimes claimed, it seems doubtful that anyone ever thought that agents should consult the optimizing principle of beneficence in their moment-to-moment deliberations. Philosophers have readily seen that it would not be for the best for agents to continually consult the principle, trying to figure out the expected benefits associated with each available action; rather, it is better if agents usually act on standing motivations and rules of thumb that themselves seem optimal in the long run.[2]

The absurdity of trying to consult the collective principle from moment to moment is even more evident. Thus the main practical role of the collective principle must be to provide a background standard against which agents assess their standing motivations and deliberative rules of thumb.

Now of course this does not mean that the collective principle is a version of rule- or motive-utilitarianism. The idea is that one should apply the collective principle to all decisions one makes, including those of which standing rules of thumb to live by most of the time, which standing motivations to try to discard or acquire, and which action to perform in a particular case where one's rules of thumb or standing motives seem likely to lead one astray.[3]

The role of rules of thumb and standing motivations requires some brief further explanation, though what I will say is neither novel nor peculiar to the collective principle. Indeed I will begin by describing the operation of the principle under full compliance, and so these comments apply without change to the optimizing principle.

Let us suppose that the collective principle of beneficence is the only moral principle there is: "collective utilitarianism" is the correct or best moral theory. Under full compliance with collective utilitarianism, we operate for the most part by rules of thumb and standing motives because it would be counterproductive to assess, moment by moment, whether it is for the best to, say, keep a promise, or refrain from violence, or devote a disproportionate amount of attention to our closest associates; in the vast majority of cases, it will be optimal to do these things. But sometimes it is for the best to break a promise, use violence, or favor strangers over our children, and if we do not do so, we act wrongly. Now on some such occasions of acting wrongly we will have acted on a motive it would have been wrong for us to try to give up—an intrinsic aversion to violence, for example. Such cases would count as blameless wrongdoing, in the sense explained in section VI of chapter 2. On other occasions no strong motive will be involved. Rather, one simply will have acted on a rule of thumb without engaging in the deliberations necessary to see that the rule gave the wrong answer in this particular instance.

There are two possibilities in this second kind of case. Acting on the rule of thumb may either be a case of blameless wrongdoing, or it may be simple wrongdoing. It will be the former if there were no signs at the time of acting that ought to have alerted the agent that the rule of thumb was unreliable in this particular instance. The kind of sign in question would be, most prominently, salient evidence of unusually large benefits from acting contrary to the rule—breaking the promise would prevent someone being injured, for example.[4] In such a case, the agent ought not to have followed the rule of thumb, but rather deliberated about what to do, and, since this was not done, the wrongdoing was not blameless.

Now this kind of account is familiar in the utilitarian tradition, and I do not intend to either develop it fully or try to defend it here. What does need to be discussed is how this familiar account of the role of a principle of beneficence in agents' deliberation needs to be supplemented to incorporate agents' deliberation under partial compliance with the collective principle. Clearly enough, agents need additional information under partial compliance, both when they are assessing their rules of thumb and standing motives in a cool hour, and when they are deliberating in the exceptional case.[5]

In addition to information about the size of the benefit each available action, or possible rule of thumb or motive, would bring about in the actual world, the collective principle requires agents in situations of partial compliance to estimate the size of the benefits different available actions, rules, or motives would bring about in a world of full compliance. Having thus figured out what they and others would be doing under full compliance, they must then estimate how well-off they would be in that counterfactual world so that they can in turn estimate their actual-world level of required sacrifice. Of course these counterfactual questions cannot be answered with anything approaching precision. Agents will have to rely on rough guesses, though sometimes they will also be able to make use of the more informed estimates of experts in, say, the field of development economics.

It bears emphasizing that agents will need to attend to questions of institutional design. Optimal political institutions do not spring up overnight, and so full compliance from now on does not imply their existence. But under full compliance our highest priority would be the establishment of such institutions, and so individual agents will need to have a sense of what their establishment would mean for them, both in the immediate transitional period and in the long run. Thus to comply with collective utilitarianism, moral agents must be political agents, too.[6]

In general, the aim would be to hit on a pattern of motives and rules of thumb that will lead us to act roughly as well as we can at roughly the level of sacrifice that would bring our level of expected well-being down to what it would be under full compliance. And for the exceptional case, where our rules of thumb seem unreliable, we aim to act as well as we can in that particular case for roughly the level of sacrifice that would bring our level of well-being down to what it would be under full compliance from that point on.

To illustrate with the example that is at the heart of the problems of beneficence discussed in this book, consider the rule of thumb that would govern the level of direct financial giving from the better-off to the worse-off. A collective utilitarian in the contemporary world would need to try to figure out the kind of life she would be living if everybody, including her, complied with the theory. Any conclusion is of course very speculative, but various assessments of optimal rates of transfer for development purposes have been made, and a rich person can do no better than rely on estimates such as these in order to come up with a sense of how much worse-off she would be under full compliance.[7] She then knows that she is required to transfer funds for the benefit of others, sustaining loss—measured against the baseline of an optimally prudent life in the factual status quo—to the point where her level of expected well-being matches her full-compliance estimate. She will also know to direct the relevant amount of funds where it will do the most good. As further information is acquired, the relevant figures will change, so the rule of thumb governing the transfer of funds will need to be sensitive to significant developments in the overall global level of well-being as well as developing accounts of how best to promote it.[8]

Clearly there would be no consensus about the amount of sacrifice the collective principle requires. For one thing, different people will estimate their own counterfactual full compliance levels of well-being in different ways, and the danger of self-serving optimism in this assessment is obvious. It is natural to suggest here a deliberative rule of thumb that agents err toward pessimism in their assessments of their full-compliance levels of well-being. In effect, such a rule tells us to err on the side of supererogation rather than on the side of acting wrongly.

The inherent vagueness in the operation of the collective principle is troubling, but it is only superficially so in comparison to the indeterminacy displayed by limited principles of beneficence. For the problem we uncovered for limited principles of beneficence in chapter 4 was not just that we could not find a precise limit to required sacrifice, or even that we could find no consensus on a best rough guess—though it is worth noting that those versions of the limited principle that employ a multiplying factor would not seem to be any easier to implement in practice than the collective principle. The main problem with limited principles was rather that we had no normative criterion to guide our thinking about limits to required sacrifice. The collective principle provides us with a clear criterion. Though our estimates of what level of sacrifice would satisfy the criterion will be rough and contentious, we know what we are trying to guess at, and this opens the space for good-faith argument about what kind of life would satisfy the principle in practice. There was no such space in the case of the limited principles; there the vagueness went to the heart of the normative idea behind the principles.

I will not add more detail to this very rough sketch of how the collective principle might provide a practical standard that real agents could use in their lives; obviously enough, much more would need to be said before we could say that we knew what life according to the collective principle would be like. My aim here is merely to indicate the structure of the operation of the collective principle, so that we have an idea of the practical role it might plausibly play. If the general structure is plausible, there is no need to consider all the details here. After a brief sketch of the operation of the third-person rider to the collective principle, I will turn to consider two characteristics of the general structure that are potentially cause for concern.

II. The Third-Person Rider

The third-person rider tells agents that action that is otherwise optimal, and falls within the required level of sacrifice for the agent, is not required if it would bring a loss to another person such that the resulting level of well-being for that person is less than it would be under full compliance. So if we imagine that it is optimal for Robin Hood to redistribute wealth from some very poor people to some extremely poor people, this would not be required if the very poor people were already less well off than they would be under full compliance, or if the loss caused by the redistribution would bring their levels of well-being down below what they would be under full compliance. Once again, we are here required to make rough guesses about levels of well-being under full compliance.

The third-person rider does not rule out the possibility of required killings or theft. But killing or theft would be required only in those cases where the unfortunate victim would, under full compliance, be required to sustain an equivalent sacrifice. Thus the third-person rider does substantially modify the requirements that would otherwise be generated by the collective principle of beneficence.

The third-person rider comes into its own in the context of institutional design. Collective utilitarianism requires us to design our social institutions so as to promote overall expected weighted well-being. But institutions that impose losses on people such that their post-loss well-being is less than it would be under full compliance are not required. In the institutional context, it would seem that problems of implementation of collective utilitarianism are much less serious. This is mainly because governments are in the business of projecting how different policies would play out in respect of the welfare of their people. On the other hand, collective utilitarianism does also require national governments to form views about how things would be for their population, and the rest of the world, under worldwide full compliance.

III. Doing and Allowing

Deontological constraints against doing harm prohibit most acts that harm people even if the result would be optimal—a net gain in expected well-being. Utilitarianism prohibits only those acts that harm others that are not optimal; but it prohibits *all* such acts. Collective utilitarianism prohibits some but not all nonoptimal acts that harm. Because it permits some nonoptimal harmings, collective utilitarianism would not appear to be a plausible theory.

To see first how collective utilitarianism prohibits some nonoptimal harmings, consider a fairly well-off complying agent who asks herself whether she can assault someone and steal his money for her own use, thus doing more harm than good. If her expected well-being as an optimally prudent person in the factual status quo, where she can expect to succeed in her assault and robbery, is higher than it would be under full compliance, where of course she does not assault and rob, and higher by an amount greater than the loss she suffers if she refrains from harming, then she is not permitted to do the deed.

But now consider those people who even if they never complied with collective utilitarianism in the actual world but rather acted with optimal prudence would nevertheless remain worse-off than they would be under full compliance; think, for example, of the very poor who would benefit greatly from the beneficence of others under full compliance. Such people need no sacrifice to bring their level of well-being down to what it would be under full compliance, and are thus required to sustain no sacrifice at all. This means that they are permitted to kill and pillage as suits their interests (so long as, that is, not killing and pillaging involves a sacrifice) until the point where their expected well-being if they continued not to comply would be higher than it would be under full compliance. Only then will they be required to sustain a sacrifice. It is true that the third-person rider ensures that killing and pillaging will never be *required* where it would bring the level of well-being of the victim below what it would be under full compliance; but collective utilitarianism does nothing to prohibit action that violates the rider. While it seems plausible to say that those who are worse-off noncomplying than they would be under full compliance never have to do anything positive to benefit others, the idea that they never have to refrain from doing harm if refraining would be at all burdensome seems very implausible.

Because in this book I have not taken a stand on the status of deon-tological constraints, the implausibility of collective utilitarianism is of no immediate concern. The main point is to establish the viability of the collective principle of beneficence as a plausible account of that part of our morality that concerns making things impersonally better. Obviously enough, if the collective principle of beneficence is thought to be part of a pluralistic theory along with standard deontological constraints, the implausible result just introduced does not obtain.[9]

However, it is worth investigating whether there is some more modest modification of collective utilitarianism that could block this result. Recall from chapter 5 the idea of a constraint against imposing unrequired sac-rifice.[10] As I noted, this suggestion has implications that some would find troubling. If it is permissible for A to save five others even though B's death is a foreseeable consequence of the action, and there is a constraint against imposing unrequired sacrifice, then it follows that B is required to sacrifice himself voluntarily. As we saw in chapter 5, this implies that in the trolley case, the one person would be required to redirect the trolley onto himself. This result is not obviously absurd, however, and indeed I believe it starts to look rather plausible when we remember that B's fail-ure to sacrifice himself would certainly count as a case of blameless wrongdoing, since his motive of self-preservation in emergency situations is surely not one he should try to rid himself of.

It is worth noting, moreover, that the constraint against imposing un-required sacrifice does not seem to have the paradoxical implications that ordinary deontological constraints are alleged to have. It is said to be paradoxical that I am prohibited from carrying out one killing for the sake of preventing five other killings.[11] Whether or not that is so, the equivalent case for the constraint against imposing unrequired sacrifice does not seem to be paradoxical at all. A is prohibited from imposing a loss on B that he is not required to sustain voluntarily, even if this would prevent C from imposing equally burdensome unrequired losses on D and E. This is not paradoxical if we understand that the point of the constraint is to give effect to limits on individual agents' responsibility.[12] For there is nothing paradoxical in the fact that B is in the first place not required voluntarily to sustain the sacrifice needed to stop C. And since this is so, it is hard to see how paradox emerges once we move to the third-person perspective and say that no one else can impose this loss on B, either. Indeed, if there is paradox to be found here, it would be in the idea that A can do something prima facie objectionable to B, namely, impose a loss on him that he is not required to impose on himself and does not want to impose on himself, for the sake of achieving an end that B could voluntarily promote, but is not required to promote.

I cannot here try to provide a full defense of the constraint against imposing unrequired sacrifice. But I believe it has enough prima facie plausibility for us to be able to introduce a theory that we might call "constrained collective utilitarianism" as a possible alternative to both collective utilitarianism and the pluralistic theory that comprises the collective principle and familiar deontological constraints. Constrained collective utilitarianism consists in just two principles—the collective principle of beneficence and the constraint against imposing unrequired sacrifice. It has some rather appealing features. It holds, for example, that while Robin Hood may not take from the very poor (who are worse-off as optimally prudent people than they would be under full compliance) to give to the extremely poor, even if this would make things better overall, he may take from the rich to give to the poor. A utilitarian Robin would always prefer, where possible, to take from the rich than from the very poor because of the diminishing marginal value of money. But the constrained collective utilitarian Robin has an additional reason: the rich would not be so rich under full compliance, and in not giving the money to the extremely poor themselves, they are failing in their responsibilities; Robin is merely acting as an enforcer of their own prior obligations. The same is not true if he takes from the very poor. Robin is required to take from the rich, to give to the extremely poor, but prohibited from taking from the very poor.

Again, this is not the place to investigate further the plausibility of constrained collective utilitarianism. To do that properly we would need to consider its *relative* plausibility; the pluralistic theory comprising the collective principle of beneficence and familiar deontological constraints would be the strongest competitor. To undertake this comparison we would have to discuss the deep issues associated with deontology generally, and this cannot be done here. It does seem, however, that constrained collective utilitarianism is not clearly implausible at first glance.

Another issue concerning the distinction between doing and allowing harm should be mentioned. Suppose that there is a civil war in some country, and a relief effort to assist refugees is organized. As someone who complies with the collective principle of beneficence, you are already promoting expected weighted well-being up to the limit of your required sacrifice—refraining from harming people and perhaps actively helping some people as well. When you hear about the relief effort, you conclude that this does not increase your level of required sacrifice at all, for under full compliance the civil war would stop, the refugees would be allowed to return to their homes, and they would not need anyone's assistance. This result may seem implausible.[13]

We should first be clear about what the claimed problem is here. It is not the case that the collective principle never requires agents to be beneficent where the need for that beneficence is caused by violence and thieving: agents are always required to do whatever will make the outcome best—up to the required level of sacrifice. The problem, if there is one, is that increased *need* for beneficence due to violence and thieving does not influence the determination of the required level of sacrifice by way of the appeal to full compliance. Now of course the whole point of the collective principle is that increased need for beneficence that is due to others not being beneficent does not increase the level of required sacrifice for complying agents. We distinguish between needs caused by people failing to be beneficent and needs caused by natural phenomena. But the objection just presented is, in effect, that this basic idea is plausible only where the noncompliance of the others consists in allowing as opposed to doing harm.

There seem to be two rather interesting explanations of the initial intuitive power of this objection. The first is that people who are actively doing harm might appear to us to be less well qualified for the title "responsible agent" than people who are merely allowing harm. That is, we might be inclined to think of those who are doing harm more as forces of nature than as responsible members of the group that aims to promote well-being. If so, we do not count them into our full-compliance ideal. But of course it is not remotely plausible to deny responsible agency to all harm-doers, and so this line of thought can be quickly rejected. It is true that there are people whose extreme viciousness might count as evidence of a lack of responsible agency; and it does follow that such people should not be included as part of the relevant group when we ask ourselves what things would be like under full compliance. But people such as this make up but a small proportion of the world's harm-doers.

The second reason for the initial plausibility of the objection we are considering is probably more important as an explanation. When my noncompliance with a principle of beneficence consists in doing harm, I am also, in most cases, in violation of some deontological constraint. It is thus not surprising that even with our attention focused on beneficence we intuitively regard the doing of harm as more seriously wrong than the allowing of harm. And since we do have these different responses to the two kinds of noncompliance, it is in turn not surprising that the attitude endorsed by the collective principle—I will carry out what I am responsible for but not what others are responsible for—seems more acceptable to us where the others' responsibility is to not allow harm rather than to not do harm. In effect, the idea is that complying agents need not concern themselves with the less important responsibilities of others but must concern themselves with the more important responsibilities of others.

Though easy to understand, this line of thought is confused. The question is whether a complying agent can idealize away from the harming behavior of others when determining her full-compliance responsibility. The thought we have uncovered is that she cannot, because that kind of noncompliance is so seriously wrong. The mistake here is to transfer the sense that noncompliers act more wrongly when they do harm than when they allow harm to the question of what complying third parties are responsible for. If the question is whether A can legitimately fail to sustain sacrifice for the sake of benefiting B, it does not matter whether B's foreseeable needs are due to C foreseeably doing harm or allowing harm.* A's concern is with the effects of C not doing what she is required to do, not with the seriousness of C's wrongdoing. In any case, when thought about directly, it is not clear why responsibility should *more* easily transfer from C to A, the *more* wrong C's noncompliance.

Consider one final case. Suppose that instead of considering whether to contribute to some effort to alleviate the effects of a war, someone is considering whether to take part in a military operation to stop a war. Since under full compliance there would be no war, this person assumes away the war when determining what her full compliance responsibilities and level of well-being would be, and thus the fact of the war does not increase her level of required sacrifice in the actual world. Here again, any sense that there is something amiss with the operation of the principle is based on confusion. In addition to the confusion identified in the previous paragraph, a negative reaction to the way the collective principle operates in this case seems to be due to a sense that it is more important to put a stop to harming behavior than it is to meet the needs of people to whom harm has either been done or allowed to befall. Once again, if we face the point directly, we see the implausibility of the distinction. Scanlon rightly notes that it is no more important to save someone from murder than from a forest fire.[14] The extra wrongness, if there is any,

---

*Suppose in our initial case of the refugees that the civil war could be stopped by some retired general who still commands the loyalty of one of the armies. This general has no stake in the conflict; he simply can't be bothered getting involved. On the line of thought we are now considering, the existence of this general makes all the difference to the responsibility of people considering whether to contribute to the refugee relief effort; for now we can say that if the general were not failing in his responsibility not to allow harm, there would be no need for the relief effort, and we do not have to shoulder the general's properly allocated responsibility.

that comes from doing harm as opposed to allowing harm does not transfer to third parties in this way.

IV. Rescue

We can help other people enormously without ever coming close to them or having much precise information about their plight.[15] It is mainly because of the possibility of this kind of impersonal beneficence that the optimizing principle makes such extreme active demands on most people.

But there are also cases where we can greatly benefit a person whose desperate plight is vividly present to our consciousness. What we can call rescue situations are, paradigmatically, sudden, unexpected, serious harm–threatening emergencies that arise in the agent's immediate vicinity; the standard example is that of being easily able save a child from drowning in a shallow pond.[16] Considered abstractly, it would seem that cases where a person is required to effect a rescue are simply instances of required beneficence, and thus that they raise no special normative issues. But our intuitive reactions to rescue cases are rather different from those that we have to cases of impersonal benefiting. We tend to feel that assistance is uncontroversially required in an emergency situation where our quick action can save a particular person from death or severe harm. Furthermore, we accept that the required sacrifice in such cases can be very high, at least in financial terms. Here is an example from Shelly Kagan.[17] For years some astronomers have been planning an observation that must take place at sea at a particular date and time; many hundreds of thousands of dollars have been spent in preparation. Just as they are about to take their readings, they receive a Mayday signal. If they rescue the sailors in distress, the project will come to nothing. But, as we intuitively think, rescue they must. This is in stark contrast to the commonsense thought that a person who abandons her research project and donates the money to OXFAM, thus saving very many lives, would be acting well beyond the call of duty.

It would be nice if the collective principle of beneficence not only yielded a plausible account of the requirements of impersonal or general beneficence but also comported with commonsense reactions to rescue cases. But it is not so. Indeed, a variation on the child in the pond case has been offered as a counterexample to the fundamental motivation for the collective principle. If we have two potential rescuers and two drowning children, but one rescuer fails to do her share, doesn't the good rescuer have to rescue both children? Doesn't this case undermine the basic idea that, when it comes to beneficence, complying agents should not have to take up the slack left by the noncompliance of others—and thus show that we should never have embraced the compliance condition in the first place?[18]

The first point to note is that the collective principle may fail to give the "right" answer even in the standard rescue case. If I (a well-off person in the actual world) pass by a child in a pond and ask myself what life would be like for me under full compliance with the collective principle, the answer would probably be that my clothes would soon be wet and perhaps my important appointment missed. This negative impact on my well-being under full compliance in turn increases the level of sacrifice now required of me. But it does not follow that what I should now do is rescue the child in the lake. Perhaps the extra amount of sacrifice could be put to better use in the form of an extra contribution to OXFAM.[19] The underlying point here is that needs that arise in the context of emergencies are not treated specially by the collective principle. These needs are certainly taken into account when figuring out the level of required sacrifice, but when the time comes to act, agents should, as always, direct their required level of sacrifice where it will do the most good.

Since this is so, we can see that the collective principle will in fact sometimes give the "right" answer in the two-rescuer case, requiring the good rescuer to take up the slack: so long as he remains within his required level of sacrifice, the only question is whether rescuing children is a better use of his resources than something else. The number of potential rescuers around is relevant for determining our agent's full-compliance level of sacrifice—if there are as many rescuers as victims, then our good agent's required level of sacrifice is increased by the whole pond scenario less than it would be if there were fewer rescuers than victims. But the presence of noncomplying potential rescuers has no impact on the question of what the complier should do for his required level of sacrifice. And if the cost of rescue is that of throwing a life preserver, it is hard to imagine that there is anything better that could be done for the price.

The larger point here is that even a two-rescuer case in which the collective principle does give the "wrong" answer does not raise the special and deep objection to the compliance condition that it seemed to. There are many rescue cases where the collective principle departs from common sense—just because under partial compliance with the collective principle, required sacrifice is limited and rescue contexts are accorded no special weight. There is no special problem raised by the two-rescuer case in particular. Indeed, perhaps most troubling is what the collective principle (and also constrained collective utilitarianism) implies about the rescue obligations of people who are very poor in the actual world. Optimally prudent very poor people, we have imagined, would be better off under full compliance; the upshot is that they are not required to sustain even trivial losses in order to rescue drowning people.

Now limited principles of beneficence do no better at matching common sense on rescue cases. Thus if we imagine a principle that requires agents to sustain sacrifice up to some yearly limit, rescue will not be required once the limit is reached. Even if, under a more sophisticated limited principle, required sacrifice does not give out but rather approaches zero asymptotically, and moreover always takes into account the amount of good a given sacrifice could do, the distinction between *rescuing* and saving far-off or otherwise inconspicuous lives will still be lacking.[20] If required sacrifice for the sake of beneficence gives out at some point, and rescue cases are subsumed under the general category of beneficence, then requirements to rescue must give out at some point too. Any limited principle of beneficence designed to match common sense about rescue cases will turn out to be *very* much more demanding than common sense when it comes to general beneficence. Suppose that a sophisticated limited principle holds that one is always required to sustain a very small sacrifice to save a life; the principle thus matches common sense about many rescue cases. But we also know that *each* ten dollars at my disposal can be put to lifesaving uses.[21]

If people had unlimited resources, the optimizing principle of beneficence would always give the "right" answer in rescue cases. But since people do not have unlimited resources, the optimizing principle of beneficence departs from common sense in the rescue context, too. If I am wearing my only suit as I pass by the pond, and without this suit I cannot earn my high salary, most of which is automatically siphoned off to OXFAM, I should not rescue the child. Wouldn't it be for the best to save the child and simply buy another suit? Not if the cost of a suit would allow OXFAM to save more than one life. Once again, the problem is clear: a general principle of beneficence, whether optimizing or not, directs people to put a given resource to the best use; rescue contexts get no special treatment. Commonsense morality tells us, by contrast, that rescuing has strict priority over general beneficence.

In the face of all this, the natural thought is that the morality of rescue is distinct from that of general beneficence; we should recognize that rescue contexts are governed by some special obligation to rescue. But if the compliance condition is right, this would only relocate the problem. For though a special obligation to rescue would be a distinct moral principle that governs rescue cases, and so the collective principle of beneficence would not need to satisfy commonsense intuitions about rescue cases, any special obligation to rescue would itself have to comply with the compliance condition. A special obligation to rescue would be what I earlier called a group-relative but agent-neutral moral principle, in respect of which questions about the responsibility of complying agents under partial compliance would be appropriate.[22]

It might seem that this confirms that rescue contexts do raise a special problem for the compliance condition in particular, a problem distinct from those apparently faced by the limited and optimizing principles of beneficence. For those principles of beneficence can be relieved of the problem so long as some special obligation to rescue is plausible. But this comparative advantage in fact holds only for defenders of the optimizing principle (or the charity view). Common sense contemplates rather severe demands in rescue contexts. As we saw in chapter 3, defenders of limited principles of beneficence owe us an explanation of why extreme demands are objectionable only when they come from a principle of beneficence; this task seems even more difficult when we add the special obligation to rescue to the list of principles from which extreme demands are acceptable—after all, a special obligation to rescue is still in form a principle of beneficence, requiring us to help a stranger in need.

In any case, it turns out that it is far from easy to describe a plausible special obligation to rescue. In his recent book *Living High and Letting Die*, Peter Unger argues that the weighty distinction we make in our intuitive moral thought between rescue cases and nonrescue cases cannot be justified by any plausible normative criteria. Such factors as physical or social proximity, to name but two of the nine factors Unger considers, do not, he claims, survive a moment's reflection.[23] But the force of Unger's argument comes not just from abstract reflection on the plausibility of the various possible distinguishing factors but also from his ability to construct, for each factor, a case that seems to prompt the wrong intuitive response. Thus to those who suppose that physical proximity is what underlies the stronger obligation to help in a rescue case, Unger might respond by pointing to an example like that of our astronomers, who we may assume are hundreds of miles from the sailors in distress.[24] So Unger's point is twofold: the factors we might think serve to mark out rescue contexts as morally special are not plausible considered on their own, and in any case commonsense moral reactions do not consistently track any one such factor or collection of them.

If there is no distinct moral category comprising rescue cases, we would expect some explanation of the widespread belief that there is. Unger suggests that in most of the cases where we readily accept a stringent obligation to meet the needs of others, those needs are very conspicuous to the agent.[25] He further claims that while "our basic moral values" support a stringent general duty of beneficence that does not distinguish between rescue cases and nonrescue cases, our "futility thinking"—roughly the thought that anything we can do to help will be a mere drop in the ocean—blinds us to this obligation in most cases. In some few cases, however, the needs of the victim are sufficiently conspicuous to us to break the hold of the futility thinking.[26] This is why commonsense morality acknowledges the underlying stringent obligation of beneficence in rescue contexts only. But of course conspicuousness as such has no moral weight; so we must accept the underlying basic commitment to a stringent principle of general beneficence—in effect, the optimizing principle.[27]

Though I of course do not follow Unger's argument all the way to the optimizing principle, his claim that commonsense reactions to rescue cases track conspicuousness does seem plausible.[28] And overall, though we cannot say that he has proven that there is no special obligation to rescue, we can say that he has shifted the burden of proof to the side of anyone who would defend the commonsense view.[29] I myself doubt that the idea of a special obligation to rescue can be defended. But even if there is no special obligation to rescue—and so the optimizing principle of beneficence gains no comparative advantage over the collective principle—it would be desirable if we could explain away the apparent implausibility of the implications of the collective principle of beneficence in rescue cases. In so doing, we would at the same time be offering some further diagnosis of the commonsense but (by hypothesis) mistaken idea that rescue contexts generate distinct and stringent duties to act.

We can start by setting out in more detail the way the collective principle operates in rescue cases. For most people, a rule of thumb that easy and cheap rescues ought to be performed would probably be endorsed by the collective principle. It would do more good in the long run if agents simply performed such rescues without reflection rather than began deliberation about their new level of required sacrifice at the rescue scene; the expected costs of engaging in the deliberation would probably exceed the expected benefits. Of course on some occasions it would be better to employ the extra sacrifice in some other way than in performing the rescue, and so the person who acts on the rule of thumb acts wrongly. But if I am right about the appropriate rule of thumb for easy and cheap rescues, this will usually be blameless wrongdoing.

Not all rescues are easy and cheap. What do we say about the astronomers? A rule of thumb that tells agents to perform all rescues where the expected benefit exceeds the expected harm to the agent is not likely to be required by the collective principle. For if an agent does contribute an enormous amount to a rescue operation that saves some few people, this will be at the expense of some very great benefit that the same sacrifice could have achieved if otherwise employed. It would seem, then, that when faced with a case involving great loss to the rescuer, an agent should indeed respond by factoring the increased need for his beneficence into his level of required sacrifice. If our astronomers are very well-off (and so their level of required level of sacrifice is high), it would seem that they may be required to let the shipwrecked sailors drown and contribute an amount equivalent to the cost of the loss of their experiment wherever it would do most good. (Of course, they are not prohibited from rescuing the sailors as well.)

Now for some people not even a rule of thumb that easy and cheap rescues be performed will be required. These are the very poor, already mentioned, of whom no sacrifice at all is required. Here we have the starkest contrast between the deliverances of the collective principle and our ordinary intuitive reactions to most rescue cases. "It doesn't matter how badly off someone is, and how unjustly so," it will be said, "if one person can easily and cheaply prevent a child from drowning at her feet, it would be monstrous if she failed to do so. But the collective principle holds that failing to rescue will be permissible in many such cases, even when it is not a question of doing more good elsewhere. This cannot be right."

We need to move beyond rules of thumb and consider agents' motives and character. For in fact actual people are typically motivated to perform all kinds of rescues, not just easy and cheap ones—typical astronomers will be very strongly inclined to respond to the Mayday call. The relevant motives are ones that come naturally to people; they do not need to be inculcated. Indeed, they are motives the possession of which makes a person better-off. Ordinary fellow feeling and a concern that harm not come to creatures with whom one is interacting, motives whose absence would make ordinary day-to-day personal relationships very difficult, are enough to lead a person to perform even rescues that are quite costly or dangerous. It is true that people are moved to rescue perfect strangers, not just those with whom they are interacting on a personal level. But one thing that most beneficiaries of what common sense holds to be a stringent duty to rescue have in common, Unger plausibly tells us, is that their needs are highly conspicuous to the agent. This is a characteristic that they share with those people who interact personally with the agent. It is not surprising that once someone's needs have become conspicuous to us, for whatever reason, the motives typically characteristic of more personal relationships become engaged.

These basic motives characteristic of even fairly casual personal relationships are not only motives that make their possessors better-off; they also are motives that, under most circumstances, make everyone else better-off as well.[30] Thus, even though the possession of such motives will on occasion lead a person to act wrongly, they are not motives it would be better to try to abandon, and so such wrongdoing would be blameless. Indeed, the ability to comply with the collective principle in a case like that of the astronomers would display a sufficiently undesirable character that a spectator would be struck more with this fact than with the rightness of the action.

The same general point applies to the case of the two rescuers. In any actual such case, a person inclined to rescue the first child would very likely also be strongly inclined to rescue the second. In doing so, she may act beyond the call of duty, but she acts on motives she ought not to try to rid herself of. And again, the person who did stop short with her fair share of the rescue load would stand out for having a highly undesirable character; this would be a case of "blameworthy right-doing."

Now of course it might be possible to fine-tune our motives such that we can distinguish between needs that are conspicuous because of some relationship between the agent and the victim, and needs that are conspicuous for any other reason. I am here only suggesting that as we in fact are, powerful motives to help seem to be engaged whenever needs become conspicuous.[31]

I can now offer a speculation about commonsense reactions to rescue cases. It seems plausible to think that our strong negative reaction to failures to rescue is based not so much on a sense that the agent acted terribly wrongly but on a sense that his emotional indifference to the victim's plight shows him to have an appalling character. Moreover, part of our feeling that such a person is appalling may be based simply on our knowledge that he is not someone with whom we would want to have personal dealings. Hume convincingly argued that our emotional reactions to human qualities do not fall into clear categories, and that to the extent that they do, our strongest concern is by no means always with the strictly moral qualities.[32] It is therefore quite plausible to think that the "what a monster" response to a nonrescuer reports more our concern not to have anything to do with the kind of person who can leave a particular, salient, fellow human being die than with an especially strong judgment of wrongdoing.

If I am right about the importance of the agent's character to our intuitive reactions to rescue cases, it would support the neglected possibility that the obligation *to act* in rescue cases is not as uniformly stringent as we have thought. The more plausible this neglected possibility, the more plausible, too, is the operation of the collective principle in rescue cases. This, obviously enough, would add to the overall appeal of the principle. But it bears repeating that rescue cases are a problem for everyone. Or almost everyone: *if* a plausible special obligation to rescue can be described, then those who embrace either the optimizing principle of beneficence or no principle of beneficence at all (charity) will face no further problems; these, however, are views about beneficence we have very good independent reasons to reject.

V. A Relatively Plausible
Overall View?

In this book I have tried to show that the compliance condition offers a more plausible diagnosis of the apparent absurdity of the demands of the optimizing principle of beneficence than does the idea of over-demandingness. I have also tried to show that the collective principle of beneficence is, relatively speaking, the most plausible principle of beneficence, all things considered. Of course these two aims are mutually reinforcing, since the collective principle is born of the compliance condition and the plausibility of the collective principle, considered on its own, shores up the plausibility of the compliance condition. No one of my many arguments is likely to convince a reader that I have achieved either of my two aims; what I hope is that all the arguments taken together might seem to make up a more convincing overall view than the relevant alternatives.

NOTES

Chapter One

1. Jean Drèze and Amartya Sen, *Hunger and Public Action* (Oxford: Clarendon Press, 1989), 275–76, make much the same point: "The persistence of widespread hunger is one of the most appalling features of the modern world. The fact that so many people continue to die each year from famines, and that many millions more go on perishing from persistent deprivation on a regular basis, is a calamity to which the world has, somewhat incredibly, got coolly accustomed. It does not seem to engender the kind of shock and disquiet that might be reasonable to expect given the enormity of the tragedy. Indeed, the subject often generates either cynicism ('not a lot can be done about it'), or complacent irresponsibility ('don't blame me-it is not a problem for which I am answerable')."

2. Henry Sidgwick, *The Methods of Ethics*, 7th ed. (London: Macmillan, 1907; repr., Indianapolis: Hackett, 1981), 252.

3. See ibid., 434. "The Utilitarian doctrine," Sidgwick says, "is that each man ought to consider the happiness of any other as *theoretically* of equal importance with his own, and only of less importance *practically*, in so far as he is better able to realize the latter" (252).

4. See John Rawls, *A Theory of Justice* (Cambridge, Mass.: Harvard University Press, 1971), 3, 7, 54–55; Rawls, *Political Liberalism* (New York: Columbia University Press, 1993), Lecture VII, "The Basic Structure as Subject."

5. See Liam B. Murphy, "Institutions and the Demands of Justice," *Philosophy & Public Affairs* 27 (1998): 251–91. In disagreeing with Rawls on this issue, I of course do not deny that institutional action will almost always be the most effective means by which to promote people's well-being.

6. For the distinction between ideal and nonideal theory, or, what is the same thing, between full-compliance and partial-compliance theory, see Rawls, *A Theory of Justice*, 8–9, 245–46.

7. "If it is wrong for me to act in my own interest whenever I could instead do something that would serve the interest of others more than any act open to me could serve my own interest, then arguably I am only rarely allowed to act in my own interest. This is absurd, and a view of morality of

which this is a consequence is surely wrong" (Joseph Raz, "A Morality Fit for Humans," *Michigan Law Review* 91 [1993]: 1297). See also Bernard Williams, "Persons, Character and Morality," in *Moral Luck*, (Cambridge: Cambridge University Press, 1981), 14: "A man who has such a ground project will be required by Utilitarianism to give up what it requires in a given case just if that conflicts with what he is required to do as an impersonal utility-maximizer when all the causally relevant considerations are in. That is a quite absurd requirement."

8. I first encountered this line of thought in Derek Parfit, *Reasons and Persons* (Oxford: Clarendon Press, 1984), 30–31 (two pages that were the primary inspiration for this entire book).

The same basic idea is found in L. Jonathan Cohen's article "Who Is Starving Whom?" *Theoria* 47 (1981): 65–81, and in Carlos Rosenkrantz, "Igualitarismo y Libertarianismo: Política no antropología," *Revista del Centro de Estudios Constitucionales* 7 (1990): 193–203. Cohen defends the view that the duty of a rich person to contribute to famine relief "is only to play a fair part in the performance of what is collectively obligatory" (76); for a disagreement I have with Cohen, see chap. 7, note 18. Dan W. Brock, in "Defending Moral Options," *Philosophy and Phenomenological Research* 51 (1991): 912, briefly alludes to the same concern, which he labels the "Why me? objection." See also Charles Fried, *Right and Wrong* (Cambridge, Mass.: Harvard University Press, 1978), 130; Henry Shue, *Basic Rights: Subsistence, Affluence, and U.S. Foreign Policy*, 2d ed. (Princeton, N. J.: Princeton University Press, 1996), 114–19.

9. See Derek Parfit, *Equality or Priority?* (The Lindley Lecture, The University of Kansas, 1991). The phrase "weighted beneficence," which does not appear in this publication, comes from Parfit, "On Giving Priority to the Worse Off" (unpublished ms., 1989).

10. See the references in note 4 and *A Theory of Justice*, 115, 333–37.

11. See the references in note 6.

12. Rawls, *A Theory of Justice*, 334.

13. See G. A. Cohen, "If You're an Egalitarian, How Come You're So Rich?" forthcoming in the published version of his 1996 Gifford Lectures; Murphy, "Institutions and the Demands of Justice."

Chapter Two

1. Richard Brandt, *A Theory of the Good and the Right* (Oxford: Clarendon Press, 1979), 276. Essentially the same objection is made by Kurt Baier in *The Moral Point of View* (Ithaca, N.Y.: Cornell University Press, 1958), 203–4. Others who have made the objection are too numerous to mention.

2. The objection does not, however, seem to have been of much concern to nineteenth-century critics of utilitarianism; for a survey see J. B. Schneewind, *Sidgwick's Ethics and Victorian Moral Philosophy* (Oxford: Clarendon Press, 1977), chaps. 4 and 5. The reason for this is perhaps that it was typically taken for granted that truly extensive beneficence was beyond the power of most people.

Mill discusses the objection that utilitarianism sets a standard "too high for humanity" in requiring that people "shall always act from the inducement of promoting the general interest of society"; see John Stuart Mill, *Utilitari-*

anism (1861), ed. George Sher (Indianapolis: Hackett, 1979), 17. As stated, this is not the over-demandingness objection, since it concerns the motives the objector supposes a utilitarian agent must have, and not the losses that compliance with the theory would bring; it nevertheless seems likely that the objectors Mill had in mind were at least in part concerned about excessive demands. In any case, part of Mill's response is to say that most people very rarely have it in their power to promote happiness on an extended scale (19). In a later work, Mill himself criticizes Comte for in effect proposing an excessively demanding morality: "It does not perceive that between the region of duty and that of sin there is an intermediate space, the region of positive worthiness." See John Stuart Mill, *Later Speculations of August Comte* (1865), in *The Positive Philosophy of Auguste Comte* (New York: Henry Holt and Co., 1875), 129; for discussion, see Mark Strasser, *The Moral Philosophy of John Stuart Mill* (Wakefield, N.H.: Longwood Academic, 1991), chap. 7.

3. Though as we will see in note 32, this influence is rather indirect.

4. See W. D. Ross, *The Right and the Good* (Oxford: Clarendon Press, 1930; repr., Indianapolis: Hackett, 1988), 27. Others who embrace the optimizing principle of beneficence as part of a pluralist moral conception are Samuel Clarke (see *A Discourse of Natural Religion* [1706], rpt. in D. D. Raphael, ed., *British Moralists: 1650–1800*, vol. 1 [Indianapolis: Hackett, 1991], 207–9); and perhaps Godwin (see William Godwin, *Enquiry Concerning Political Justice* [1798] [Harmondsworth: Penguin, 1976]).

5. Imagine a moral theory that ranks beneficence second in importance to more or less any benefit that could be bestowed on a family member. Since benefits to family members are typically not nearly as burdensome to the agent as benefits to strangers, wouldn't it be true to say that such a theory makes only moderate demands, and thus true that the optimizing principle of beneficence, as it occurs in this theory, is not extremely demanding at all? No, for even this theory has the potential to impose extreme demands—think of the unfortunate agent with no family.

6. The relevant literature is enormous. Two prominent recent works are Drèze and Sen, *Hunger and Public Action*, and Robert Cassen and associates, *Does Aid Work?* 2d ed. (Oxford: Oxford University Press, 1994).

7. In a letter asking for contributions written in the mid-1990s, the chair of the U.S. Committee for UNICEF noted that oral rehydration therapy cost fourteen cents a dose, and thus that a twenty-five-dollar contribution could save the lives of 179 children. See Peter Unger, *Living High and Letting Die: Our Illusion of Innocence* (New York: Oxford University Press, 1996), for extensive discussion of such cases, and of our obligations upon receiving such letters; see also Peter Singer, *Practical Ethics*, 2d ed., (Cambridge: Cambridge University Press, 1993), chap. 8. For an evaluation of the effectiveness of humanitarian aid, with proposals for improvement of current aid practices, see Cassen and associates, *Does Aid Work?*, and United Nations Development Programme, *Human Development Report 1994* (New York: Oxford University Press, 1994), chap. 4.

8. See Parfit, *Reasons and Persons*, 30–31.

9. See, e.g., Peter Railton, "Alienation, Consequentialism, and the Demands of Morality," *Philosophy & Public Affairs* 13 (1984): 160–63; Thomas Nagel, *The View from Nowhere* (New York: Oxford University Press, 1986), 206–7; Scheffler, *Human Morality*, chap. 8.

10. Railton, "Alienation, Consequentialism," 161; on these advantages, see also Shelly Kagan, *The Limits of Morality* (Oxford: Clarendon Press, 1989), 393–99.

11. Cf. Railton, "Alienation, Consequentialism," 161: "A consequentialist theory is therefore likely to recommend that accepting negative responsibility is more a matter of supporting certain social and political arrangements (or rearrangements) than of setting out individually to save the world." See Murphy, "Institutions and the Demands of Justice."

12. See Sidgwick, *The Methods of Ethics*, 431, 434. For recent versions of this argument, see R. M. Hare, *Moral Thinking: Its Levels, Method and Point* (Oxford: Clarendon Press, 1981), 201–3; and Frank Jackson, "Decision-Theoretic Consequentialism and the Nearest and Dearest Objection," *Ethics* 101 (1991): 461–82. The argument was once put to me with great conviction and zeal by Isaac Levi.

13. See the references given in notes 6 and 7 and also Brad Hooker, "Brink, Kagan, Utilitarianism and Self-Sacrifice," *Utilitas* 3 (1991): 268–69, which includes a discussion of some other attempts to show that the optimizing principle of beneficence is not extremely demanding.

14. Some remarks of Onora O'Neill are relevant:

In arguing for a reconsideration of imperfect obligations and of charity I am well aware that no general duty of beneficence, such as Utilitarianism may entail, has been established. Nothing has been said about obligations to please others or to make them happy, let alone to maximize happiness. In the sense in which the phrase is generally used there is here no "over-load of obligations" problem. Charity as here constructed is a much narrower duty than beneficence; it is concerned only with meeting agency-threatening needs.

See O'Neill, "The Great Maxims of Justice and Charity," in *Constructions of Reason* (Cambridge: Cambridge University Press, 1989), 233; the phrase "over-load of obligations" is due to James Fishkin, *The Limits of Obligation* (New Haven, Conn.: Yale University Press, 1982), passim.

15. More fully, the claim is that we are required to "provide the condition in which people will enjoy the basic capacities to take advantage of the opportunities available in their society"; see Joseph Raz, "Duties of Well-Being," in *Ethics in the Public Domain* (Oxford: Clarendon Press, 1994), 18. I will not try to present Raz's position in full. It should, however, be noted that Raz himself does not claim that the limits on what one person can do to promote the well-being of another render principles of beneficence undemanding, though, as we will see later, he does believe that his theory of well-being is relevant in a different way to the extent of demands.

16. James Griffin, *Well-Being: Its Meaning, Measurement and Moral Importance* (Oxford: Clarendon Press, 1986), 185.

17. Kagan's argument is directed against a person he calls "the moderate," who accepts a "pro tanto [overridable] reason to promote the good" but also believes that there are limits to the sacrifice one is morally required to sustain; see *The Limits of Morality*, 15–19. He seeks and fails to find a rationale that would make the commitment to options compatible with the commitment to the pro tanto reason to promote the good; see generally ibid., especially chaps. 1, 7–9.

18. Among philosophers, Kagan, in ibid., chap. 10, Singer, in *Practical Ethics*, 242–46, and Unger, in *Living High and Letting Die*, chap. 6, are impor-

tant exceptions. Hare is a more complicated case; see note 47. Of course, as explained in sec. I, there are defenders of utilitarianism who reject my account of its demands.

19. Fishkin, *The Limits of Obligations*, 14, presents as an uncontroversial "element of the basic structure of individual morality" that "there are limits to the sacrifice which can be demanded of any individual as a matter of duty or obligation."

20. See Thomas W. Pogge, *Realizing Rawls* (Ithaca, N.Y.: Cornell University Press, 1989), 5 n, for a strong statement of this point.

21. Samuel Scheffler convinced me of this point.

22. See Kagan, *The Limits of Morality*, chap. 8; the phrase "motivational condition" is Kagan's.

23. See J. L. Mackie, *Ethics: Inventing Right and Wrong* (Harmondsworth: Penguin, 1977), 129–34.

A motivational condition (or, equivalently, James Griffin's "Requirement of Psychological Realism"; see *Well-Being*, 127) might instead be grounded in a commitment to some version of the "internalism" requirement on moral judgment that stipulates that agents can be truly said to be subject to some moral requirement only if they have, or are capable of developing, the motivation to comply with it; see Kagan, *The Limits of Morality*, 277, and references given there.

A third kind of argument is found in Brad Hooker's defense of rule-consequentialism: he rejects the optimizing principle in part because of the "costs of inculcating and sustaining" a highly demanding rule; see "Rule-Consequentialism," *Mind* 99 (1990): 76–77; and "Rule-Consequentialism and Demandingness: A Reply to Carson," *Mind* 100 (1991): 269–76.

24. See Kagan, *The Limits of Morality*, chap. 8.

25. Griffin, *Well-Being*, 7. What I am calling the "general account" of well-being corresponds to what Griffin later calls "the rough, broad, everyday notion of well-being that is used outside of moral theory" (40), except that I do not see why the general account should be any rougher than accounts suited to particular moral contexts.

26. See Griffin, *Well-Being*, 40–41. It may be wondered why I assume that if a particular context requires an account of well-being different from the general account, that account will be a restricted version of the general account. The reason is the theoretical primacy of the general account. If there are facts about individual well-being, this account presents them. While we can imagine that in some practical contexts we may be concerned with some but not all aspects of individual well-being, as defined in the general account, if in some contexts we go *beyond* this account then we will, by definition, no longer be talking about well-being.

27. See T. M. Scanlon, "Preference and Urgency," *Journal of Philosophy* 72 (1975): 655–69, cf. Scanlon, "Value, Desire, and the Quality of Life," in Martha C. Nussbaum and Amartya Sen, eds., *The Quality of Life* (Oxford: Clarendon Press, 1993), 191–92; for Scanlon's most recent views on these issues, see *What We Owe to Each Other* (Cambridge, Mass.: Harvard University Press, 1998), chap. 3. See also Nagel's discussion of "reasons of autonomy" in *The View from Nowhere*, 166–71.

28. Griffin's list of (in effect) substantive goods includes accomplishment, enjoyment, and "deep personal relations"; see *Well-Being*, 67.

29. A version of this idea was suggested to me by Derek Parfit.

30. See Raz, "Duties of Well-Being," 27–28. Of course this idea is not necessarily compatible with all possible substantive good theories of well-being; but neither is it clearly incompatible with the most plausible of such theories. Making beneficence one's project would, for example, bring accomplishment, knowledge of certain sorts, and so forth.

31. Some comments of Susan Wolf made this clear to me.

32. The main argument in Williams, "A Critique of Utilitarianism," in J. J. C. Smart and Bernard Williams, *Utilitarianism: For and Against*, 77–150 (Cambridge: Cambridge University Press, 1973), concerns the way in which the moral requirements facing a utilitarian agent are objectionably (as Williams sees it) mediated by the choices that others make; for discussion and criticism, see Nancy Davis, "Utilitarianism and Responsibility," *Ratio* 22 (1980): 15–35. (My own concern with unfair demands under partial compliance, discussed in chap. 5, has some affinity with this argument.) Williams explicitly states that his argument does not concern "the question of how limits are to be placed on one's apparently boundless obligation, implied by utilitarianism, to improve the world," though he adds that "answers are needed to that, too" ("A Critique of Utilitarianism," 109–10). The main argument in "Persons, Character and Morality" does, however, respond to a very particular aspect of the problem of over-demandingness, namely, the extreme demand made when a person is morally required to give up a "ground project"—a project that is "closely related to his existence and which to a significant degree give[s] meaning to his life" (12).

33. See Jackson, "Decision-Theoretic Consequentialism."

34. Some special goods are "lexically prior" to all other aspects of well-being if no amount of the other goods could outweigh certain minimal losses in the special goods. For discussion of the idea of lexical priority in moral theory, see Rawls, *A Theory of Justice*, 42–43.

35. See the "one thought too many" passage in Williams, "Persons, Character and Morality," 17–18; and Michael Stocker, "The Schizophrenia of Modern Ethical Theories," *Journal of Philosophy* 73 (1976): 453–66. A collection of relevant articles is Lawrence C. Becker et al., "Symposium on Impartiality and Ethical Theory," *Ethics* 101 (1991): 698–864.

36. Williams, "Persons, Character and Morality," 17–18. As Derek Parfit comments (personal communication, August 31, 1997): "It's odd that Williams gives, as the thought that the person's wife might hope he was having, that he is saving her because she is *his wife*. She might have hoped that he saved her because she was *Mary*, or *Jane*, or whatever. That she is his wife seems one thought too many."

37. See Scheffler, *Human Morality*, chap. 3.

38. For a Kantian response to the problem, see Barbara Herman, "Integrity and Impartiality," *The Monist* 66 (1983): 233–50; and Herman, "Agency, Attachment, and Difference," *Ethics* 101 (1991): 775–97.

39. See Parfit, *Reasons and Persons*, 27–28; see also Sidgwick, *The Methods of Ethics*, 432–33; Hare, *Moral Thinking*, 197; R. M. Adams, "Motive Utilitarianism," *Journal of Philosophy* 73 (1976): 467–81. This line of thought is most fully and explicitly developed as a reply to the alienation objection in Railton, "Alienation, Consequentialism."

Another reason that it would not make the outcome best if we were all pure do-gooders is that constantly thinking in terms of the best outcome would be counterproductive: it would be too time-consuming and might lead us astray, since we tend in the heat of the moment to overestimate the benefits that our preferred action will bring. Therefore, it would be better if we all had some settled dispositions not to kill, cheat, and so forth. See, e.g., Hare, *Moral Thinking*, 35–39; also relevant is Sidgwick, *The Methods of Ethics*, 480–92. If utilitarianism did require constant deliberation about how to act optimally, this would make agents' lives intolerable, and thus would be another source of extreme demands; see Owen Flanagan, *Varieties of Moral Personality* (Cambridge, Mass.: Harvard University Press, 1991), 33–35.

40. Railton, "Alienation, Consequentialism," 151.

41. Ibid., 141.

42. See Parfit, *Reasons and Persons*, 30.

43. In this section I elaborate a suggestion made to me by Derek Parfit. The arguments here connect with a number of controversial issues in moral psychology about which I attempt to remain neutral.

44. This paragraph follows Parfit, *Reasons and Persons*, sec. 14.

45. By contrast, motive utilitarianism is restricted in this way; it holds just that each agent ought to have the motives his having which will make the outcome best; see Adams, "Motive Utilitarianism." When I benefit my brother, my motives could not be better, and thus I am open to no condemnation from motive utilitarianism.

46. Sidgwick, *The Methods of Ethics*, 428.

47. This suggestion should be distinguished from Sidgwick's suggestion (ibid., 492–93) that utilitarians should praise people who sustain great loss to promote the good, but not blame those who fail to do so. Sidgwick's position on actions "beyond the call of duty" is that "it is always wrong for a man knowingly to do anything other than what he believes to be most conducive to Universal Happiness," but that it is typically best not to blame such wrongdoing if acting rightly would have brought great loss to the agent. As we have seen, this is not Parfit's blameless wrongdoing.

We should also distinguish here Hare's discussion of supererogation in *Moral Thinking*, 198–203. In addition to repeating Sidgwick's point that it would not be in accordance with utility to blame failures to sustain great loss for the sake of promoting utility, Hare offers another reason that it would not make the outcome best if we all were pure do-gooders: in trying to do too much, we may fail and end up doing less good than we would have done if we had set our sights lower. In Hare's two-level version of utilitarianism, the intuitive level (level-1) principle of beneficence with the highest "acceptance utility" would not be very demanding. Nevertheless, at the level of critical thinking (level-2), the optimizing principle of beneficence always prevails. Hare would deny that there is a single answer to the question, When it would be optimal to do more than my level-1 principle requires, would my failure to do so be wrong (despite its not being in accordance with utility to blame me) or not? He appears to believe that the most one can say is that such actions are level-1 right though level-2 wrong; see further Hare, "Comments," in Douglas Seanor and N. Fotion, eds., *Hare and Critics* (Oxford: Clarendon Press, 1988), 222–23, 261.

48. This limitation was mentioned by Derek Parfit when he made the suggestion that this section elaborates.

49. See Unger's discussion (*Living High and Letting Die*, 149–50) of the limited extent to which a "decent" family life interferes with our ability to bestow great benefits on strangers.

50. See p. 14.

51. See Michael Slote, *Common-Sense Morality and Consequentialism* (London: Routledge and Kegan Paul, 1985), chap. 2.

52. See Scheffler, *Human Morality*, 98.

53. See ibid. Jonathan Bennett distinguishes the "tight reins" of utilitarianism from its excessive "thwarting of desires," in *The Act Itself* (Oxford: Clarendon Press, 1995), 143–50.

54. The example of career choice was used by Ronald Dworkin, in discussion, to illustrate (what I call) the problem of confinement; I am indebted to Dworkin and Thomas Nagel for convincing me of the importance of the problem of confinement.

55. I owe this example to Thomas Nagel.

56. I owe this suggestion to Christopher Eisgruber.

57. Sen defends the idea that freedom of choice (or more precisely, in his terms, "capability to function") may contribute directly to a person's well-being in *Inequality Reexamined* (Cambridge, Mass.: Harvard University Press, 1992), chap. 3; see also Sen, "Capability and Well-Being," in Nussbaum and Sen, *The Quality of Life*, 30–53. However, Sen does not argue that a person's freedom of choice may be reduced by morality itself.

58. See Slote, *Common-Sense Morality and Consequentialism*, chap. 2. A similar position is taken by Brock, "Defending Moral Options."

59. See Kagan, *The Limits of Morality*, 236–38, and "Replies to My Critics," *Philosophy and Phenomenological Research* 51 (1991): 922–24.

60. The notion of moral autonomy perhaps makes most sense if we accept a Freudian division of the psyche; we could think of the superego as constraining the (moral) autonomy of the rest of the psyche. For moral philosophical discussions of the Freudian account of the superego, see Scheffler, *Human Morality*, chap. 5, and Russell Grigg, "The Ethics of Desire," *Analysis* (Melbourne Centre for Psychoanalytic Research) 3 (1991): 29–35.

61. How significant the special losses flowing from confinement might be, compared with the more mundane losses I focused on in introducing over-demandingness, is unclear without further discussion. But it would surely be implausible to claim that the over-demandingness objection is concerned *only* with losses due to confinement. Thus it would be implausible to think that it is only if these special losses can be defended as such that there is a problem of over-demandingness at all.

62. In discussion, Ronald Dworkin used the term "ethical space" for what I believe is the same idea.

63. See Nagel, *The View from Nowhere*, esp. chaps. 9 and 10. One of Scheffler's arguments in *The Rejection of Consequentialism*, rev. ed. (Oxford: Clarendon Press, 1994), might seem to fit in here. Scheffler is concerned to find a motivation for what he calls an "agent-centered prerogative," which is a permission for agents to refrain from performing the optimal action in some circumstances. The motivation he suggests is the "liberation strategy." This is one way of accounting for the moral importance of the personal point of view. To the fact that people do not typically adopt the impersonal perspective, but rather value their own interests out of proportion to the weight they receive in an impersonal assessment, the liberation strategy responds by insisting that a moral theory should reflect this fact by allowing agents to promote their own interests out of proportion with their impersonal value. See pp. 57–62.

This line of thought does not address confinement, however, where the problem concerns my options for action and what determines them. Rather, it responds to the fact that we tend to *care* disproportionately for our own interests and to the normative idea that moral theories should in some way reflect this. Scheffler offers his argument as an interpretation of Williams's critique of utilitarianism.

64. See Amartya Sen, *Collective Choice and Social Welfare* (San Francisco: Holden-Day, 1970), chaps. 7 and 7*; Parfit, *Reasons and Persons*, sec. 146.

65. This might be what Bennett has in mind when he notes, in his discussion of utilitarianism's "tight reins," that "any space that is left, whether large or small, is uncomfortable. Each gap between what is required and what is forbidden is kept open by opposing moral pressures rather than the absence of any—the tense calm at the centre of a hurricane rather than the relaxed peace of a halcyon day" (*The Act Itself*, 145).

66. I am persuaded by Scheffler's argument, in *Human Morality*, chap. 2, that morality must be seen as pervasive. Does it make sense to regard such trivial actions as brushing my teeth as morally assessable? Yes. What if someone is choking in the next room? What if I had promised not to brush my teeth? What if I am already late for an appointment, or taking my children to school?

Chapter Three

1. On the two versions, see chap. 2, sec. IV.

2. This position was originally suggested to me by Derek Parfit.

3. See Godwin, *Enquiry Concerning Political Justice*, bk. VIII, chap. 2. On Godwin's view, when I pass by a beggar who needs my shillings more than I do, I am, morally speaking, stealing them from him.

4. As Gisela Striker suggested to me.

5. Holly Smith Goldman suggests a "minimal justice" baseline for assessing the demands of distributive justice; I take the example of the thief and stolen goods from her; see "Rawls and Utilitarianism," in H. Gene Blocker and Elizabeth H. Smith, eds., *John Rawls' Theory of Social Justice: An Introduction* (Athens: Ohio University Press, 1980), 356–57.

6. Though not by F. M. Kamm; see *Morality, Mortality*, vol. 2, *Rights, Duties, and Status* (New York: Oxford University Press, 1996), 109.

7. "Apart from Aristotle, who made a desperate attempt to justify it by arguing that it was natural and just, the Greeks did not generally approve of slavery as a just institution. They regarded it as a great calamity for the person enslaved, and a few explicitly said that it was unjust. They accepted it because they could not imagine how the civilized way of living they cherished might be possible without slaves." See Gisela Striker, "Are We Any Better?" review of Bernard Williams, *Shame and Necessity*, *London Review of Books*, August 19, 1993, 17; Striker here summarizes Williams, *Shame and Necessity* (Berkeley and Los Angeles: University of California Press, 1993), 106–17. H. D. F. Kitto believed that "Athens from (say) 480 to 380 was clearly the most civilized society that has yet existed"; see *The Greeks* (Harmondsworth: Penguin, 1951), 96. This means that there was a lot to lose.

8. See p. 28.

9. I owe this suggestion to Charles Larmore.

10. For different versions of this point I am indebted to Gerald Doppelt, Charles Larmore, and Lawrence Sager.

11. It would not do to insist in response that all theorists agree that *some* parts of morality should be treated as settled. It is indeed hard to dispute the standard example of it being wrong to torture for fun. But it would be wrong to think that we could find our baseline in the area of agreement between, say, all moral conceptions that have some degree of plausibility and historical support (a possibility suggested to me by Michael Smith). For it is in fact misleading in this context to say that utilitarians believe that torturing for fun is wrong. To adapt some words attributed to Shelly Kagan (in Parfit, "On Giving Priority to the Worse Off"), utilitarians believe that (1) it is wrong to choose an action with less expected benefit than some other available action, and (2) that's all. It would be arbitrary, and prejudicial, to use one implication of the utilitarian principle to set the baseline for assessing the demands flowing from its other implications.

12. See the discussion of the "costs of a morally decent life" in Unger, *Living High and Letting Die*, chap. 6.

13. A partial exception may be Williams, who suggests that any moral principle that requires the abandonment of a "ground project" is objectionable; see "Persons, Character and Morality," 14.

It is the asymmetry between our intuitive reactions to the demands of beneficence and the demands of other parts of commonsense morality that lies behind Kagan's and Kamm's objection to the "hybrid" theory proposed by Scheffler in *The Rejection of Consequentialism;* see Kagan, "Does Consequentialism Demand Too Much?" *Philosophy & Public Affairs* 13 (1984): 239–54; and Kamm, "Supererogation and Obligation," *Journal of Philosophy* 82 (1985): 118–38; see also Kagan, *The Limits of Morality*, chap. 1 and p. 79; and Kamm, *Morality, Mortality*, 2:109. A hybrid theory contains no deontological constraints but allows agents to favor their own interests rather than always choose the optimal action. The objection made is that this allows agents to actively harm others for (nonoptimal) personal gain. Essentially the same objection is raised by Jonathan Bennett to his own similar proposal for a less demanding version of utilitarianism in "Morality and Consequences," in S. M. McMurrin, ed., *The Tanner Lectures on Human Values*, vol. 2 (Salt Lake City: University of Utah Press, 1981), 78–81; for a fuller discussion, see Bennett, *The Act Itself*, chap. 9.

14. See Kagan, *The Limits of Morality*, 79. The remainder of this section benefited from the criticism of Shelly Kagan and Larry Temkin.

15. As Kamm points out; see *Morality, Mortality*, 2:109.

16. In a brief discussion (ibid.), Kamm points out that it is possible to object to cost X for act Y while accepting cost X for act Z. That is so, but we would expect to be able to say why Z justifies a higher price than Y. She draws an analogy to refusing to pay X for a VCR while happily paying that much for a car; but here the justification is clear, since cars have a higher market value than VCRs and are also, for most people, more important (have a higher "use value"). If deontological constraints are in some sense "worth more" than beneficence, we need to be told what that sense is.

17. A point noted by Warren S. Quinn, a defender of the distinction between doing and allowing; see "Actions, Intentions, and Consequences: The Doctrine of Doing and Allowing," in Bonnie Steinbock and Alistair Norcross,

eds., *Killing and Letting Die*, 2d ed. (New York: Fordham University Press, 1994), 357.

18. See the essays in Steinbock and Norcross; see also Bennett, *The Act Itself*.

19. Cf. Raziel Abelson, "To Do or Let Happen," *American Philosophical Quarterly* 19 (1982): 226–27.

20. See, e.g., Richard Trammell, "Saving Life and Taking Life," in Steinbock and Norcross, *Killing and Letting Die*, 292; H. M. Malm, "Between the Horns of the Negative-Positive Duty Debate," *Philosophical Studies* 61 (1991): 194; Kamm, *Morality, Mortality*, 2:87–109; cf. Bruce Russell, "On the Relative Strictness of Negative and Positive Duties," *American Philosophical Quarterly* 14 (1977): 87–97.

21. See, e.g., Trammell, "Saving Life and Taking Life," 292; Jean Beer Blumenfeld, "Causing Harm and Bringing Aid," *American Philosophical Quarterly* 18 (1981): 328–29; H. M. Malm, "Directions of Justification in the Negative-Positive Duty Debate," *American Philosophical Quarterly* 27 (1990): 322; cf. Bennett, *The Act Itself*, 161–63.

22. For example, if Christine Korsgaard's argument in "The Reasons We Can Share," in *Creating the Kingdom of Ends* (Cambridge: Cambridge University Press, 1996), 275–310, were persuasive, no principle of beneficence would be defensible, whatever its demands. Similarly, Kamm's argument, in *Morality, Mortality*, 2:228–30, that we are not "for" promoting the good, is a fundamental attack on requirements of beneficence.

23. Criticism by Derek Parfit helped me find the notion of compliance appropriate for my discussion.

24. See chap. 2, sec. III and the work of Raz there referred to; see also Scheffler's discussion of the "resonance" of morality in *Human Morality*, chap 4.

25. Conversations with Stephen Perry and Lewis Kornhauser helped me greatly with the following discussion.

26. See Parfit, *Reasons and Persons*, pt. 3, esp. pp. 329–42, and the discussion in "Comments," *Ethics* 96 (1986): 832–72; see also Nagel, "Equality," in *Mortal Questions*, 124–25 n.

27. See chap. 2, p. 19.

28. Sibylle Fischer convinced me of the importance of this idea; it has affinities with the idea that principles of distributive justice should not allocate more resources to those who have "chosen" to develop expensive tastes, see, e.g., Richard Arneson, "Equality and Equal Opportunity for Welfare," *Philosophical Studies* 56 (1989): 77–93.

29. Kamm distinguishes active and passive loss; see *Morality, Mortality*, 2: 215. Scheffler makes in effect the same distinction in *The Rejection of Consequentialism*, 38–39. I count as a passive demand only those losses that flow to a person from others acting as they are *required* to by a moral theory; losses flowing from action that is merely permissible according to some theory are not rightly regarded as demands of that theory. (I am indebted here to Jeff McMahan.) If this seems wrong, consider passive benefits—the benefits a person receives from others' compliance with a moral theory (discussed later in the text). It would seem very odd to count the benefits a person receives from others merely acting as they are permitted to by a moral theory as benefits of those others' compliance with the theory.

30. See chap. 1 for discussion of the relevance of the issue of the demands of beneficence to the topic of distributive justice.

31. Thomas Nagel, "Libertarianism Without Foundations," *Yale Law Journal* 85 (1975): 145–46.

32. I became much clearer about this issue after conversations with Richard Arneson and Lawrence Sager.

33. The world of full compliance is indeterminate, too, since there is more than one way in which one can act as required by a moral theory—as we saw in chap. 2, all plausible moral conceptions leave scope for the merely permissible. But this indeterminacy is very much less than that we confront when thinking about a world in which people do not act as required.

34. See David Gauthier, "Justice and Natural Endowment: Toward a Critique of Rawls's Ideological Framework," in *Moral Dealing: Contract, Ethics, and Reason* (Ithaca, N.Y.: Cornell University Press, 1990), 150–70; and Rawls's reply in *Political Liberalism*, Lecture VII, secs. 7–8.

35. See Allan Gibbard, "Constructing Justice," *Philosophy & Public Affairs* 20 (1991): 270.

36. A legitimate political system, on Nagel's account,

is one which reconciles the two universal principles of impartiality and reasonable partiality so that no one can object that his interests are not being accorded sufficient weight or that the demands made on him are excessive. What makes it reasonable for someone to reject a system, and therefore makes it illegitimate, is either that it leaves him too badly off by comparison with others (which corresponds to a failure with respect to impartiality), or that it demands too much of him by way of sacrifice of his interests or commitments by comparison with some feasible alternative (which corresponds to a failure with respect to reasonable partiality). (Nagel, *Equality and Partiality* [New York: Oxford University Press, 1991], 38–39)

37. Nagel says that

to provide a ground for *reasonable* rejection [of a proposed system] the alternative would have to depend not on the arbitrary assignment of greater advantages to certain individuals or groups, but on a different balance between the weight of personal and impartial egalitarian claims in the design of social institutions. . . . (The thought that one could be a hereditary monarch, or that one's profession could be heavily subsidized at public expense, does not establish a feasible alternative by comparison with which it would be reasonable to reject [a proposed system]). (Ibid., 173 n)

Note that this restriction on what are qualifying feasible alternatives is essential for the question of demands to play an independent role in the contractualist story. If demands were assessed relative to a person's me-theory, a proposed moral theory would count as more demanding the worse-off the person would be under it. This would mean that the appeal to demands would simply duplicate the other concern in Nagel's contractualist decision procedure, namely, the relative levels of well-being of different people.

38. "If sacrifice is measured by comparison with possible alternatives rather than by comparison with the status quo, the situations of possible winners and possible losers are symmetrical" (ibid., 84). Note that by "status quo" Nagel means the existing system of justice, i.e., the normative status

quo—the demands of laissez-faire on the poor are measured not against prevailing laissez-faire social systems but against some feasible alternative under which they do better. Nagel's baseline of feasible alternatives does not abstract from the *factual* status quo. As a result, the untalented rich may be able to claim great comparative losses that the untalented poor cannot, even using the baseline of feasible alternatives; the untalented rich can point to social systems in which they know they will (continue to) do very well, but the untalented poor cannot. While social contingencies such as a person's wealth can legitimately affect the assessment of demands for the purposes of the over-demandingness problem, it seems to me at least open to question whether this is appropriate within Nagel's contractualist framework.

39. "The poor may recognize that the rich are not unreasonable to resist more than a certain level of sacrifice, in light of their constellation of motives, while at the same time the poor may reasonably refuse to accept the resulting degree of benefit as sufficient, even in light of the recognition that the rich can reasonably refuse more" (ibid., 172). Nagel is skeptical about the prospects of egalitarianism in the domestic context, too, where he says that the results of the contractualist method are "far from clear" (ibid., 83); however, Nagel's skeptical discussion of domestic egalitarianism focuses more on problems of incentives and motivation than on the problem of excessive demands; see chaps. 9–11.

40. Nagel interprets egalitarian impartiality as inclining us "to favor the alternative that is least unacceptable to the persons to whom it is most unacceptable" (ibid., 68). I am suggesting, in effect, that we could reinterpret the problem of over-demandingness along the same lines; Nagel himself does not do this. Furthermore, this is only one of several possible reinterpretations of the problem; one could, for example, look not just to the size of the demands but also to the number of people on whom demands are made. The remarks in the text would, I believe, apply to the other possibilities as well.

41. Sidgwick makes a similar point:

"If . . . we take an actual man—let us say, an average Englishman— and abstract his morality, what remains is an entity so purely hypothetical, that it is not clear what practical purpose can be served by constructing a system of moral rules for the community of such beings." (*The Methods of Ethics*, 468)

Derek Parfit brought this passage to my attention.

Chapter Four

1. See Scheffler, *The Rejection of Consequentialism*, 5. Scheffler uses the label "agent-relative permissions" in his introduction to *Consequentialism and Its Critics* (New York: Oxford University Press, 1988), 5; Kagan prefers the term "option," see *The Limits of Morality*, 3.

2. The precise form of the prerogative Scheffler offers is quite complex; see *The Rejection of Consequentialism*, 20. Scheffler glosses this statement of the prerogative in a later article as follows:

Suppose, in other words, that each agent were allowed to give M times more weight to his own interests than to the interests of anyone else. This would mean that an agent was permitted to perform his preferred act (call it P), provided that there was no alternative A open to him, such that (1) A would produce a better overall outcome than P, as judged from an impersonal standpoint which gives equal weight to everyone's interests, and (2) the total net loss to others of his doing P rather than A was more than M times as great as the net loss to him of doing A rather than P. (Samuel Scheffler, "Prerogatives Without Restrictions," appendix to *The Rejection of Consequentialism*, 169)

This seems to be equivalent to the following formulation, which I, at least, find easier to grasp: an agent is permitted to perform any of the actions that, compared with the optimal (in impersonal terms) action available to her, are at least M times better for her than they are worse in impersonal terms. As Scheffler notes, other prerogatives are possible. But the differences among the various prerogatives need not concern us—the points I make in the text would apply to any prerogative that makes use of a multiplying factor. Scheffler does not, in any case, take himself to have defended his preferred prerogative against the possible alternatives.

3. See *The Rejection of Consequentialism*, 57–62.

4. He does this most clearly in *Human Morality*, which does not discuss the prerogative. But concern with over-demandingness is certainly present in *The Rejection of Consequentialism*. Scheffler says: "If the unrestricted responsibility for producing optimal outcomes that consequentialism assigns to individuals is thought to be objectionably demanding, then the natural solution is to allow agents not to promote such outcomes when it would be unduly costly or burdensome for them to do so" (20). He then goes on to present the agent-centered prerogative.

5. Scheffler's account of moderate morality could be criticized, along the lines of the previous chapter, for treating the demands of all kinds of moral principles alike. But this does not undermine its usefulness for us as an account of moderate beneficence.

6. Scheffler, *Human Morality*, 100.

7. Ibid., 26.

8. Ibid., 115, 102.

9. Though see the discussion of "heroism" in the next chapter.

10. I here adapt a suggestion made by Jeff McMahan that is similar in some respects to one made by Derek Parfit, discussed in sec. III.

11. As noted in note 47 to chap. 2, "two-level" utilitarians, such as R. M. Hare, have available a criterion that will determine the shape of the "run-of-the-mill" principle of beneficence (which is the "level-one" principle, or the rule of thumb to be used in everyday deliberation): we should adopt that run-of-the-mill principle with the highest "acceptance utility"; see Hare, *Moral Thinking*, 201–3. That is, the right limit to the demands of the principle of beneficence that we appeal to in our everyday deliberations is the limit that it would be optimal for such a principle to employ. This approach offers a clear criterion for the everyday principle, but since it rejects any limit to demands at the reflective or second level of moral thinking, it denies that there is any intrinsic objection to extreme demands and thus does not provide the kind of criterion I am asking for. On Hare's approach to the issue of the demands of beneficence, the rare person who would do more good if she accepted the optimizing principle of beneficence as her principle for everyday deliberation should accept such a principle, and there would be no objection to the extreme demands it imposed on her.

12. For discussion of eudaimonist ethics, see Gisela Striker, "Greek Ethics and Moral Theory," in *Essays on Hellenistic Epistemology and Ethics* (Cambridge: Cambridge University Press, 1996), 169–82.

13. Scheffler discusses such a view under the title "the ideal of purity"; "the intuitive idea" here is that "morality's concerns are specific, distinctive, and in particular, sharply to be distinguished from the standpoint of the individual agent's interests" (*Human Morality*, 101). He goes on (see, e.g., 102) to link the ideal of purity with the view that morality is stringent, thus presenting the ideal of purity as supporting a particular view about the degree of acceptable conflict between self-interest and the moral life. This seems to me to be wrong; the ideal of purity is rather a rejection of that question. Moreover, stringency is not even contingently guaranteed by purity—everything depends on what one believes the content of morality to be.

14. Ibid., 102.

15. Included in Scheffler's statement of the moderate position (quoted in the text, p. 66) is the claim that morality, while not stringent, nevertheless "imposes costs—sometimes very great costs—on agents." It is hard to see how one could reach this view about the role of morality in human life other than by reflecting on one's prior moral convictions. If general stringency is unacceptable, why are occasional very great costs all right? And it is not a coincidence, furthermore, that the arguments Scheffler considers for the stringency of morality are in fact arguments for a particular moral theory, namely, utilitarianism; see chap. 6 of *Human Morality*. I am in complete agreement with Scheffler's rejection of attempts to derive the truth of utilitarianism from some alleged formal property of morality. But it is misleading to describe these arguments as attempting to establish the stringency of morality, as if the claim were that being potentially very demanding were part of the very nature of morality. On the contrary, the extreme demands of utilitarianism could naturally be regarded as regrettable; moreover, many utilitarians offer arguments, some of which I considered in chapter 2, to show that their moral theory is not as demanding as it may seem.

16. See Slote, *Common-Sense Morality and Consequentialism*, chap. 5.

17. See p. 5. I thank Jeff McMahan for dissuading me from thinking that Slote's view differed from the charity view.

18. See Immanuel Kant, *The Metaphysics of Morals*, Ak. VI, 393–94, 454, translated by James W. Ellington in Kant, *Ethical Philosophy* (Indianapolis: Hackett, 1983), 52–53, 118–19. For discussion, see Thomas E. Hill Jr., "Kant on Imperfect Duty and Supererogation," *Kant-Studien* 62 (1971): 55–76; Marcia Baron, "Kantian Ethics and Supererogation," *Journal of Philosophy* 84 (1987): 237–62. For a dissenting interpretation, see David Cummiskey, *Kantian Consequentialism* (New York, Oxford University Press, 1996), chap. 6.

My remarks about the minimalism of the duty of beneficence Kant himself discusses are of course compatible with the derivation of much more robust duties of beneficence from elsewhere in Kant's moral philosophy. See, in this connection, Cummiskey, *Kantian Consequentialism*; Nagel, *Equality and Partiality*, chap. 5.

19. I owe this suggestion to Derek Parfit. (The idea of scalar wrongness is introduced by Frances Howard-Snyder and Alistair Norcross in "A Consequentialist Case for Rejecting the Right," *Journal of Philosophical Research* 18 [1993]: 113, but then rejected, pp. 113–23.)

20. In passing, Brian Barry makes a related suggestion: "I think it is fairly clear that there is a greater obligation [of 'humanity'] the more severe the distress, the better off the potential helper would still be after helping, and the higher the ratio of benefit to cost." "Humanity and Justice in Global Perspective," in J. Roland Pennock and John W. Chapman, eds., *Nomos XXIV: Ethics, Economics, and the Law* (New York: New York University Press, 1982), 225.

21. See Garrett Cullity, "Moral Character and the Iteration Problem," *Utilitas* 7 (1995): 293–95.

22. Some deontological wrongdoing, such as stealing and promise-breaking, may be less wrong on account of cost to the agent.

23. Less plausible still is Slote's "scalar consequentialism"—as opposed to his proposal for scalar beneficence as one principle among many; see Slote, *Common-Sense Morality and Consequentialism*, chap. 2. Recall that on Slote's scalar view we cannot say of any action that it is, simply, wrong; rather, we rank actions as more or less good depending on the size of the benefit they bring about. But the point to make about gratuitous killing or torture is not that we could be doing better. And we cannot even say that gratuitous killing stands out among actions we could perform because we could do *a lot* better than that. Given the open-ended nature of potential beneficence in our current situation of partial compliance and great need, anyone living a fairly typical life could also be doing *a lot* better.

Chapter Five

1. I use the version of Nagel's distinction between agent-neutral and agent-relative reasons that Parfit gives in *Reasons and Persons*, 27, 143. On this version all principles of beneficence, including limited principles of beneficence and the collective principle of beneficence, are agent-neutral, since they give all agents the same aim. On Nagel's own version of the distinction, these principles might count as agent-relative, since their formulation may seem to include "an essential reference" to the agent subject to the principle; see *The View from Nowhere*, 152–53. On the other hand, the reference to the agent that these principles involve might be thought to be inessential. The main point for my purposes is that while some of these principles specify the degree of sacrifice required by each agent, and in that sense mention the agent and require her to take into account a fact about herself when figuring out what the principle requires, they nevertheless give all agents the same aim—promoting well-being. The illustration of the intuitive contrast between an agent-relative and an agent-neutral principle offered in the text applies without strain to the collective and limited principles of beneficence.

2. See the references given in chap. 1, n. 8.

3. See chap. 2, sec. I.

4. Cf. chap. 3, sec. III.

5. See chap. 3, sec. II.

6. See chap. 3, secs. II and IV.

7. See Robert H. Myers, *Self-Governance and Cooperation* (Oxford: Oxford University Press, 1999), chap. 2, esp. pp. 59–68; Myers, "Prerogatives and Restrictions from the Cooperative Point of View," *Ethics* 105 (1994): 128–52; Larry Alexander, "Scheffler on the Independence of Agent-Centered Prerog-

atives from Agent-Centered Restrictions," *Journal of Philosophy* 84 (1987): 277–83. (Alexander discusses a constraint against forced supererogation, to use Myers's phrase, which is narrower than a constraint against forcing unrequired action.)

8. In "Should the Numbers Count?" *Philosophy & Public Affairs* 6 (1977): 293–316, John Taurek argues, in effect, from (1) a constraint against imposing unrequired sacrifice and (2) our apparent acceptance of a limit to active demands (the one is not required to direct the trolley onto herself), to the conclusion that third parties are not permitted to redirect the trolley away from the five and toward the one. Conversely, Unger can be seen as arguing from (1) a constraint against imposing unrequired sacrifice and (2) the widespread belief that a third party is permitted to redirect the trolley onto the one, to the conclusion that the one is required to redirect the trolley onto herself. Unger proposes:

> *The Reasonable Principle of Ethical Integrity.* Other things being even nearly equal, if it's all right for you to *impose losses on others* with the result that there's a significant lessening in the serious losses suffered by others overall, then, if you're to avoid doing what's seriously wrong, you *can't fail to impose equal or smaller losses on yourself*, nor can you fail to accept such losses, when the result's *an equal or greater* significant lessening of such serious losses over-all.

He adds that "when there's no fussing over niceties of formulation, this precept is embraced by anyone with even a modicum of moral decency"; see 139–40.

9. I will further discuss the constraint against imposing unrequired sacrifice in chapter 7.

10. Parfit, *Reasons and Persons*, 30–31, argues that the objection to act-utilitarianism he there discusses supports a move to ideal-collective utilitarianism. In what follows I borrow terminology from his discussion.

11. See Brandt, "Fairness to Indirect Optimific Theories in Ethics," *Ethics* 98 (1988): 341–60; Hooker, "Rule-Consequentialism," and "Rule-Consequentialism and Demandingness."

12. As I did when I wrote "The Demands of Beneficence," *Philosophy & Public Affairs* 22 (1993): 267–92, noting, p. 279, that the ideal collective theories satisfied a version of the compliance condition that concerned only active demands.

13. This formulation of the collective principle reflects criticism of earlier versions by Thomas Pogge and Tim Mulgan. As already indicated, chap. 2, footnote to p. 14, I favor a weighted principle of beneficence, but I do not defend this in this book.

14. My interest in the distribution of compliance effects descends from an interest in the distribution of demands that was due to a discussion of the issue in an early draft of Scheffler's *Human Morality;* some of this discussion survives on pp. 98–99. From the start, Thomas Pogge tried to make me see that the distribution of (active) demands was not of importance in itself. In moving to a discussion of the distribution of compliance effects, I have, many years later, finally gotten the point. Amélie Oksenberg Rorty, "King Solomon and Everyman: A Problem in Coordinating Conflicting Moral Intuitions," *American Philosophical Quarterly* 28 (1991): 181–94, is also in effect a discussion of the distribution of moral demands.

15. I owe the points in this paragraph to Derek Parfit.

16. Cohen, "Who Is Starving Whom?" 76. Shelly Kagan pointed out to me that Cohen's assertion about unclaimed benefits may seem wrong—for suggesting that it would be better to waste the leftover goods than to distribute them among those who already have received their fair share. I take Cohen to have in mind situations where the unclaimed benefits would not be wasted. They might return, as it were, to general revenue: if the town decides that each person who wants one should have a free bicycle, it does not follow from the fact that some do not want one that others can have more than one. Or the unclaimed benefits might stay with the distributor: a person who promises to spend two hours helping each of his friends has not committed himself to helping one of them for four hours if another declines the help. There is an asymmetry here between burdens and benefits, insofar as burdens, as such, should be "wasted" if they can be. (But don't the unaccepted burdens of compliance with the collective principle of beneficence in fact end up somewhere—with the people who would have been benefited if the noncompliers had complied? To say this is misleading, for reasons given in the text, p. 92, and n. 19.)

17. For this objection I am indebted to Shelly Kagan and, especially, Larry Temkin.

18. See further chap. 6, sec. II.

19. The objector could reply that the victims are in a sense worse-off because of the requirements the collective principle makes under partial compliance insofar as the collective principle does *not* require the better-off compliers to take up some of the slack left by others' noncompliance. In other words, though the collective principle does not impose an additional passive burden on the victims in the move from full to partial compliance, it can be faulted for not requiring compliers to convey additional passive benefits. But this continues to misconstrue the idea of fairness embodied in the compliance condition. The compliance condition comes into play once we have a common aim, and constrains the allocation of responsibility for pursuit of that aim. In the case of principles of beneficence, the aim is the promotion of well-being. There is no sense in which the victims of noncompliance under the collective principle can be said to be taking on more than their share of the responsibility for the promotion of well-being. The common aim of promoting well-being would be better achieved if the compliers took up some of the slack, but if the compliers do not do this, they are not transferring responsibility for the promotion of well-being to the victims of noncompliance. By contrast, when the optimizing principle of beneficence requires compliers to take up some of the slack, it is transferring responsibility.

20. Robert E. Goodin, in a passage attacking the kind of view embodied in the compliance condition, distinguishes between "primary" and "secondary" responsibility; see *Protecting the Vulnerable* (Chicago: University of Chicago Press, 1985), 134–35. Though he contemplates the possibility that secondary responsibility is not always triggered by the mere unwillingness to act of the person with primary responsibility (152), it is clear that in Goodin's central case of "protecting the vulnerable," secondary responsibility *is* automatic. "Those able to help, albeit not as well as those with primary responsibility, retain a residual responsibility to do so in case the others default. . . . The limit of this responsibility is, quite simply, the limit of the vulnerable agent's needs and of the responsible agent's capacity to act efficaciously—no more, but certainly no

less" (134–35). It is clear that for Goodin failures in secondary responsibility are wrong in just the same way as failures in primary responsibility.

21. Nagel, *The View from Nowhere*, 177.

22. By "substantive" here, I have in mind an aim more concrete than Scanlon's suggested motivation to act according to principles that no one could reasonably reject—for example, the aims of well-being, equality, or freedom; for Scanlon's contractualism, see *What We Owe to Each Other*, chaps. 4 and 5.

23. See Gibbard, "Constructing Justice"; Allen Buchanan, "Justice as Reciprocity Versus Subject-Centered Justice," *Philosophy & Public Affairs* 19 (1990): 227–52; the main objections to such views were set out in Robert Nozick, *Anarchy, State, and Utopia* (New York: Basic Books, 1974), 223. Gibbard characterizes Rawls's theory of justice (justice as fairness) as an instance of justice as fair reciprocity, and Rawls endorses this characterization in *Political Liberalism*, 17 n.

24. My characterization of collective beneficence may sound similar to Donald H. Regan's description of morality as a community or cooperative enterprise in chapter 12 of *Utilitarianism and Co-operation* (Oxford: Clarendon Press, 1980). It is in fact very different, however, for Regan is concerned with cooperation among complying agents only; on his picture, when someone ceases to comply, she is no longer part of the cooperating group. His "cooperative utilitarianism" directs each agent to "co-operate, with whoever else is co-operating, in the production of the best consequences possible given the behavior of non-co-operators" (124). In my terms, we could say that Regan's view addresses agents with individually held aims to promote well-being who may be able to better achieve their aims through cooperation with each other. A further conception of morality as a cooperative enterprise—more similar to but also distinct from my own account of beneficence as a collective undertaking—is presented in Myers, *Self-Governance and Cooperation*.

25. Jeremy Waldron and Marcus Willaschek helped me here.

26. See David Hume, *A Treatise of Human Nature*, edited by L. A. Selby-Bigge; 2d ed., ed. P. H. Nidditch (Oxford: Clarendon Press, 1978), bk. III, pt. III, sec. III.

27. In the grenade case, taken from J. O. Urmson, "Saints and Heroes," in A. I. Melden, ed., *Essays in Moral Philosophy* (Seattle: University of Washington Press, 1958), 202–3, we can assume that the agent was the only one who saw the grenade in time, and that there was no option of throwing someone *else* on the grenade! See R. A. Duff, "Absolute Principles and Double Effect," *Analysis* 36 (1975–76): 79, cited by Kagan, *The Limits of Morality*, 145. Griffin, (*Well-Being*, 185), refers to Oates and his famous parting words, "I am just going outside and may be some time" (364 n. 57) when discussing the possibly extreme demands of utilitarianism.

28. See Unger, *Living High and Letting Die*, 150–57.

29. The case resembles Nozick's example of ten Robinson Crusoes; *Anarchy, State, and Utopia*, 185.

30. See pp. 4, 7–8.

Chapter Six

1. In the first footnote to p. 14.

2. Changing the baseline level of expected well-being in this way would be distorting if we were interested in determining *degrees* of inequality with

any precision. For discussion of different ways to understand degrees of in-equality, see Sen, *On Economic Inequality*, enlarged edition (Oxford: Clarendon Press, 1997); and Larry S. Temkin, *Inequality* (New York: Oxford University Press, 1993).

3. See generally Sen, *On Economic Inequality*, 15–18.

4. See Rorty, "King Solomon and Everyman."

5. As Larry Temkin pointed out, equality could be achieved by handicap-ping the better-off. But even this route to equality would take time, and so it remains true that equality of compliance effects would not be achieved im-mediately upon full compliance with the theory.

6. Unless, perhaps, those inequalities also benefit all people; this is the formula offered by Rawls, *A Theory of Justice*, 75 ff.

7. See further the references given in chap. 5, note 23.

8. Could a view about the fair distribution of compliance effects be based on the "priority view" about the distribution of well-being—the view that benefits to worse-off people matter more (see chap. 2, footnote to p. 14)? No, because the view that benefits to worse-off people matter more is not based in some idea of fairness.

9. Sidgwick, *The Methods of Ethics*, 416–17. Sidgwick prefaces the quoted words with "as we saw"; the passage he has in mind is probably the discussion of equality and justice (266–68), to which Rawls refers in his discussion of "formal justice" in *A Theory of Justice*, 58. I follow also the discussion of H. L. A. Hart, *The Concept of Law*, 2d ed. (Oxford: Clarendon Press, 1994), 157–67; on p. 158 Hart notes that his discussion of justice could as well be cast as a discussion of fairness.

10. Sidgwick does not make this broader point.

11. See Sidgwick, *The Methods of Ethics*, 267–68.

12. Ibid., 416.

13. Could there be conflicting supplementary rules coming from these two different perspectives? It would seem so, wherever the aim of the agent-neutral principle in question was not the promotion of general well-being (on general well-being, see chap. 2, sec. III). Then we would have one supple-mentary rule telling us to break ties by aiming at equality of whatever it is that the principle aims at, and another telling us to aim at equality of ex-pected well-being (compliance effects). Presumably this conflict would be re-solved by reflecting on which object of distribution was more important—that aimed at by the principle, or compliance effects understood in terms of well-being.

14. Trenchant criticism by Shelly Kagan helped me to improve this and the next two sections.

15. In this kind of case this new supplementary rule could conflict with the one introduced earlier requiring A to act so as to promote equality of compliance effects. This conflict would have to be resolved by deciding on a ranking between the two considerations of fairness; see note 13.

Chapter Seven

1. See pp. 41–47, 81–83.

2. For discussion and references, see chap. 2, secs. V and VI.

3. See Parfit, *Reasons and Persons*, sec. 10.

4. See Richard B. Brandt, *Facts, Values, and Morality* (Cambridge: Cambridge University Press, 1996), 151–52.

5. Tim Mulgan, "Two Conceptions of Benevolence," *Philosophy & Public Affairs* 26 (1997): 62–79, criticizes the collective principle of beneficence as offered in my "The Demands of Beneficence" (under the name "cooperative principle of beneficence") on grounds that turn in large part on the information agents applying the principle would need. For my response, see "A Relatively Plausible Principle of Beneficence: Reply to Mulgan," *Philosophy & Public Affairs* 26 (1997): 80–86.

6. This is true not just for collective utilitarianism but also for a pluralistic theory that includes the collective principle of beneficence along with some independent principles of political justice that apply only to the design of institutions: to know what life would be like under full compliance with the overall theory, agents would need to know what institutions their society would be aiming at in that case.

7. See, e.g., United Nations Development Programme, *Human Development Report 1997* (New York: Oxford University Press, 1997), 112, and references there cited, for an estimate of the total cost of eradicating global poverty. Of course, the aim of the collective principle of beneficence is not limited to the eradication of poverty.

8. The gap between the idealized assessment of required sacrifice and the nonidealized assessment of how to do most good means that a person might have to increase her giving locally—where it will do most good—even if locally things are getting better. For things may be getting much worse far away, and that affects the measure of her required sacrifice because it affects what her level of well-being would be under full compliance. I am indebted to Joseph Raz for this point, though unlike him I do not see in it an objection to the collective principle.

9. If the collective principle was part of a wider theory, references to full compliance in the statement of the principle would need to be understood as full compliance with the overall theory.

10. See pp. 83–84.

11. See Nozick, *Anarchy, State, and Utopia*, 30; Scheffler, *The Rejection of Consequentialism*, chap. 4.

12. See also Myers, *Self-Governance and Cooperation*, 63–67.

13. Muhammad Ali Khalidi, Tim Mulgan, Robert Myers, and Wayne Proudfoot all pressed this on me. The answer to the objection I offered in "The Demands of Beneficence" was wrong, as I explain in "A Reasonably Plausible Principle of Beneficence," 85–86.

14. As quoted in Parfit, *Reasons and Persons*, 47.

15. This section has benefited greatly from Shelly Kagan's comments.

16. See Peter Singer, "Famine, Affluence and Morality," *Philosophy & Public Affairs* 1 (1972): 229–43; Kagan, *The Limits of Morality*, 3–4, 231–32, and throughout. F. M. Kamm, in "Faminine Ethics: The Problem of Distance in Morality and Singer's Ethical Theory," in Dale Jamieson, ed., *Singer and His Critics* (Oxford: Blackwell, 1999), 177–96, shows that the relevant category of cases is actually broader than my definition in the text, which follows other discussions of the topic, suggests. What she calls the problem of distance in morality is summed up, as "whether we can justify our intuition that we have a greater responsibility to take care of what is going on in the area near us

or near our efficacious means, whether this involves needy victims, threats, or means belonging to victims" (195). Since I am skeptical about the moral relevance of proximity, I will not try to take into account Kamm's points about the location of means and threats.

17. Shelly Kagan, personal communication, February 4, 1992.

18. James Rachels mentions this case to show "the fallacy of supposing that one's duty is only to do one's fair share, where this is determined by what would be sufficient *if* everyone else did likewise," in "Killing and Starving to Death," *Philosophy* 54 (1979), rpt. in Jan Narveson, ed., *Moral Issues* (Toronto: Oxford University Press, 1983), 157; see also Singer, "Famine, Affluence, and Morality," 233. Note that even if the collective principle of beneficence does not require the complying agent to take up the slack left by the noncomplier and rescue the second drowning child, that would not mean that, if there is but one child and many noncomplying potential rescuers, the "responsibility" or blameworthiness of each noncomplier is proportionately reduced by the availability of other potential rescuers (as Rachels's discussion, in "Killing and Starving to Death" suggests). For if there is one child to be rescued, and many potential rescuers, the collective principle requires each such person to do what would be best in the circumstances (up to the required level of sacrifice), which may mean that each should have started out to perform the rescue, holding back only if it became clear that someone else was in a better position to help. If none of the people starts out to perform the rescue and none of them is evidently better placed than the others to effect the rescue, it is not inaccurate to say that each of them is responsible for the death. On this point I differ with Cohen ("Who Is Starving Whom?" 75), who says that "if there are a hundred independent defaulters . . . , and one death, each carries a hundredth of the responsibility, not the whole of it." See also Goodin, *Protecting the Vulnerable*, 135. The problem of the division of blame when many people are in a position to do something good that can only be done by one person but no one acts is quite different from the question of the responsibility of complying agents to sustain sacrifice that, if others were also participating, would not be necessary.

19. In "The Demands of Beneficence," 291, I give an incorrect account of the operation of the collective ("cooperative" in that article) principle in rescue cases. Thomas Nagel pointed out my mistake, which I here correct.

20. See chap. 4, pp. 67–68.

21. Note that the principle Singer reaches as a generalization of the commonsense view about what we should do when we confront the child in the pond (*Practical Ethics*, 230)—"If we can prevent something bad without sacrificing anything of comparable significance, we ought to do it"—is as demanding in the actual world as the optimizing principle of beneficence.

22. See chap. 5, sec. VII, p. 94.

23. See Unger, *Living High and Letting Die*, chap. 2; for a list of the nine factors, see pp. 53–54. Unger himself does not use the description "rescue case."

24. The case Unger actually offers to make this point involves the motorist's equivalent of a Mayday signal; see the case of "The CB Radios" (*Living High and Letting Die*, 34–35). Responding to this case, Kamm ("Rescue and Harm: Discussion of Peter Unger's *Living High and Letting Die*," *Legal Theory* 5 [1999]: 10; "Faminine Ethics," 184) reports her belief that "our intuitive responses *do*

change, and we sense a reduced obligation, once we take account of the fact that what is costlessly 'near by car' may be farther away than what is near if I am not in a car." For what it is worth, my own intuitions agree with Unger's (and "most" of the people he has asked about the case, see p. 35). To keep the case pure, I find it helpful to imagine a motorist in the Australian outback, with no other potential rescuers to be found for several hundred miles: it seems to make no difference to the commonsense rescue obligation whether the motorist comes across the victim in person, or instead hears over the radio that he is fifty miles off the track. It is, incidentally, perhaps no surprise (as Philip Pettit remarked to me) that Australia's Northern Territory has one of the most stringent "duty to rescue" laws in the world—certainly in the common law world— providing for up to seven years imprisonment for "callous" failures to rescue; see *Criminal Code Act* sec. 155.

25. See Unger, *Living High and Letting Die*, 28–29, 77–79.

26. See ibid., 77–78; once again, I cast Unger's position in my own terminology.

27. Unger in effect embraces the optimizing principle of beneficence without considering alternative principles of beneficence with apparently more reasonable demands; see ibid., chap. 6.

28. Though see Kamm, "Rescue and Harm," 8–11. Another possibility that seems plausible is that we intuitively accept an obligation to rescue in precisely those cases where even ideal social institutions could not have prevented the need from arising. For further relevant discussion, see Murphy, "Beneficence, Law, and Liberty: The Case of Required Rescue" (unpublished ms., 1999). Our unconscious thought might be that even under ideal institutions rescue obligations would continue often to fall to individuals, and so we should accept them as our responsibility. (Thus I think Kamm may be right to limit her discussion of rescue cases to "accidents" that do not raise issues of "basic justice," since basic justice would presumably be dealt with by ideal institutions; see "Rescue and Harm," 10–11.) Once again, this would not justify treating rescue contexts as special; I offer it only as an alternative diagnosis of the (by hypothesis) mistaken belief that rescue contexts generate special obligations. This diagnosis is compatible with Unger's appeal to the factor of conspicuousness, for where the kinds of needs that cannot be prevented in advance by ideal institutions can be met by an individual, those needs are likely to be conspicuous because sudden, unexpected, and so forth. It is noteworthy that when Unger considers "The Thought of the Governments" (*Living High and Letting Die*, 40), he dismisses it not with an example that shows that common sense allows us to ignore inconspicuous needs that would have arisen even under an ideal government, nor with one that shows that common sense requires us to act in a conspicuous case where the needs would not have arisen under an ideal government, but by (correctly) pointing out that the mere fact that the government *could* have prevented the problem from arising doesn't mean that we, in our actual world, have no obligation at all to deal with it.

Though both this diagnosis and Unger's appeal to conspicuousness and futility thinking seem plausible, in the end (as I explain later in the text) I think that commonsense reactions to rescue cases probably reflect not judgments of right and wrong action at all, but rather judgments of good and bad character.

29. For some preliminary arguments, see Kamm, "Faminine Ethics," 198–200, and "Rescue and Harm," 19–20. A different argument that is sometimes made is that rescue contexts could be the subject of a mutually beneficial ex ante bargain. I do not find this a plausible option. In the first place, the bargain could only be hypothetical, and, as has often been pointed out, it is not clear why hypothetical bargains should have any moral force at all; see, e.g., Ronald Dworkin, *Taking Rights Seriously* (Cambridge, Mass.: Harvard University Press, 1977), 150–52. Second, such an argument requires strict unanimity, and this seems rather dubious. Imagine a well-guarded billionaire who never swims or takes personal risks. Such a person's resources might well be called on in emergencies (imagine some variation on Unger's case, "Bob's Bugatti,"*Living High and Letting Die*, 136) while his chances of needing a stranger's assistance are close to zero; see, e.g., Parfit, *Reasons and Persons*, 109.

30. See chap. 2, sec. V.

31. See Kagan's discussion of vivid beliefs, *The Limits of Morality*, 283–91.

32. See Hume, "Of Some Verbal Disputes," appendix IV to *Enquiry Concerning the Principles of Morals*, ed. L. A. Selby-Bigge; 3d ed., ed. P. H. Nidditch (Oxford: Clarendon Press, 1975).

BIBLIOGRAPHY

Abelson, Raziel. "To Do or Let Happen." *American Philosophical Quarterly* 19 (1982): 219–28.

Adams, R. M. "Motive Utilitarianism." *Journal of Philosophy* 73 (1976): 467–81.

Alexander, Larry. "Scheffler on the Independence of Agent-Centered Prerogatives from Agent-Centered Restrictions." *Journal of Philosophy* 84 (1987): 277–83.

Arneson, Richard. "Equality and Equal Opportunity for Welfare." *Philosophical Studies* 56 (1989): 77–93.

Baier, Kurt. *The Moral Point of View*. Ithaca, N.Y.: Cornell University Press, 1958.

Baron, Marcia. "Kantian Ethics and Supererogation." *Journal of Philosophy* 84 (1987): 237–62.

Barry, Brian. "Humanity and Justice in Global Perspective." In J. Roland Pennock and John W. Chapman, eds., *Nomos XXIV: Ethics, Economics, and the Law*, 219–52. New York: New York University Press, 1982.

Becker, Lawrence, et al. "Symposium on Impartiality and Ethical Theory." *Ethics* 101 (1991): 698–864.

Bennett, Jonathan. "Morality and Consequences." In S. M. McMurrin, ed., *The Tanner Lectures on Human Values*, vol. 2, 45–116. Salt Lake City: University of Utah Press, 1981.

———. *The Act Itself*. Oxford: Clarendon Press, 1995.

Blumenfeld, Jean Beer. "Causing Harm and Bringing Aid." *American Philosophical Quarterly* 18 (1981): 323–29.

Brandt, Richard B. *A Theory of the Good and the Right*. Oxford: Clarendon Press, 1979.

———. "Fairness to Indirect Optimific Theories in Ethics." *Ethics* 98 (1988): 341–60.

———. *Facts, Values, and Morality*. Cambridge: Cambridge University Press, 1996.

Brink, David O. "Utilitarian Morality and the Personal Point of View." *Journal of Philosophy* 83 (1986): 417–38.

Brock, Dan W. "Defending Moral Options." *Philosophy and Phenomenological Research* 51 (1991): 909–13.

Buchanan, Allen. "Justice as Reciprocity Versus Subject-Centered Justice." *Philosophy & Public Affairs* 19 (1990): 227–52.

Cassen, Robert, and associates. *Does Aid Work?* 2d ed. Oxford: Oxford University Press, 1994.

Clarke, Samuel. *A Discourse of Natural Religion* (1706). Reprinted in D. D. Raphael, ed., *British Moralists: 1650–1800.* vol. I, 224–61. Indianapolis: Hackett, 1991.

Cohen, G. A. "If You're an Egalitarian, How Come You're So Rich?" 1996 Gifford Lectures. Forthcoming, Harvard University Press, 2000.

Cohen, L. Jonathan. "Who Is Starving Whom?" *Theoria* 47 (1981): 65–81.

Cullity, Garrett. "Moral Character and the Iteration Problem." *Utilitas* 7 (1995): 289–99.

Cummiskey, David. *Kantian Consequentialism.* New York: Oxford University Press, 1996.

Davis, Nancy. "Utilitarianism and Responsibility." *Ratio* 22 (1980): 15–35.

Drèze, Jean, and Amartya Sen. *Hunger and Public Action.* Oxford: Clarendon Press, 1989.

Dworkin, Ronald. *Taking Rights Seriously.* Cambridge, Mass.: Harvard University Press, 1977.

Fishkin, James. *The Limits of Obligation.* New Haven, Conn.: Yale University Press, 1982.

Flanagan, Owen. *Varieties of Moral Personality.* Cambridge, Mass.: Harvard University Press, 1991.

Fried, Charles. *Right and Wrong.* Cambridge, Mass.: Harvard University Press, 1978.

Gauthier, David. "Justice and Natural Endowment: Toward a Critique of Rawls's Ideological Framework." In *Moral Dealing,* 150–70. Ithaca, N.Y.: Cornell University Press, 1990.

Gibbard, Allan. *Wise Choices, Apt Feelings.* Cambridge, Mass.: Harvard University Press, 1990.

———. "Constructing Justice." *Philosophy & Public Affairs* 20 (1991): 264–79.

Godwin, William. *Enquiry Concerning Political Justice* (1798). Harmondsworth: Penguin, 1976.

Goldman, Holly Smith. "Rawls and Utilitarianism." In H. Gene Blocker and Elizabeth H. Smith, eds., *John Rawls' Theory of Social Justice,* 346–94. Athens: Ohio University Press, 1980.

Goodin, Robert E. *Protecting the Vulnerable.* Chicago: University of Chicago Press, 1985.

Griffin, James. *Well-Being.* Oxford: Clarendon Press, 1986.

Grigg, Russell. "The Ethics of Desire." *Analysis* (Melbourne Centre for Psychoanalytic Research) 3 (1991): 29–35.

Hare, R. M. *Moral Thinking.* Oxford: Clarendon Press, 1981.

———. "Comments." In Douglas Seanor and N. Fotion, eds., *Hare and Critics* 199–293. Oxford: Clarendon Press, 1988.

Hart, H. L. A. *The Concept of Law.* 2d ed. Oxford: Clarendon Press, 1994.

Herman, Barbara. "Integrity and Impartiality." *The Monist* 66 (1983): 233–50.

———. "Agency, Attachment, and Difference." *Ethics* 101 (1991): 775–97.

Hill, Thomas E., Jr. "Kant on Imperfect Duty and Supererogation." *Kant-Studien*, 62 (1971): 55–76.

Hooker, Brad. "Rule-Consequentialism." *Mind* 99 (1990): 67–77.

———. "Brink, Kagan, Utilitarianism and Self-Sacrifice." *Utilitas* 3 (1991): 263–73.

———. "Rule-Consequentialism and Demandingness: A Reply to Carson." *Mind* 100 (1991): 269–76.

Howard-Snyder, Frances, and Alistair Norcross. "A Consequentialist Case for Rejecting the Right." *Journal of Philosophical Research* 18 (1993): 109–25.

Hume, David. *A Treatise of Human Nature* (1739). Edited by L. A. Selby-Bigge; 2d ed., edited by P. H. Nidditch. Oxford: Clarendon Press, 1978.

———. *Enquiries Concerning Human Understanding and Concerning the Principles of Morals*(1777). Edited by L. A. Selby-Bigge; 3d ed., edited by P. H. Nidditch. Oxford: Clarendon Press, 1975.

Jackson, Frank. "Decision-Theoretic Consequentialism and the Nearest and Dearest Objection." *Ethics* 101 (1991): 461–82.

Kagan, Shelly. "Does Consequentialism Demand Too Much?" *Philosophy & Public Affairs* 13 (1984): 239–54.

———. *The Limits of Morality*. Oxford: Clarendon Press, 1989.

———. "Replies to My Critics." *Philosophy and Phenomenological Research* 51 (1991): 919–28.

Kamm, F. M. "Supererogation and Obligation." *Journal of Philosophy* 82 (1985): 118–38.

———. *Morality, Mortality. Vol. 2, Rights, Duties, and Status*. New York: Oxford University Press, 1996.

———. "Faminine Ethics: The Problem of Distance in Morality and Singer's Ethical Theory." In Dale Jamieson, ed., *Singer and His Critics*, 162–208. Oxford: Blackwell, 1999.

———. "Rescue and Harm: Discussion of Peter Unger's *Living High and Letting Die*." *Legal Theory* 5 (1999): 1–44.

Kant, Immanuel. *The Metaphysics of Morals*. In *Ethical Philosophy*, trans. James W. Ellington. Indianapolis: Hackett, 1983.

Kitto, H. D. F. *The Greeks*. Harmondsworth: Penguin, 1951.

Korsgaard, Christine. "The Reasons We Can Share." In *Creating the Kingdom of Ends*, 275–310. Cambridge: Cambridge University Press, 1996.

Mackie, J. L. *Ethics*. Harmondsworth: Penguin, 1977.

Malm, H. M. "Directions of Justification in the Negative-Positive Duty Debate." *American Philosophical Quarterly* 27 (1990): 315–24.

———. "Between the Horns of the Negative-Positive Duty Debate." *Philosophical Studies* 61 (1991): 187–210.

Mill, John Stuart. *On Liberty* (1859). In *Three Essays*, ed. Richard Wollheim, 1–141. Oxford: Oxford University Press, 1975.

———. *Utilitarianism* (1861). Edited by George Sher. Indianapolis: Hackett, 1979.

———. *Later Speculations of August Comte* (1865). In *The Positive Philosophy of Auguste Comte*, 113–82. New York: Henry Holt and Co., 1875.

Mulgan, Tim. "Two Conceptions of Benevolence." *Philosophy & Public Affairs* 26 (1997): 62–79.

Murphy, Liam B. "The Demands of Beneficence." *Philosophy & Public Affairs* 22 (1993): 267–92.

———. "A Relatively Plausible Principle of Beneficence: Reply to Mulgan." *Philosophy & Public Affairs* 26 (1997): 80–86.

———. "Institutions and the Demands of Justice." *Philosophy & Public Affairs* 27 (1998): 251–91.

———. "Beneficence, Law, and Liberty: The Case of Required Rescue." Unpublished ms., 1999.

Myers, Robert H. "Prerogatives and Restrictions from the Cooperative Point of View." *Ethics* 105 (1994): 128–52.

———. *Self-Governance and Cooperation.* Oxford: Oxford University Press, 1999.

Nagel, Thomas. "Libertarianism Without Foundations." *Yale Law Journal* 85 (1975): 136–49.

———. "Equality." In *Mortal Questions*, 106–27. Cambridge: Cambridge University Press, 1979.

———. *The View from Nowhere.* New York: Oxford University Press, 1986.

———. *Equality and Partiality.* New York: Oxford University Press, 1991.

Nozick, Robert. *Anarchy, State, and Utopia.* New York: Basic Books, 1974.

O'Neill, Onora. "The Great Maxims of Justice and Charity." In *Constructions of Reason*, 219–33. Cambridge: Cambridge University Press, 1989.

Parfit, Derek. *Reasons and Persons.* Oxford: Clarendon Press, 1984.

———. "Comments." *Ethics* 96 (1986): 832–72.

———. "What We Together Do." Unpublished manuscript, 1988.

———. "On Giving Priority to the Worse Off." Unpublished manuscript, 1989.

———. *Equality or Priority?* The Lindley Lecture, The University of Kansas, 1991.

Pogge, Thomas W. *Realizing Rawls.* Ithaca, N.Y.: Cornell University Press, 1989.

Quinn, Warren S. "Actions, Intentions, and Consequences: The Doctrine of Doing and Allowing." *Philosophical Review* 98 (1989): 287–312. Reprinted in Steinbock and Norcross, 355–82.

Rachels, James. "Killing and Starving to Death." *Philosophy* 54 (1979): 159–71. Reprinted in Jan Narveson, ed., *Moral Issues*, 154–66. Toronto: Oxford University Press, 1983.

Railton, Peter. "Alienation, Consequentialism, and the Demands of Morality." *Philosophy & Public Affairs* 13 (1984): 134–71.

Rawls, John. *A Theory of Justice.* Cambridge, Mass.: Harvard University Press, 1971.

———. *Political Liberalism.* New York: Columbia University Press, 1993.

Raz, Joseph. "A Morality Fit for Humans." *Michigan Law Review* 91 (1993): 1297–314.

———. "Duties of Well-Being." In *Ethics in the Public Domain*, 3–28. Oxford: Clarendon Press, 1994.

Regan, Donald H. *Utilitarianism and Co-operation.* Oxford: Clarendon Press, 1980.

Rorty, Amélie Oksenberg. "King Solomon and Everyman: A Problem in Coordinating Conflicting Moral Intuitions." *American Philosophical Quarterly* 28 (1991): 181–94.

Rosenkrantz, Carlos. "Igualitarismo y Libertarianismo: Política no antropología." *Revista del Centro de Estudios Constitucionales* 7 (1990): 193–203.

Ross, W. D. *The Right and the Good*. Oxford: Clarendon Press, 1930. Reprint, Indianapolis: Hackett, 1988.

Russell, Bruce. "On the Relative Strictness of Negative and Positive Duties." *American Philosophical Quarterly* 14 (1977): 87–97.

Scanlon, T. M. "Preference and Urgency." *Journal of Philosophy* 72 (1975): 655–69.

———. "Value, Desire, and the Quality of Life." In Martha C. Nussbaum and Amartya Sen, eds., *The Quality of Life*, 185–200. Oxford: Clarendon Press, 1993.

———. *What We Owe to Each Other*. Cambridge, Mass.: Harvard University Press, 1998.

Scheffler, Samuel. *Consequentialism and Its Critics*. New York: Oxford University Press, 1988.

———. *Human Morality*. New York: Oxford University Press, 1992.

———. *The Rejection of Consequentialism*. Rev. ed. Oxford: Clarendon Press, 1994.

Schneewind, J. B. *Sidgwick's Ethics and Victorian Moral Philosophy*. Oxford: Clarendon Press, 1977.

Sen, Amartya. *Collective Choice and Social Welfare*. San Francisco: Holden-Day, 1970.

———. *Inequality Reexamined*. Cambridge, Mass.: Harvard University Press, 1992.

———. "Capability and Well-Being." In Martha C. Nussbaum and Amartya Sen, eds., *The Quality of Life*, 30–53. Oxford: Clarendon Press, 1993.

———. *On Economic Inequality*. Enlarged edition. Oxford: Clarendon Press, 1997.

Shue, Henry. *Basic Rights*. 2d ed. Princeton, N.J.: Princeton University Press, 1996.

Sidgwick, Henry. *The Methods of Ethics*. 7th ed. London: Macmillan, 1907. Reprint, Indianapolis: Hackett, 1981.

Singer, Peter. "Famine, Affluence, and Morality." *Philosophy & Public Affairs* 1 (1972): 229–43.

———. *Practical Ethics*. 2d ed. Cambridge: Cambridge University Press, 1993.

Slote, Michael. *Common-Sense Morality and Consequentialism*. London: Routledge and Kegan Paul, 1985.

Steinbock, Bonnie, and Alistair Norcross, eds. *Killing and Letting Die*. 2d ed. New York: Fordham University Press, 1994.

Stocker, Michael. "The Schizophrenia of Modern Ethical Theories." *Journal of Philosophy* 73 (1976): 453–66.

Strasser, Mark. *The Moral Philosophy of John Stuart Mill*. Wakefield, N.H.: Longwood Academic, 1991.

Striker, Gisela. "Are We Any Better?" Review of Bernard Williams, *Shame and Necessity*. *London Review of Books*, August 19, 1993, 17–18.

———. "Greek Ethics and Moral Theory." In *Essays on Hellenistic Epistemology and Ethics*, 169–82. Cambridge: Cambridge University Press, 1996.

Taurek, John. "Should the Numbers Count?" *Philosophy & Public Affairs* 6 (1977): 293–316.

Temkin, Larry. *Inequality*. New York: Oxford University Press, 1993.

Trammell, Richard. "Saving Life and Taking Life." *Journal of Philosophy* 72 (1975): 131–37. Reprinted in Steinbock and Norcross, 290–97.

Unger, Peter. *Living High and Letting Die*. New York: Oxford University Press, 1996.

United Nations Development Programme. *Human Development Report 1994*. New York: Oxford University Press, 1994.

———. *Human Development Report 1997*. New York: Oxford University Press, 1997.

Urmson, J. O. "Saints and Heroes." In A. I. Melden, ed., *Essays in Moral Philosophy*, 198–216. Seattle: University of Washington Press, 1958.

Williams, Bernard. "A Critique of Utilitarianism." In J. J. C. Smart and Bernard Williams, *Utilitarianism*, 77–150. Cambridge: Cambridge University Press, 1973.

———. "Persons, Character and Morality." In *Moral Luck*, 1–19. Cambridge: Cambridge University Press, 1981.

———. *Shame and Necessity*. Berkeley and Los Angeles: University of California Press, 1993.

Wolf, Susan. "Moral Saints." *Journal of Philosophy* 79 (1982): 419–39.

———. "Above and Below the Line of Duty." *Philosophical Topics* 14 (1986): 131–48.

INDEX

145n.26, 149n.18, 150n.1,
156n.19
on the demands of justice, 54–
56
nonideal theory, 5, 8, passim
Norcross, Alistair, 149n.19
Nozick, Robert, 153nn.23, 29, 155n.11

O'Neill, Onora, 138n.14
over-demandingness, problem of, 6, 9,
15–16, 34–62
choice of baseline for, 34–41
and commonsense morality, 37–43,
55, 68
and the compliance condition, 97–
101
losses vs. absolute level
interpretation, 20–21, 61–62,
66
summary of objections to, 59–61,
69–70

Parfit, Derek, 11, 14, 18, 22–23,
136nn.8–9, 137n.8, 139n.29,
140n.36, 143n.2, 145nn.23,
26, 147n.41, 148n.10,
149n.19, 150n.1, 151n.10,
152n.15, 154n.3, 158n.29
on blameless wrongdoing, 23–25
partial compliance, responsibility
under. *See* responsibility
passive effects, 48–59
past noncompliance, 45–47, 77, 112–
15
Perry, Stephen, 145n.25
Pettit, Philip, 157n.24
Pogge, Thomas W., 139n.20, 151nn.13–
14
Proudfoot, Wayne, 155n.13
prudence, 17

Quinn, Warren S., 144n.17

Rachels, James, 156n.18
Railton, Peter, 23, 137n.9, 138nn.10–
11
Rawls, John, 4–5, 8, 112, 135n.6,
140n.34, 146n.34, 153n.23,
154nn.6, 9

Raz, Joseph, 14, 136n.7, 140n.30,
145n.24, 155n.8
Regan, Donald H., 153n.24
rescue, 40, 87, 127–33
responsibility
distribution of, 75–77, 88–90, 94,
102–14
under partial compliance, 7, 75–84,
88–102, 114–16
Rorty, Amélie Oksenberg, 151n.14,
154n.4
Rosenkrantz, Carlos, 136n.8
Ross, W. D., 10
Russell, Bruce, 145n.20

Sager, Lawrence, 144n.10, 146n.32
scalar wrongness, 70–73
Scanlon, T. M., 17–18, 126, 153n.22
Scheffler, Samuel, 9, 26, 32, 137n.9,
139n.21, 140n.37, 142nn.60,
63, 144n.13, 145nn.24, 29,
151n.14, 155n.11
on the agent-centered prerogative,
64–65
on moderate morality, 65–69
Schneewind, J. B., 136n.2
Sen, Amartya, 135n.1, 137n.6,
142n.57, 143n.64, 154nn.2–3
Shue, Henry, 136n.8
Sidgwick, Henry, 4, 10, 13, 24–25,
107–9, 114, 140n.39, 147n.41
Singer, Peter, 137n.7, 138n.18,
155n.16, 156nn.18, 21
Slote, Michael, 29–30, 71, 142n.51,
150n.23
Smith, Michael, 144n.11
Stocker, Michael, 140n.35
Strasser, Mark, 137n.2
Striker, Gisela, 143nn.4, 7, 149n.12

Taurek, John, 151n.8
taxation, and compliance effects, 47–
48, 50, 52, 60, 78, 82–84
Temkin, Larry, 144n.14, 152n.17,
154nn.2, 5
Trammell, Richard, 145nn.20–21

Unger, Peter, 130–32, 137n.7,
138n.18, 141n.49, 144n.12,
151n.8, 153n.28

United Nations Development
  Programme, 137n.7, 155n.7
unrequired sacrifice, constraint on
  imposing, 83–84, 88, 123–24
Urmson, J. O., 153n.27
utilitarianism
  collective, 119–23
  constrained collective, 123–24
  defined, 6

Waldron, Jeremy, 153n.25
well-being
  and demands, 16–20
  different conceptions of, 13–18
Willaschek, Marcus, 153n.25
Williams, Bernard, 10, 20–22, 64,
  136n.7, 143n.7, 144n.13
Wolf, Susan, 9, 140n.31
world poverty, 11

DA